Homeward Bound

Homeward Bound

AMERICAN VETERANS
RETURN FROM WAR

Richard H. Taylor
with Sandra Wright Taylor

PRAEGER SECURITY INTERNATIONAL
Westport, Connecticut • London

Library of Congress Cataloging-in-Publication Data

Taylor, Richard, 1944-
Homeward bound : American veterans return from war / Richard H. Taylor with Sandra
Wright Taylor.
     p. cm.
  Includes bibliographical references and index.
  ISBN 0–275–98385–4 (alk. paper)
    1. Veterans–United States–History.   I. Taylor, Sandra Wright.   II. Title.
  UB357.T39   2007
  305.9′06970973—dc22   2006100460

British Library Cataloguing in Publication Data is available.

Library of Congress Catalog Card Number: 2006100460
ISBN-10: 0–275–98385–4
ISBN-13: 978–0–275–98385–7

First published in 2007

Praeger Security International, 88 Post Road West, Westport, CT 06881
An imprint of Greenwood Publishing Group, Inc.
www.praeger.com

Printed in the United States of America

The paper used in this book complies with the
Permanent Paper Standard issued by the National
Information Standards Organization (Z39.48–1984).

10 9 8 7 6 5 4 3 2 1

Homeward Bound *is dedicated to all of America's veterans, and to those who waited, and still wait, for them to come home.*

By a Vietnam veteran to his father, a veteran of WWII, and to Scott and Amy, veterans of the war in Iraq.

And to my Mother, Sandy, Lynn, and Julie, who waited.

Contents

Acknowledgments

I was honored to be asked to tell the story of America's war veterans but sure I was not up to the challenge. The veterans in my family, the Vietnam veterans I hang out with, and the veterans I met at Fort Hood and in Iraq inspired me to try. My wife worried while we were apart and lived through my homecoming trials and those of her father, a son, and a daughter; but she gave the green light. For their sake and mine, I wanted to understand why homecoming dreams are so hard to realize. My research uncovered a long line of veterans with shared experiences and common fears, hopes, and dreams. Their passage from war zone to home front is a story easily missed, and I would have missed it without help.

Any mistakes, omissions, or misjudgments are mine. I am grateful for the named and unnamed whose gracious and generous assistance provided me the opportunity for this odyssey. Librarians always told me they were only doing their jobs, but without them this job could not have been done. I'm especially thankful to the smiling staff at the Cobb County, Georgia, Library System who requested unending inter-library loans. Librarians and archivists at the Library of Congress and The National Archives in Washington and Maryland were always busy, but never too much to stop, help, advise, or locate something.

To name just a few, Eileen Simon, the archivist for the Veterans' History Project, American Folklife Center in the Library of Congress, showed me a treasure of living history in the restricted stacks, public domain, and on the Internet. She took the time to answer all my questions, do research, pull records, hand-carry them to the reading room, and email links and lists of names and material. And Rachel Mears continued the support after Eileen started another project. The Veterans History Project is a valuable collection of veterans' lore and a national treasure. We owe a debt of gratitude to the sponsors, interviewers, contributors, and preservationist for saving those stories and to Congress for endowing them, notably Senators Max Cleland and Chuck Hagel. As we saluted a friend's grandson on his way to Marine Corps boot camp, Max and I pulled aside to discuss the Veterans'

History Project, Vietnam, the 1st Cavalry Division, VA hospitals, and PTSD. Max helped me realize I will never fully comprehend this complex subject.

Karen Tupek, Federal Preservation Officer at the Department of Veterans Affairs in Washington, had just returned from overseas when I showed up at her office door. She waved off a busy schedule long enough to pull and copy documents, thumb through dusty files with me, run the copier, and lead me to the department's library. The VA's library staff opened the stacks, and their kind hearts.

Librarians and archivists in the photographic records departments of both the Library of Congress and the National Archives opened a wealth of photographs that revealed messages stronger than words with inspirational stories written on the faces of real people. At a reunion of the First Cavalry Division at Fort Hood, I found Master Sergeant Larson and Specialist Joshua McPhie in the division's public affairs office. Joshua spent hours, with the sergeant's permission of course, showing me thousands of homecomings and helping me pick a few special ones to represent the division I love.

Collection specialist Carrie Cutchens at the First Cavalry Division's Museum found time to save photos during the museum's busiest day of the year. While she copied them, she showed me a blue horse blanket from General Custer's cavalry regiment, donated by an old trooper who proudly wore his doughboy uniform to the cavalry reunion.

Dr. Heather Ruland-Staines, Senior Editor of History and Military Studies at Praeger Press, suggested this project and allowed me to miss deadline after deadline to continue the research, stretching out the writing when affairs of life intruded. When I called her to say I was taking it with me to Baghdad, she only wanted to know if I could email it to her.

To Sandy I owe everything. She hung with me through Vietnam and afterwards when things weren't much better. She traveled from post to post, to Germany, to Belgium, and waited for me to come home from the Philippines. She allowed me to go to the battlefield in Iraq and promised to back me up to ensure this project was completed. She allowed me to lose myself in the stories and challenged me to tell them better. She tweaked my words, criticized my punctuation, and pointed out my errors. I love her for that, and for much more. All the while, she lived with seeing a daughter go to Iraq, then a son, and now a husband. And in her spare time she completed her Masters in Creative Writing. Sandy gave the story life and made me a better man.

Many veterans and their families exposed heartwarming, sometimes heart-breaking, personal stories. Sometimes they told them willingly and sometimes held something back; I understand completely. Their stories were in their written words, books, diaries, journals, and letters, or captured in their photographs. Without them there would be no book; there would be no country. Thank you for your service and welcome home!

Introduction

World War II, Korean War, Vietnam War, and Iraq War vets marched together past the Marietta town square on the Fourth of July, but they left no lasting footprints on the pavement when they were gone. Only a few yards away, Rebels had pursued Yankees north toward Chattanooga in the Great Locomotive Chase 140 years before. Only *The General* remains now; footprints of Rebel and Yankee soldiers washed away long ago and only their spirits remained. On this day a stranger stepped from the crowd, grabbed a wrinkled hand, and whispered, "Thank you!" Their wars were over but they carried tradition with them. They followed a familiar route, a timeless road that stretches from Lexington through New Orleans to Manassas, from Berlin and Manila to Seoul, on to Saigon, Kabul, Baghdad, . . . and back to this place, home.

They answered the bugle's call, left hearth and home behind, and when their duty was done they came home. This book is a tribute to their sacrifices, dreams, expectations, disappointments, and achievements. And it is for those who waited for them, lived with them afterwards, and for those whose veterans never came home. Some were hurt by their experiences, others made stronger. All they did was keep us free.

Turning civilians into soldiers has been tested, refined, and proven to work; changing them back is more complicated. In 1918, they called it "five years of fighting and ninety-five years of winding up the wire." Tracing the long line of veterans is a glimpse into history, a taste of sociology, a touch of psychology, but consists mostly of legends of human strengths and frailties. Their stories are in the broad generalities and individual portraits of real people searching for the way home. Homecoming is not a Norman Rockwell cover on *The Saturday Evening Post*; it is a real test of human endurance, an illusive quest, containing both troubles and joy.

There is no average soldier and there is no common veteran. The members of one community, or one military outfit, are all different people with different experiences, different homes, different hopes, and different outcomes. But those who speak for us all in these pages do so eloquently. They are the veterans of America's wars.

1

Born of Revolution

A scrappy band of patriots risked everything in 1775 when they pointed muskets at British troops and fired. They staked their lives, fortunes, and honor on freedom for themselves, their families, and their wavering neighbors. They took a bold stand with only the slimmest chances of success. After the smoke cleared from that first battle, some lay dead, others fought on—but many doubted their wisdom. But those who fought on, those few brave patriots saw a better way of life and were unafraid to seize it. They marched to the call of freedom but the shadows of war followed them home, and that is the basis for this account. *Homeward Bound* is the continuing chronicle of American veterans coming home, what they face, what they bring with them, and how they are received.

IN THE BEGINNING

The colonies had veterans long before the first shots at Lexington, before the United States was a country. Traditions from early colonial history became enduring values for the Continental Army and part of American culture. Early pioneers who crossed the Atlantic, searching for a better life, found conditions in the colonies difficult. The first settlements in Virginia barely survived the harsh winters, starvation, disease, and hostile natives. But there was no turning back; they clung to life as other colonies were added along the eastern seaboard after 1607.

Early settlers sought to coexist peacefully with the numerous Indian tribes but skirmishes between them were common. Settlers stayed ever vigilant for Indian attacks, carrying muskets and knives to defend themselves and their homes while clearing fields to raise crops, but some were wounded defending their families or their neighbors. In 1686, Plymouth County in the Virginia Colony decided to support anyone disabled fighting the Pequot. That practice was adopted by other colonies and became the beginning of veterans programs in the colonies.

The Hills and the Early Indian Wars

Peter Hill was a planter and assemblyman in York County, Maine, settling with his family near the Saco River in 1648. Hill was dissatisfied with Maine's government and encouraged County York to secede from the Maine Colony and merge with Massachusetts. His efforts failed, but he continued to shape his world into one more to his liking, better still for his heirs.

Peter's third son, Samuel, commanded a packet hauling supplies from Boston to forts further east during the early Indian wars. Samuel was promoted to captain but the French and Indians captured him in 1701 and imprisoned him in Canada for several years. In 1704 the French sent him to Boston to arrange an exchange of prisoners. He never forgot those experiences and in a letter home in January 1706, he warned his brother John to be mindful of "the enemy lurking in the woods."

Brother John had been mustered to fight in King William's 10-year Indian war in 1689. Indians raided a settlement at Salmon Falls and many of the settlers were killed or captured. Most of Hill's family moved to safety, leaving John to defend Fort Saco. His mother stayed with him until his father implored him to hire a boat and bring her out by river because land travel was not safe. Peter Hill cautioned his son to be very careful for his mother, because they lived in dangerous times.

In 1692, Indians attacked a fort at York and John barely escaped an ambush. He rallied the men and women of the garrison to defend it, men firing muskets and women passing ammunition and reloading. After his strong leadership, he was promoted to captain and married Mary Frost in 1694. But tragedy struck in 1696 when his father died; the next year Indians killed his father-in-law. The times were indeed dangerous.

The early Indian wars were mostly undeclared and disconnected conflicts that extended from the earliest settlements until well into the late 1800s. The early wars involved alliances of Indians, British, Spanish, French, and colonials pitted against one another; later Mexicans and Indians opposed American western expansion. Fortunately for some of the wounded Indian fighters, their colonies or communities elected to provide some lasting support, but mostly they were on their own to survive as best they could.[1]

Seeds of Rebellion

England clutched the colonies tightly as part of a global empire to fill the king's coffers, but profits were too small in colonies barely subsisting. Instead of providing riches, supporting a remote government overseas and protecting it from Indian raiders, French encroachers, and Spanish conquistadors, drained the treasury. Colonists became increasingly intolerant of hard-edged governors and higher taxes, but the king wasn't prepared to give up his troublesome subjects.

Local militia units, consisting of intensely parochial home guards, wanted no part of British territorial conflicts with the French and the Spanish. When the

French and Indians defeated Lieutenant Colonel George Washington's Colonial Regiment at Fort Necessity in 1754, the king realized he could not rely only on local troops. He sent a professional from London to take charge.

General Loudon sailed for the colonies in 1756 to lead 14,000 soldiers against French incursions from Canada. He expected to enlist at least 9,000 of them from the colonies and bring the others from England. But in the first year he managed to sign only 1,200 colonials; after 2 years recruiting he was still shorthanded, so he called for 11,000 British soldiers from England to make up the difference.

England and France signed the Treaty of Paris in 1763, leaving fifteen British regiments in the colonies, 10,000 troops stretched all the way from Canada to Florida. Maintaining the overseas contingent was expensive, so the king decided to pay for it with new taxes on the colonies, infuriating hard-pressed settlers. Taxes, arrogant governors, and British troops to back them up became intolerable. The Sons of Liberty demonstrated their opposition by dumping tea into Boston Harbor. By 1775 both sides had become intransigent; there was no backing down.

First Blood

British General Thomas Gage recognized the situation for what it was and decided to regain control by destroying the rebels' military stockpiles in Concord. He ordered sixteen companies of grenadiers and infantry from Boston to quell what he considered a minor dispute. British Lieutenant Colonel Francis Smith commanded his red coats to move during the cover of night to surprise the colonists early next morning, but partisans saw them and sent Paul Revere to Lexington on horseback to warn the colonists. He arrived at midnight to wake the town.

The colonials had only a militia of armed citizens to oppose Smith's regulars. One militia company planned to stop them from reaching their supplies by holding Concord Bridge. Militia Captain John Parker mustered 130 of his men and stood by at Lexington Commons for the first showdown, but he sent a messenger to Boston for reinforcements. Parker also sent scouts to find and report on the progress of the British troops. When the scouts did not return, he reasoned the British were still far away and dismissed his men, subject to recall.

They wandered home to sleep or hung out at the local tavern to await the next move. But the scouts had not returned because the British infantry had captured them all except Thaddeus Brown. Brown hid until he was able to run to Lexington with the shocking news: the British were only one-half mile away.

Dawn was breaking when Parker hastily summoned his minutemen but only half had returned when the red-jackets appeared. Parker saw he was outnumbered by five to one, so he prudently ordered a retreat. As they withdrew a single shot was fired. Scattered musket fire answered from both sides until the British mounted a heavy volley followed by a bayonet charge. The colonials fled, leaving behind eight dead and ten wounded. First blood was spilled.

Smith pressed his men hard to Concord but bands of gathering minutemen sniped at them along the way. British troops returned fire as best they could. Smith eventually reached Concord; his men quickly destroyed most of the weapons and ammunition and began a hasty withdrawal to the safety of Boston. By then, reports of fighting spread between communities. The minutemen formed small bands and ambushed the British, forcing them through a bloody gauntlet all the way back. Smith reported to General Gage: "On our leaving Concord to return to Boston, they began to fire on us from behind the walls, ditches, trees, etc., which as we marched increased to a very great degree. . . . "[2]

General Gage reviewed the results and was stunned. He had lost 250 regulars—killed, wounded, or missing—at the hands of the unruly minutemen; they had lost half as many. From the tiny villages of Lexington and Concord, the first sound of war rattled through Boston and was heard clearly in London.

The poorly organized militia knew what they had done meant war, one impossible for them to win. Colonial patriots were long on courage but seriously short on manpower, and even they were untrained, disorganized, and ill equipped. They lacked arms and supplies and were unprepared to face a real army in the field. Both colonists and loyalists doubted the wisdom of a war for independence at all, much less under such circumstances. Only a third of the colonists favored war, a third opposed it, and the others were undecided. But the will, courage, and determination of a few prevailed over the weak and wavering.

They had started an unwinnable war and faced dreadful consequences if they lost. Before the fighting ended, it spread from Boston—north to Quebec and south all the way to Georgia. Every major city was occupied, every seaport was raided, and most frontier outposts were hit by Indian war parties. The war was too long, too bitter, and too cold; but losing was not an option.

FORMING A MILITARY

The Continental Congress authorized an army on June 14, 1775, to save their necks from the king's gallows. Local militias had started the shooting and remained under state governors, but operational control of all forces was handed to a single commander to unify their efforts. George Washington was made a general to command the new army and the militias. The Continental Army, which existed only on paper, was asked to defeat a traditional British professional army and navy. Congress promised pensions to any soldier disabled in the war to encourage enlistments, drawing on the traditions of a former colony, the Commonwealth of Virginia. But well-meant promises proved difficult to keep.

The new country also needed a navy. Congress had no funds to purchase ships, so instead commissioned private citizens to sponsor their own ships and crews and become U.S. ships and navy captains. The private fleet needed able men but the sparsely populated states, already strapped with quotas for the army, were unable to raise crews. So Congress allowed the private ship-owners, privateers, to keep captured bounties for compensation; over a thousand privateers sailed under those terms. A Corps of Marines was established on November 10, 1775, to fight as infantry at sea. But the formation of a private fleet complicated determining a date of origin for the navy. October 13, 1775, was later established.

The amalgamated navy fought surprisingly well, capturing or sinking over 600 English vessels. John Paul Jones, a Scotsman and private sailor in the colonies when war broke out, became a privateer. Jones encountered the British HMS *Serapis* while at sea on the *Bonhomme Richard*. The British captain called for Jones to surrender, but he replied, "I have not yet begun to fight!" He lashed the *Richard* alongside *Serapis* and his crew scrambled over the side to fight the British hand to hand. His audacity inspired a new country also just beginning to fight.

The war stretched through five bitter winters, and when Cornwallis eventually surrendered at Yorktown in October 1781, fighting did not end. The British still held five major posts within the United States, and Spain controlled vast regions in Florida. European powers encouraged the Indians to continue attacking isolated American outposts. The victory at Yorktown was highly significant, but the results were tenuous.

Many citizens and some politicians still opposed an organized military and a strong central government even after the victory at Yorktown. The minutemen had started a fight they could never finish but the Continental Army, shored by Washington's strength and leadership, won the war and the nation's independence. Despite such incredible success, a standing army was still not popular with independence-minded people. The citizen militia had always been a facet of colonial life, preserving order and protecting against threats while living as neighbors. Militiamen were prominent citizens and admired for serving; Continental Army soldiers often came from other states and were as foreign as the British who had previously occupied their homes. Washington understood the Continental regulars represented the only chance for victory; the militia, though essential, lacked their training and discipline to follow through. The colonists had long opposed King George's army, but now they had one of their own to feed, clothe, billet, and pay.

Nathaniel Holms

When war began, the community of Petersbourg, New Hampshire, went with the rebels and selected Nathaniel Holms as their representative soldier. Holms joined the local militia but returned home as soon as his obligation ended, satisfied he had done quite enough. Although the war was going badly, he was anxious to resume a normal civilian life. But the new Continental Army needed regulars. So Congress levied the states with quotas distributed to communities. When army recruiters demanded conscripts, Holms' friends and relatives encouraged him to go for the sake of the community. He had no family of his own to support and was already trained to fight, but he knew well the dangers and the hardships and worried about his financial future. Soldiers' wages were notoriously low, if paid at all. He could earn more at home, buy some land, start a family, and follow his dreams.

His sister pleaded with him; if he didn't go, her husband would have to. Still he resisted; his clothes were tattered from militia duty, shoes worn through from long marches, and he just didn't want to go again. His brother-in-law offered to make up the difference between army wages and civilian pay and his sister sheared four lambs and dyed the wool, spun it into thread, and made cloth for a new uniform. Then she sent her husband into town to purchase new shoes.

Nathaniel Holms marched reluctantly back to the front, leaving his dream behind. He went for the sake of his sister, his community, for family and friends, not for the abstract concept of national independence. He fought for his regiment, his honor, and the companions marching by his side.[3]

Revolutionary Women

While the men were away, women shouldered the heavy work of plowing, blacksmithing, tanning, making soap or candles, hunting, plowing, harvesting, and repairing leaky roofs. After the war, most of them willingly returned to the equally hard, traditional work of running a household. Through it all, they clung to the vague hope that their sacrifices would amount to something some day.

American women served as a volunteer quartermaster corps for the Continental Army. Some went straight to the front to nurse the sick and wounded; others made uniforms, raised funds, and melted pewter into musket balls. Some wives followed their husbands into battle, reloading their muskets, hauling water, or cooking. Some even buried their husbands or sons where they fell, marking their graves with loose stones and sticks before going home alone to pick up the pieces of their lives.

A few women fought alongside the men, like Molly Pitcher at the Battle of Monmouth. Those who stayed home alone were without much protection and sometimes were abused by English troops occupying their farms or homes; they learned to shoot to protect themselves and their property. But despite their contributions to victory, the Revolution did little to improve their lives.

ENDING THE BEGINNING

Resisting tyranny began long before that fateful spring of 1775, but the defiant stand at Lexington marked the end of wavering; war was certain after that. The militia that shot first needed the Continental Army to finish it. The Continentals were poorly equipped and trained throughout the war and were narrowly victorious, but they were persistent and very fortunate against a far superior military. They came out bloodied, bruised, and starved, but they stood shoulder to shoulder at Yorktown in tattered uniforms and watched Lord Cornwallis surrender his shining sword. The band played *The World Turned Upside Down*, and in that historic moment the world was indeed transformed.

Victory did not show in their faces as joy but as grim reality. Nearly eight hard years had been required to reach that momentous day, but the nation they created was on the brink of economic collapse. The trials ahead of the bone-weary veterans would prove as difficult as those passed. Independence brought only the opportunity to face new adversities alone. Life, liberty, and happiness were still to be pursued—dreams not yet realized.

In that hot summer of 1783, weary veterans dissembled and drifted away from an army that needed them no more, could afford to pay them no longer, nor could feed them. No parades distinguished their going out and no celebrations awaited them at home. After forging a nation with bayonets and muskets, they trekked homeward alone to reassemble the pieces of their disrupted lives. They started back with only their muskets, the shirts on their backs, and the useless promissory notes in their pockets. Determination had sustained them through the worst of it and was all they had left. They knew about war, but faced uncertainty in peace.

They wore ragged, torn uniforms as they straggled away and carried the same hunger that had gnawed their guts through bitter winters. They were poorer than before, but when they reached home their hopes for a brighter future were sobered by reality. The new nation staggered under heavy debts to pay for the long war; the treasury was empty and payments were due. The nation's founders debated how to assemble a viable government.

Demobilization was an inglorious end for those who served. Some left penniless but others stayed on, waiting for pay or the next meal. But Congress could not meet the payroll. So even they were sent away with only their muskets, tattered clothes, and 4 months' pay in promissory notes that matured in 6 months. Few could wait that long to eat, so they sold the script to speculators for a fraction of the value. Men in the Pennsylvania Line revolted and officers mutinied at Newburgh; dispirited soldiers heightened fears of keeping a standing army. The army and navy were reduced precipitously just when a viable defense was needed most to protect the vulnerable new country.

Veterans returned to the results of years of neglect: crops strangled by weeds, farm buildings and property in disrepair, pewter shops emptied for musket shot. If they were fortunate, a neighbor offered a meal and they accepted knowing their next one might be long in coming. When the sun rose they rolled up their sleeves and went to work, or into town looking for work. Surviving the postwar economy meant scratching out a living one day at a time, lofty ideals supplanted by bare necessities.

The Constitution was not yet ratified and the government had nothing to offer them, but nothing was expected. Employment and subsistence were the responsibilities of individuals, not for government concern. Individual rights carried independent responsibilities, so public concerns for those who marched to war and limped home afterwards were muted.

After the dust settles, historians write about sweeping movements of armies, maneuvers of corps, artillery, and reserves, dates, victories, defeats, all the drama of battles and their political consequences. But those on the ground with muskets never know the full context until later; common soldiers are reluctant to pick up a quill to write about crawling in mud with shots cracking overhead, of their anguish, fears, or dashed hopes. Historians tell us why nations go to war, but why men fight, what they expect, their hopes for the future, or how they endure the pain is another matter. Those answers must come from carefully listening to their words, reading their letters, journals, and memoirs, from knowing them before and after. Their real stories are found between the lines and in their hearts; perhaps there is some indication in their eyes.

Joseph Martin

Joseph Plumb Martin was one revolutionist who shared his life as a soldier and veteran. When the first shot was fired at Lexington, Martin was enjoying his carefree youth, reluctant to leave it. But innate exuberance for adventure drove the 15-year-old to join the Connecticut militia on July 6, 1776. During a 6-month enlistment, he saw action at Brooklyn, Harlem, and White Plains, New York. His spirit of adventure satiated, his duty tour ended none too soon. He missed his fanciful youth and was anxious to recapture it.

Martin pocketed the 4 shillings travel money and walked 52 miles home to Prospect, New York, where his paternal grandparents waited for him with arms opened wide. He passed the winter with them but in April, when the weather improved, he grew restless and realized he actually missed the action. Continental Army recruiters came to Prospect with cash incentives, so he reenlisted. He was offered a choice of a regular 3-year enlistment or serve for the duration. He thought the war was almost over, so he signed on for the duration. He was wrong. Martin fought with the army from 1777 to 1783, becoming a noncommissioned officer before he was finally discharged.[4]

Joseph Martin was among the weary soldiers trudging home in the summer of 1783, returning to weedy fields and insatiable creditors. The soldiers had no jobs, many had no shoes or shirts and no money; the paper script was nearly worthless. The blessings of a hard-won liberty were elusive. Those who followed the fife and drum into battle, returned home to find their land confiscated by their own local governments for debts unpaid. The nearly useless script was not enough to offset back taxes and debts. Instead of the freedom they won, they had debtors' prison.

Cincinnatus

George Washington led the Continental Army to victory and was elected first president of the United States under the ratified Constitution; he took office on

April 30, 1789. One of his first responsibilities was to settle the $42 million war debt to foreign and domestic creditors. Debts owed to the veterans who saved the nation would have to wait. The injustice of it even touched Washington; he asked for no pay as commander but requested reimbursement for over 8,000 pounds of out-of-pocket expenses. Washington was shorted more than 10 percent. Baron von Steuben, Thomas Paine, and the widow of Alexander Hamilton faired no better— all victims of budget shortfalls. They were in good company with the common soldiers.

Henry Knox, chief of artillery during the war and one of Washington's top military advisors, was appointed the first Secretary of War. Knox received a ribbon for his service, but he wanted other officers to have more than a symbol. He wanted an organization to recognize them, to preserve the strong bonds forged by the war. As a group they could assist needy and deserving comrades without relying on civilians or the government for support. Knox drew up a constitution for the Society of Cincinnati and presented it to other officers at von Steuben's headquarters on May 13, 1783. They designed a badge to recognize members of America's first veterans' organization.

But the society was stunned by vitriolic opposition to their group, especially by the strong words from many of the nation's founders, who deemed their organization a relic of the European caste system they had rebelled against. They were suspicious of officers as a noble class. The society intended only to honor and help officers who served, but restrictions on membership made it appear elitist, and advocating pensions seemed self-serving. George Washington intervened, changed the terms of the organization, and preserved it for a time.

Luke Day and Daniel Shays

Private creditors demanded hard cash for debts and would not accept the promissory notes paid to discharged soldiers. In Massachusetts, debtors were regularly hauled into court, where they risked losing all their property; if they had no property, they faced prison.

Luke Day had been a valiant captain in the army but after the war was trapped between creditors and the courts. Day only knew to fight back and led a march on debtors' court to shut it down. As long as the doors were closed no property could be taken; no one could be thrown in jail until appeals could be heard. Day's stance in Massachusetts spawned others in Vermont and Connecticut. The tactics worked for a while, but within 2 years most appeals were denied and the courts resumed confiscating their property or their freedom.

Daniel Shays was another local hero, wounded and decorated for valor at Bunker Hill and Stony Point. Lafayette himself presented Shays a ceremonial sword, but Shays valued more the old sword he carried in battle, so he sold Lafayette's for cash to pay off some of his debts. Shays was fiercely independent and refused to join the Society of Cincinnati though they might have helped him. He didn't want help; he wanted only independence, and he wanted justice.

Massachusetts Governor Bowdoin was increasingly disturbed by the obstinacy of veterans like Shays and Day, and requested Secretary Knox resolve the annoying veteran problem. Knox requested $500,000 from Congress to pay a thousand special troops for the mission, but the nation was still broke; Congress refused the funds.

Bowdoin turned in desperation to General Benjamin Lincoln to raise private money for a mercenary army of college students, willing veterans, and former slaves. Lincoln agreed to do it. When Shay's little army marched to Springfield Arsenal for arms and ammunition, Lincoln's troops blocked their way. Shay's rebellion ended without a single shot being fired in anger, but three of his followers were killed by preemptive artillery fire from Lincoln's guns.

Daniel Shays, Luke Day, and others had nowhere to turn. They were trapped between an ailing national economy and their own personal poverty, both created by the war that brought independence. Those poor veterans had fought to rid the country of one tyranny only to find it replaced by another.

LOOKING BACK

Through blistering days and freezing nights, on forced marches or around campfires, on lonely picket lines or seasick on rolling seas, the patriots imagined a better future. The harsher the conditions, the more vivid were their hopes and dreams. They tabulated their limited assets and planned to increase them through opportunity and hard work. Their meager possessions were usually limited to a plow, a mule, and a hard life with a strong woman. They did not want taxes, large armies, or government interference. The Revolution had been for freedom but their campfire dreams seemed little more than smoky fantasies during the postwar depression.

By mid-August, 1783, the army was reduced to only 700-strong, the last navy ship sold off by 1785. Disbanding units broke up friendships forged of adversity, leaving the strong disoriented. Joseph Martin recalled leaving his friends: ". . . my anticipation of the happiness I should experience upon such a day as this was not realized . . . there was as much sorrow as joy. . . . In short, the soldiers . . . were a band of brothers. . . ."[5]

Martin said farewell to his friends and turned toward home, determined to make a go of it. No happiness awaited his arrival. His grandparents had died during the long war and the community turned its back. Martin spent his life trying to recapture his lost youth and the dreams that sustained him through Valley Forge. He longed for a share of what he had earned although his friends opposed pensions for veterans while complaining about the destitute men in the streets. Veterans with empty pockets found few chances to earn a decent living. Yet merchants who avoided service had become wealthy. Even some who dodged serving, deserted, or even fought for the British lived quite well. Scoundrels were generally better off financially and were more socially acceptable than the veterans who won the war. But the ones who stayed warm, dry, and well fed during the winter of Valley Forge were the first to complain.

Kirtland Griffin

Kirtland Griffin had been an infantryman at Ticonderoga before becoming a privateer in the navy; as such, he was taken prisoner by a British man-of-war and confined at Mill Prison in England for over 2 years. Benjamin Franklin, then Ambassador to France, negotiated an exchange of British and French prisoners in 1779, including Griffin. When Griffin was released, he was taken to France, but getting back home from there without fare for passage was his problem to solve. He found John Paul Jones in port and signed onto his crew for his return voyage. That was how Griffin happened to be with John Paul Jones' on the *Richard* during his famous sea battle.

During the voyage home, Jones spied the *Serapis* and the battle ensued. Griffin and his mates scrambled over the enemy ship's bulkhead and he faced an enemy sailor swinging a blade. He blocked a deathblow with his own sword just as a shipmate thrust a bayonet into the enemy.

Griffin continued his journey home after the battle, but in Boston he was charged $70 for breakfast because his script had depreciated so much. When he reached home to Guilford, Connecticut, he met and married Rosanna Parmele and settled down for a long domestic life. The year was 1781, and the British had not yet given up the fight. One Sunday as Griffin sat in church with his new bride, a courier interrupted the service with news that the British were landing nearby. The sermon ended abruptly as men rushed out to repulse the landing.

Griffin looked for a ride and spotted a local Tory mounting his horse to hurry home. Griffin asked politely to borrow the horse, but the Tory refused. With encouragement from a lady of the choir, he grabbed the Tory's foot and toppled him from his saddle. Griffin jumped on the horse and galloped to meet the British at the shoreline. The converging congregation convinced the British to sail away to a more passive landing site.

Griffin lived in Guilford for several years before moving his growing family to Paris, New York. They were among the first settlers to build the town from an untamed wilderness. There he rediscovered a religious passion instilled by a pastor who had visited him regularly in Mill Prison. He become active in his church, a civil magistrate, and was highly respected in his community. He remained a revered father, a loving husband, and a loyal friend to many until his death.

Griffin's descendents kept his sword as a treasured souvenir of his exploits and displayed it for the community on his birthday each year of his life. While he was alive his family and friends gathered around him every year on his special day, March 15, the anniversary of his release from prison. That day became a local holiday as businesses closed while people gathered to listen to Griffin recount his life at Ticonderoga, in Mill Prison, and with John Paul Jones. Those close to him knew the exact moments in his stories when he would burst into tears.[6]

A PLACE FOR THEIR BONES

Discharged men headed first for home after demobilization but found their opportunities limited. Thomas Pickering, Secretary of State under John Adams, proposed solving two problems simultaneously. The United States could offer land to veterans on the western frontier as a reward while expanding the country's borders. The land would be parceled out with 1,100 acres to a major general, down to 100 acres to a private. The idea had promise. Many restless veterans followed the lure of lands out west or down south. The prospects were best in western Pennsylvania, Virginia, the Carolinas, Tennessee, Kentucky, or Georgia. When the open spaces became too congested, they moved again, stretching the boundaries further.

Joseph Plumb Martin had been well educated before the Revolution, and after the war tried teaching school in upstate New York. But he soon grew restless, bored by routine; his spirits had soared during the war years and he missed the adventure. When bounty land was offered in the Maine extremities, he started there to stake a claim, but with news of better prospects in Ohio, he angled for a better deal. Claiming the land was no easy task and soldiers of the Revolution had no one to represent them in ensuring they received a fair allocation. He gave up on the Ohio land and sold his deed to a speculator for a fraction of the value. The money was gone too soon and he regretted giving up the land; land was hope. He still wanted just "enough land to lay my bones in."[7]

Western expansion continued into the early 1800s, but the far west beckoned. William Clark and Meriwether Lewis led an expedition from St. Louis in 1803. By 1806 they had explored all the way to the northwest coast, charting overland routes and assessing the Indian situation. Lewis and Clark were awarded army rank and pay and their thirty-two volunteers and ten Indian guides were also classified as entitled veterans. After their expedition they were entrusted with 320 acres of land each. Lewis and Clark received double pay, five new uniforms, and 1,500 acres of land.

Land

Land beyond state boundaries was there for the taking. Federal, state, and territorial governments encouraged hearty men with military experience to settle in the wilderness territories to tame it. Cash was scarce but land was plentiful, and land grants became the payment of choice for veterans. Land represented opportunity and that was what they needed most. With a parcel of land, a man could grow crops, raise animals, start a family, and build fences to protect his property. Money was gone as soon as received; land was forever. It was next to life itself: a piece of earth to live out their days, a place to die in peace, a place to lay their bones. But land was slow in coming. Most waited years; some died without their family plot.

Most federal land grants were in the military territory of Ohio. A regular soldier was entitled to 100 acres, a colonel received 500. States with unclaimed land raised the ante and offered more acreage to those who stayed put. Georgia offered 200 acres to a private and 1,955 to a brigadier general; in North Carolina it was 640 and 12,000. But northeastern states like Delaware, New Jersey, New Hampshire, Rhode Island, and Vermont were already crowded and had none to spare.[8]

Seasoned veterans protected frontier settlers from Indians, and the promise of security made commercial land more attractive to civilians. Special tax incentives enticed some veterans to actually live on the land instead of selling out to speculators. Although land was a gift to deserving veterans, it came with a price: backbreaking work to carve out a farm, or build a house and barn, and to eke out a living while defending it from renegades.

Land grants frequently coincided with business interests. The Ohio Company and the Scioto Associates were developers poised to make huge profits from new communities. Such companies purchased the rights to properties adjoining land grants, then bought as much of the veterans' land as possible, amassing parcels large enough for commercial development. Those veterans who kept their land provided free protection and leadership to others just by their presence.[9]

Revolutionary War veteran William Dana tried to balance the books on his farm in Amherst, Massachusetts, and found independence was driving him into poverty. Each succeeding year he sunk deeper into debt and his Continental script was depreciating faster than the fertility of the over-worked soil. Dana made a difficult decision: he gave up farming and tried to get by as a carpenter, but that proved no more lucrative. Finally, at the age of forty-four, he decided to make a fresh start in Ohio before it was too late. There he found rich, unworked soil, planted fresh crops, plowed, and built a house where he intended to live out the remainder of his life in sparse comfort. Far from his native Massachusetts he finally found a small piece of his dream and a place to lay his bones when he died.[10]

Pensions

Back in 1778, Congress had authorized half-pay pensions for life to many of the officers of the Continental Army in a desperate attempt to hold the army together. The cost was estimated to be between $400,000 and $500,000 a year, a sum equal to all the states' contributions to the federal government. But 5 years later, Congress was shocked to learn the cost was much higher than projected and reneged even before the first payment was made. Without any authority to tax, the government had no means to pay pensions. In lieu of pensions, they issued commutation certificates worth 5 years' pay.[11]

Infirmed and destitute veterans hung about the village green in many communities until their presence became a problem for town councils. Arguments about Revolutionary War veterans raged even after the War of 1812, but pompous speeches praising their sacrifices did nothing to alleviate their plight.

The town of Peterborough, New Hampshire, agreed that Benjamin Alld was due something for his service, and that his care was an obligation for the whole community to share, but there was no precedence for how to do that. The town council convened a public auction for a services contract and Alld's personal care was awarded to the lowest bidder at the town's expense. The low bid was 96 cents a week. Benjamin Alld was rescued from the street corner and a value assigned to his sacrifice, less than a dollar a week.[12]

Veterans returning to Peterborough found a growing community—300 percent growth from 1767 to 1800. A third of the population represented the original founders and another third constituted second-generation members; the rest were newcomers. Peterborough was swept up in the same changes found everywhere. Religious pluralism replaced sectarian conformity. Minutemen defenders were seconded to a standing army, small as it was. Nationalist sentiments were beginning to take hold. The economy had transitioned from pure agrarian to industrial as farm families used their farms as collateral for textile mills and small manufacturing plants. Veterans who had served only short stints on active duty easily reintegrated into such a population and quickly reached economic and social prominence. However, Peterborough's Continental Army veterans remained in a lower status, having missed their opportunity for economic freedom.[13]

The price of war was high in lives, as well as revenue. Between 1775 and 1783, over 6,000 men had been killed in more than 1,300 land battles with over 1,000 lost in 218 naval engagements. Some 10,000 died of diseases and 8,500 prisoners died in captivity without the medical attention that might have saved them; over 8,000 returned home wounded, nearly 1,500 simply went missing. Wounded or disease-ridden veterans faced hardships earning a living. A sweat-driven economy had little to offer those who could not perform manual labor. One man found that holding 10-penny nails between his toes and driving them with a hammer in his left hand was a very painful way to support a family of five.[14]

Jeremiah Greenman

Jeremiah Greenman had not prepared himself for a trade before the Revolution. But military service presented him an opportunity to do his patriotic duty while gaining valuable skills. He served honorably, was taken prisoner three times, but through hard work and meticulous attention to detail, he climbed from private to first sergeant in his Rhode Island regiment. By the end of the war, he had been promoted to first lieutenant and served with distinction as the unit's adjutant.

Greenman was proud of his personal achievements in the army and made grand plans for his future. He had climbed the ladder of success by mastering every detail and completing each assignment with distinction. As an enlistee his only attributes were loyalty and dedication to duty, but he learned to balance accounts, write clearly, give orders and follow instructions to the letter, and he demonstrated leadership under difficult conditions. His talents presumed a bright future. When the war ended, he applied for a federal military commission but it was buried among thousands of others who were excess baggage at the prime age of twenty-five.

Greenman did not give up his hopes for a commission in the regular army, but in the short term he just needed a job. He settled in Providence, a town with great prospects in the 1780s, and used his army pay to open a small shop in partnership with an army buddy. He bought a modest house on Broad Street, married a local woman, and settled down to wait for happiness to catch up with him. But he wasn't prepared to wait that long. After a few months, he found keeping shop boring. He craved something more dramatic and made a sudden career change, commander of a commercial ship. He achieved enough success in life to satisfy most, but misplaced hopes and unfulfilled dreams still haunted him. He needed more but would have to wait for another war to know if he would find it.[15]

Veterans of Valley Forge were living icons of sacrifice and patriotic service. Their very existence represented essential concepts of duty, reciprocal obligations of citizens and country. The value ascribed to service to country and the value citizens assign their freedoms are reflected in the way veterans were considered then and now. As the United States was born of Revolution, traditions emerged there to shape our ideals of those who risked everything for our freedom.

2

British, Indians, Mexicans, and Manifest Destiny

The new United States enjoyed relative peace for 29 years between 1783 and 1812 though citizens struggled economically. Acquiring fundamentals, such as food and clothing, consumed everyone's efforts and money. While British, Indians, and Mexicans opposed the apparent destiny of the expanding United States, there were no serious threats to sovereignty and no compelling reasons to offer anything more to Revolutionary veterans.

Former European empires, stung over losing their possessions, incited Indians to attack the upstart former colonists, while the settlers negotiated with them for local treaties. Settlers and Indians used the vast uninhabited stretches between them as buffers. But as civilization spread westward across the Appalachians, the natives resisted further encroachment of tribal lands. Chief Tecumseh led the Shawnees against William Henry Harrison's troops in the Indiana Territory, inflicting heavy casualties at the Battle of Tippecanoe. Eventually Harrison's troops forced the Shawnees out and claimed the region. When Tecumseh died, Indian unity collapsed and the Shawnee, Delaware, Miami, Ojibwa, and Wyandot tribes all made peace separately.

Indians were not the only danger. European powers still held aspirations for territory and their ships obstructed commerce at sea and on major waterways. In 1798, Congress reactivated the navy and Marine Corps to protect shipping while the army was increased to over 12,000 troops. The navy engaged in an undeclared Quasi-War with France by arming over 1,000 merchant ships in addition to a 54-ship standing fleet. The Navy won most of the skirmishes for 2 years, sinking or capturing ninety-three French privateers while losing only one. But as soon as tensions eased Congress scaled back perilously to thirteen frigates with only six at sea.

THE WAR OF 1812

By the spring of 1812, the United States and England were inching toward open hostilities. Mobilizations swelled the U.S. Army to 36,000, with another 50,000 standing volunteers and a militia of 100,000. The extraordinarily long coastlines were defended from forts with gunboats cruising offshore. Twenty ships, including three 44-gun frigates and a few smaller blue water vessels, could mass to stop an invasion if they could only arrive in time, though early enough warning was doubtful. National arsenals contained only cannons and muskets, rusty remnants from the Revolution; forts were in dire need of repairs and improvement. Total military strength consisted of land and sea forces, arsenals, supplies, and forts scattered over expansive territory in isolated outposts, but there was no comprehensive and unifying national defensive concept.

The British began kidnapping merchant sailors and ships at sea, impressing them into service in their own navy. The British had never fully accepted their defeat in the Revolution, nor did they consider loss of the colonies final. The British had become too aggressive; Congress declared war again in July 1812.

Nearly two-thirds of the positions in the regular army were vacant when the war began. Troop levies were rushed to the states to bring the army up to strength quickly. Fresh recruits rushed into battle with scant training and commanders had no doctrine for employing their units. Discipline had held the Continental Army together through the Revolution, but in 1812 any semblance of order was missing. A federal peacetime logistical supply system designed for economy was not vigorous enough for the increased demands of war. Troops going to battle depended on the lowest bidding contractors for essentials.

Troops were scattered along the northern border with Canada and as far southwest as New Orleans, their ranks thinned considerably by the great distances. Campaigns were chance encounters rather than by strategic design. The army performed dismally in the early stages, chalking up more defeats than victories, but performance improved with battle experience and appointments of a new Secretary of War and new battlefield commanders. Still, it was not enough or in time to stop the invasion, occupation, and sacking of the new capital in Washington. But the U.S. army and navy, improving with hard lessons, eventually prevailed again over superior British military power. The Treaty of Ghent formally closed the War of 1812.

Although the war was officially over, fighting was not. Andrew Jackson's 3,500 men faced a frontal assault of some 6,000 British regulars at New Orleans after the treaty was signed. His men suffered only two casualties firing from behind cotton bales, to win a late, but decisive, victory. We can only speculate whether the British would have conceded had they won that battle. The triumph at New Orleans sealed the accomplishments of the Revolution and preserved the United States' integrity as a nation. An ill-equipped and ill-trained army, with their backs against the wall, had once again defeated regulars. Some who fought had been seasoned in the Revolution but they all joined the growing ranks of American veterans.

In the War of 1812, citizen volunteers again willingly marched away to take up arms, leaving families and farms behind to fight for their new country. But when the war was over and they marched home, they were again surplus and as out of place as their forebears from the Revolution. They wandered back with very little cash and hardly any possessions, but this time they held to a new hope, a future based on the vague promises of land. A parcel of land could be touched and controlled, connecting dreams with achievable opportunities. Such hopes buoyed them until they saw Revolutionary veterans still waiting for their promised land. The 1812 veterans fell to the end of the line.

They patiently waited and hoped together for a better outcome this time; the federal government was established and solvent and public attitudes towards veterans had improved. The public mood soared with the victory in 1817, improving relations with the Indians, and a reduced military naval presence on the Great Lakes. Tensions relaxed and the government had disposable money in the treasury. President Polk reported to Congress the Treasury had taken in over $24 million and had a surplus of $2.7 million. For the first time the nation had an opportunity to repay debts owed to veterans.

Hapless Heroes

Veterans of the War of 1812–1817 joined the old revolutionaries on village greens and on courthouse benches, miserable in infirmity and embarrassed by poverty. Their appearance contrasted sharply with memories of vigorous men at Yorktown and New Orleans. Heroes had been reduced to pitiful beggars waiting for a crumb. Such scenes embarrassed the entrepreneurs thriving under new commercial and agricultural opportunities paid for in blood, sweat, and tears by these old men. Images of their fathers and brothers suffering through Valley Forge did not mesh with the reality before them. The plight of the veterans was cruel and unfair, it was un-American. Sympathy for them reached politicians attuned to public sentiments; speeches about the shame of hapless heroes raised a national sense of guilt. The price of freedom included an obligation to take care of those who served. Politicians, citizens, active soldiers, and veterans coalesced around that one essential point.[1]

The Great Pension Debate

By 1817, the graying hair of Revolutionary veterans warned their time was nearly expired and soon it would be too late to show any support for them. They had been lauded, praised, and romanticized, but never rewarded. The financial condition of the treasury had always prevented it, but that was no longer an excuse to avoid doing the right thing. But there was a broader issue that was not settled, that of defining the national obligation to veterans. A national outpouring of sympathy for the old soldiers made the Revolutionary War Pension Act of 1818 possible, but opened a strident debate.

Many disagreed with the government's obligation to pay pensions to anyone and publicly opposed them. The arguments brought the plight of veterans from obscurity to national prominence. President James Monroe, a veteran of several campaigns in the Revolution, carried old wounds from the Battle of Trenton. His status as a war hero gave strength to his position favoring the veterans. He argued that pensions should certainly be paid to the destitute, the old, the infirmed, and the impoverished from the Revolution and the War of 1812. He took his case to the Fifteenth Congress in December 1817, and it was warmly received there and in the media. But others, such as Senator William Smith of Virginia, disagreed with all government support to any group of citizens and argued a military pension system was a curse on the nation, a debt on the backs of their children.

The debate over the veteran problem heated up but pensions were considered by most as the first payment for debts paid in blood. After all, the country might be at risk again and need to call for people to sacrifice once more. Some believed government was responsible to care for all the needy, some only for needy veterans—others were opposed to any government role in social welfare. All opinions represented constitutional theories but fiscal constraints were real; the cost of any payments had to be first calculated then measured against the solvency of the country. Government and the public weighed the precarious balance between sacrifice and self-interest, between each one's duties to the other. Two centuries later President John F. Kennedy still admonished, "Ask not what your country can do for you; ask what you can do for your country."

Debates swung between idealism and pragmatism in the House of Representatives, pulled members between sympathy and duty, by prohibitive cost and obligation, and the risk of setting a lasting precedence. A pension plan was passed only after members were convinced it was affordable, not based on settled principle. It was commonly believed that few of the 1812 veterans would actually apply for the pensions and most of the Revolutionary veterans were dead or would soon be. Congress figured an allowance of $20 a month for officers and $8 a month for enlisted men would amount to only $500,000. That was affordable.

Legislators appointed five former officers as a panel to prepare the pension legislation. The committee proposed half-pay pensions for veterans whose age or infirmary rendered them unable to provide for themselves. Those applying were required to demonstrate proof of their honorable service and their disability. The measure passed and veterans from the Revolution more than 30 years before were finally slated for compensation. In the March of 1818, Monroe signed the pension bill into law, under the jurisdiction of the Secretary of War. Monroe had won his case; pensions were considered compensation for losses due to military service but the government's role as a sustaining social organ was unresolved.

The Pension Act was a generous gesture but difficult to enact fairly. Payments were unevenly distributed with some shortchanged, others overpaid. Old criticisms quickly resurfaced over whether anyone should receive anything from the government. Even those favoring the payouts argued about who was entitled: whether a minuteman who rallied to protect his community for 1 hour should have the same entitlement as a long-term Continental Army veteran; or if the merchant seaman's sacrifice was as great as the widow of a drowned commissioned naval officer.

Wherever the line of eligibility was drawn, evidence was still a problem. Would missing limbs be acceptable proof of disability or would it be necessary to demonstrate financial need as well? Were official documents necessary as evidence, or would eyewitnesses suffice? Proof of service was required, but a fire in 1801 had destroyed many service records, making false claims possible. These, and a hundred other questions, were unanswered when the first payments were made. The very perception of fraud by a few criminals cast a long shadow of doubt over deserving veterans.

Monroe's bill had passed without the humiliating "proof of poverty" clause, but other problems arose almost immediately. The number of applications greatly surpassed those expected, raising the cost of the program; Congressional estimates had been wrong. Then a financial panic struck the nation's banks in 1819; money became tight and public generosity vanished. With the one-two punch of the slumping economy and the program costing six times as much as expected, popular sentiment swung away from veterans' programs.

Pressured by the fiscal crisis, Congress amended the Pension Act to curb rising costs and falling support. Physical evidence was made mandatory for a veteran to remain on the payroll and Congress encouraged Secretary of War John C. Calhoun to strike any veteran who could not prove his case. Seven thousand eligible veterans were dropped from pension rolls, reducing it from 19,000 to 12,000 with the strike of a pen. But costs were still fifteen times the original estimate. Original projections that pensions would be 1.5 percent of the federal budget ballooned to 16 percent. The new projection for the entire program came to $70 million—more than all other costs of the Revolution combined.[2]

Hard-pressed veterans, encouraged by the possibility for relief, were frustrated when the panic of 1819 wiped out the treasury's surplus that was to have funded the program. Put simply, there were too many eligible veterans so qualifications were redefined to reduce the numbers and make the program affordable. Men already deemed eligible were hence stricken from the list. They were outraged.

Politicians feared another Shays' Rebellion and wouldn't repeal the law completely. Instead, a means test was devised to restrict pensions to the most needy. Humiliated veterans were forced to prove their poverty before an administrative appeal board. Old veterans marched to the courts by the hundreds to prove their poverty and claim their entitlement. The sight of former war heroes pleading for aid in a court of appeal swung a compassionate public back to their side.

GREENMAN AND MARTIN

Joseph Plumb Martin was nearly destitute when he lined up to apply for his Revolutionary War pension in 1818. He itemized the cost of supporting five children, a sickly wife, two cows, six sheep, and a scrawny pig. The value of his possessions was assessed as $52, which entitled him to receive $8 a month. Martin managed on that for the rest of his 96 years until he died in 1850. The simple epitaph engraved on his tombstone: "A Soldier of the Revolution."[3]

Jeremiah Greenman, another soldier of the Revolution, had tried several professions but finally became a merchant sea captain. The high seas were more interesting than tending shop, but he still missed the military life. He had never forsaken his dream for an army commission, even as each application he submitted was rejected. Time passed and Greenman grew as jaded with sailing as he had tending store. Impulsively, he pulled up anchor and left his New England coastal roots for the Ohio wilderness. He staked his claim on the Promised Land late in life, in a final desperate grab for happiness.

Greenman was not happy with the Ohio tract he was assigned and traded for another on a rocky hill nearby. He was getting too old to farm but was determined to stick it out. He grew feeble and lonely on his rocky hillside farm—still missing the army life he loved—far from the sea and far from his roots in Providence.

Under the original Pension Act, Greenman had gone to the courthouse to testify for his original entitlement of $20 a month. He won his case then, but in 1821 he revised his holdings to include his new bounty land in Ohio. When Congress revised the rules for entitlement, he was one of those struck from the rolls as self-sufficient. He appealed and lost. He appealed again, and on his third application his pension was finally restored.

Greenman had been happiest during the war, when he advanced on the sole basis of his achievements. Demobilization of the army hit him hard and left him disoriented and without the commission he wanted. He might have been satisfied as a shopkeeper with a loving wife and house on Broad Street, or as a sea captain in the merchant marine, perhaps even as a marginally successful Ohio farmer, but he wasn't. He dreamed of his accomplishments and adventures in the war. He longed for the times when he was shot at and nearly killed, imprisoned, starved, shivered through frigid winters, even when he was unpaid for his services. Instead of living his dream, he spent his final days on the Ohio bounty farm, fighting the government for his meager pension, clinging to his dignity, and dreaming of what might have been.

The crusty old veteran died on his rocky farm and his family buried him there on the highest hill. They were never happy on the farm; as soon as they said a prayer over his grave they moved to Illinois. The lonely old veteran of the Revolution died without achieving the dreams of his service days. All he claimed at the end of his life was a small plot of ground to rest his bones.[4]

Earning a pension in the war was risky business. Pension applications revealed 220,000 had joined the Army, Navy, Marines, or militia for some time during the Revolution. The army suffered 26,000 fatalities, a ratio of one to ten. The percentage of deaths as a proportion of the population was four times higher than in WWII. Many were wounded; more fell to disease through contaminated water, poor sewage disposal, insect-born diseases, severe weather, and overcrowded living conditions. But they hadn't marched to war only for a pension, after all.[5]

FRONTIER FIGHTERS

During the quarter century following the War of 1812, the United States expanded its borders, insidiously transferring Indians to territories west of the Mississippi, but conflicts between the settlers and Indians did not end. Local Indian wars broke out when they resisted resettlement. Notable were the Black Hawk War in Illinois and Wisconsin and the Second Seminole War in Florida. The Seminoles evaded attempts to round them up but could not escape indefinitely. The Cherokees were also removed from Georgia, as were the Creeks from Alabama and Mississippi.

Like the Seminoles, the Creeks did not go peacefully; they attacked and massacred many of the settlers at Fort Mims, Alabama. But their leadership was divided over the question of war or peace. Andrew Jackson took advantage of their indecision and marched in with the Tennessee militia to put an end to the trouble. The Battle of Horseshoe Bend sealed United States' dominance in the South and ended Indian resistance in the lower Mississippi Valley.

By 1821 the army numbered only 6,000 troops, mostly holdovers from the War of 1812. But those who had stayed were not necessarily the best soldiers. Eastern cities were inhospitable to immigrants and they gravitated to the army to make a living on 1 shilling a day. The poor arrived in America with calloused hands and hope in their hearts, but found the same racial, religious, and cultural conflicts they fled. Yet, hard training drills at rugged frontier posts, even an occasional Indian attack, were better than the poverty or crime they escaped. As old veterans and new immigrants made horse-soldiering their career, they blended with Irishmen, Germans, and Poles; the frontier army was a good opportunity for them, although they were poorly housed, not well fed, earned low wages and their duties were mostly dull. It was a life of leisure mixed with high adventure.

Nomadic Indian tribes were independent and didn't unite to resist the westward expansion; tribes resisted for a while then moved away from trouble. When settlers caught up with them and staked claims further west the cycle was repeated. But continuous expansion brought more farms, cattle ranches, mines, and new towns. Bloodshed accompanied growth.

The army's mission on the frontier was policing the 827,000 square miles acquired with the Louisiana Purchase. Soldiers were often the only law and order in rowdy frontier towns, yet they were sometimes less disciplined than farmers and ranch hands. But they were the government, serving as revenue agents, road builders, explorers, or even pony express, security, and general-purpose troubleshooters.

Indian fighters were all but forgotten in the large eastern cities, and in Washington, D.C. The civilized world was in the east; taming the west was considered a western problem and a western opportunity. Fighting Indians was a risk they assumed in their quest for prosperity. The struggle with Indians had been a long one that involved settlers, miners, and ranchers as well as the soldiers. The only reward anyone expected was land to farm or ranch, a spot for a business, or a grubstake mine in the mountains. The land bonus for veterans lost value as land became generally available to homesteaders. Pensions were paid only to veterans of the Revolution and the War of 1812; militia, volunteers, and Indian fighters were excluded.

Managing Pensions

The Bureau of Pensions was reorganized in 1833 to run the program, insulating Congress, the War Department, and the administration from criticism, although the administration still defended the pension program and tried to reduce corruption. Pensions were allocated from the War Department's budget and consumed a considerable amount of it. Just over 8 percent of the defense budget in 1844 went for active service payrolls, while disability and retirement pensions consumed a whopping 36.8 percent. Only 55.1 percent was left for all other requirements, including roads, lighthouses, harbors and rivers, the Indian Department, and uniforms.[6]

Administration of pensions was moved again to the Interior Department in 1849, but payments were still too meager for many old soldiers and sailors. The navy had already begun helping underprivileged sailors and marines as early as 1811 with a home in Philadelphia. The army established the first Old Soldier's Home in 1851.

As early as 1814, the General Society of the War of 1812 began the first veterans' organization after the Society of Cincinnati, though it was not chartered until 1854. Through the 1840s and 1850s, veterans assembled mostly in the northeast, near where they lived. They met for camaraderie and used the gatherings to call for new legislation, mainly pensions. At the encampments, members remembered the war and tended graves of fallen comrades. They discussed better support for veterans, respect for their deeds, and the need to research and preserve the history of the War of 1812. As the celebrations for the centennial of the Revolution approached in 1876, public sentiments swung back to the old veterans and their causes.

TRADITION

The American tradition of honoring military veterans emerged slowly after the Revolution along with other national symbols, such as the Liberty Bell and the Declaration of Independence. The 100-year debate over obligations to veterans coalesced into a consensus as military service became intrinsic with national heritage. Veterans finally stood in a place of honor with the flag, monuments, cemeteries, and historic places.

Minutemen had grabbed their muskets and courageously started the Revolution. Their impetuous act made the Continental Army a necessity, since only a regular military could obtain and protect the new nation's freedom. Opposition to a standing military gave way as people came to realize the victory at Yorktown represented the essence of freedom. But veterans were more than symbols; they were the living spirit of liberty. Those who suffered through a desperate winter at Valley Forge became the old, tattered, and penniless veterans that personified the spirit of the nation. As they loitered on village greens, their humble presence demanded some sign of honor. The lasting bond between civilians and their soldiers sealed the national obligation, making future sacrifices possible.

Help came too late for many. The Pension Act required 40 years to evolve, well after the War of 1812. Scandals and cost overruns set off arguments about the role of government and its ability and authority to pay pensions. Washington and Madison prevailed only by appealing to the hearts of compassionate citizens and a sympathetic Congress. The law stood up against efforts to repeal it, upholding the tradition of honoring service.

The Societies of Cincinnati and the War of 1812 brought veterans together as bands of brothers in the tradition of comrades sticking together, helping one another, and giving back to communities more than they were given. When they huddled around warming fires at the front, slept with gnawing hunger, or stood alone on sentry duty, they dreamed of better times. They wanted to taste the freedom they risked their lives for, an opportunity to realize their dreams. Economic depression, scarce jobs, delayed pay, and broken promises disappointed. For some, such as Daniel Shays and Luke Day, the government even became the enemy. Fitting in was difficult for them; they were ignored, ridiculed, and their anxiety increased by starting over in new places. They often moved on, chasing the illusive dream, looking for a place to call home, a place to lay their bones.

WAR WITH MEXICO

The Mexican War came about over a border dispute and the manifest destiny of an expanding United States. Often overlooked or confused with the War for Texas Independence fought from 1835 to 1836, the Mexican War began on April 25, 1846, and ended nearly 2 years later on February 2, 1848, with the Treaty of Guadalupe Hidalgo. Three Mexican states of Texas, New Mexico, and Alta California, sat squarely in the path of America's westward migration after the War of 1812. For 30 years frontier settlers had fought their way westward against increasing Indian and Mexican resistance and were not about to stop.

Mexico and the United States had crossed bayonets over borders after Texas won independence with a devastating defeat at the Alamo and a decisive victory at San Jacinto. General Sam Houston's Texas army captured the Mexican President and General, Antonio Lopez de Santa Anna, and forced a peace treaty for Texas' independence. But the Mexican government never accepted the terms as final, and when Santa Anna returned to Mexico City he was removed from office and exiled. The Mexican Congress repudiated the deal, bringing Texas' status into dispute. The Texas Republic turned for protection to the United States and sought statehood as a last resort.

President Polk believed he could settle the business peacefully and acquire the land for $5 million by leveraging American claims against Mexico. He would forgive the debts if the Texas border was drawn along the Rio Grande River and included a swath of southern California. Polk expected Mexico to accept his offer, but he was wrong. Mexico annexed all of Texas in 1845, drawing the border along the Sabine River, then severed diplomatic relations, ending negotiations. Brigadier General Zachary Taylor galloped to the troubled border with a troop of soldiers. He reached Corpus Christi in late July and began building a force by training 4,300 new volunteers. Americans were riled by the Mexican intransigence and nearly 75,000 signed up for volunteer regiments. Thousands more enlisted as regulars, making a draft unnecessary.

Attempts to settle the border issues diplomatically failed. The United States sent a strong message by positioning a naval cordon off both Mexican coasts. Taylor dismissed Mexico's claim to Texas and positioned his troops on the Rio Grande. Everyone was in position awaiting the Mexican reply. It came quickly as two thousand Mexican cavalrymen forded the river and ambushed American dragoons, killing thirteen soldiers and wounding six. Taylor notified President Polk and Congress issued a formal declaration of war two weeks later. They authorized 50,000 volunteer troops to augment the regulars, raising the stakes.

The American Fort Texas occupied the north bank of the Rio Grande with Mexico's Matamoros on the south side. Mexicans hurled artillery at the American outpost for six days. Soon, Mexicans and Americans clashed on an open prairie near the coast at Palo Alto and the Americans drove them away at Resaca de la Palma. The first battles were fought on disputed Texas territory but Taylor quickly took the war into Mexico, the United States' first foreign excursion.

Mexicans took advantage of our immigrant-heavy army with Protestant-Catholic divides to entice deserters to cross over. They offered defectors from the army 320 acres of land in Mexico, citizenship, and equal or better rank in the Mexican Army. About two hundred Irish, Nordic, Scottish, and English immigrants deserted to fight against Taylor's troops at Monterey, Mexico City, Buena Vista, and Churubusco. The Foreign Legion, sometimes called the Saint Patrick's Brigade, fought desperately, fully aware of their fate if they lost. Fifty were eventually captured and hung at the end of the war.

Though much of the fighting was in northern Mexico, Taylor led his troops to victory at Monterey and Buena Vista. New American states of New Mexico and California were annexed and occupied peacefully but rebel insurrections continued for some time and had to be suppressed by force. Ground attacks deep into

Mexico were augmented by amphibious assaults into the heart of the country with coordinated naval and ground movements at Vera Cruz, Cerro Gordo, Churubusco, Molina del Rey, and Chapultepec. Marines seized the Halls of Montezuma and General Winfield Scott established his headquarters at the grand presidential palace in Mexico City.

The Treaty of Guadalupe Hidalgo marked a tentative end to decades of disputed border conflicts and 2 years of outright war. Establishing the border along the Rio Grande required military action to draw a line between the United States and Mexico. The new border was an uncertain bonus until gold was discovered in California and the gold rush drew more people westward. The United States had added more than 1 million square miles, doubling its size. Mexico's future was less clear and it was doubtful whether they would ever accept the Rio Grande as a legitimate border.

Taylor began with only a few regulars, but it was a splendid army despite its small size. He commanded one-third of the army's best-trained and equipped troops, and before the end of the war more than 31,000 regular troops, 58,000 voluntary militia, and 13,000 sailors joined them in theater. But the small professional force was not without problems. The army was short generals and used brevet colonels to fill in. Even Taylor was brevetted when he commanded an army of five regiments of infantry and dragoons. Regular infantry came straight from the Indian frontier. One battalion of artillery was converted to infantry and others were pulled from coastal defenses to replace the artillerymen. Units were poorly disposed for their missions making rapid adjustments necessary.

Fortunately, they were well trained and disciplined because Mexicans outnumbered them by 35,000 men. Still, the cocky Americans expected an easy victory; but it took longer and was more difficult than they had imagined. Perceptions from the front disillusioned the public, softening support and making recruiting of fresh volunteers more difficult as the war stretched out.

Congress had approved raising volunteers before the first shot was fired, guaranteeing federal benefits to wounded or disabled volunteers. Remuneration included half-pay for a private, or $3.50 a month, extended to widows and orphans if the volunteer was killed on duty.

Prior to the Mexican War the frontier army was a refuge for those unable or unwilling to earn an honest living. Most officers were well educated but enlisted men were generally from the lower social strata, 40 percent immigrants and one third illiterate. But nationalist sentiment for a foreign war made service fashionable. Enlistees went straight to the front with little training and found the quality of life difficult. Food was not good at the front and soldiers complained about it constantly. Sutler merchants sold groceries to augment the rations and those with money depended on locally purchased provisions to augment army chow. Soldiers foraged food wherever they could find it. Housing was primitive, treatment of disease rudimentary, and medical care was very fundamental, as it was everywhere in the 1840s; disease killed more of them than the Mexicans.

After the War

War with Mexico was popular at first, but it was costly; over one thousand men were killed and 3,600 wounded in twenty-six major battles. Nine thousand fell to yellow fever, malaria, measles, or dysentery while others died from diseases due to poor sanitation. Nearly 10,000 men were discharged for disability before completing their enlistment and as many deserted. The high desertion rate was attributed to a lack of commitment to federal service and unwillingness to endure the discomforts and dangers. The casualty rate for the Mexican War was high with 153 deaths for every 1,000 men, even higher than the Civil War, when ninety-eight of every 1,000 soldiers died.[7] Most of the dead were left in Mexico; 750 were buried at the U.S. National Cemetery near Mexico City, following battles in and around Mexico City. The cemetery near the city was well maintained but graves in outlying battlefields were unmarked, untended, soon forgotten and overgrown.

Recruiting posters promised property and money to those who served, and the army of 6,500 swelled to over 42,000 federals and 73,000 volunteers by May 1846. Due to the large number of volunteers, more were eligible for federal bounty land warrants. New western territories had to be occupied and defended, so the reward included 160 acres of unclaimed land anywhere in the United States, or one hundred dollars in script. Speculators swindled many veterans out of their land; those down on their luck were easily persuaded to sell unseen parcels for half value. The money was soon gone and they were left with only hangovers or venereal disease for their service.

Volunteers had enthusiastically responded to the bugle's call for adventure; most brought enough courage to see them through the tough times. When they were released, they were greeted with raucous homecoming celebrations, but for those who returned with high fevers, the parties were not enjoyable. The sick were mostly left unattended, the state of medical care rudimentary, and many died in quarantine.

The Aztec Club and Other Organizations

On October 13, 1847, a group of 149 officers convened during the occupation of Mexico City to form an officer's club for the entertainment of officers and their guests. The Aztec Club became a home away from home with entertainment, relaxation, and dining. Membership in the exclusive group was later extended to any officer with Mexican War service. Among the original members were two officers who would lead armies opposing: Robert E. Lee and Ulysses S. Grant.

On February 25, 1870, the Associated Veterans of the Mexican War was incorporated to preserve memories of the war, serve as a social outpost, and help those with needs. Membership was open to anyone who had served in the war and was honorably discharged. Alexander Kenaday, a former dragoon sergeant, founded another group, the National Association, in 1874 with a goal of federal legislation for an eight-dollar a month service pension.

Years after the Mexican War, old veterans infirmed by wounds, injuries, or illness were still burdened by their problems. In 1887, Captain William Blanding presented a bill to Congress on their behalf. It was passed and signed by the President and granted the eight dollars a month for survivors, or to their widows, after age 62. There were thought to be 7,500 known survivors and only 900 widows who were eligible. The scent of money attracted claims from over 17,000 veterans and 6,000 widows. Pressure from the National Association to increase the amount was refused by Congress. The cost was already too high, but there was a more compelling reason; many Mexican War veterans by then had served as Confederate soldiers. Jefferson Davis, President of the Confederacy, was a Mexican War veteran, as was General Lee. Davis renounced his entitlements to a federal pension, making it possible for other veterans and widows. Mexican War pensions peaked at 17,158 in 1890, but by 1916, only 513 veterans and 3,785 widows were still on the books. In 1897, the pay was increased to twelve dollars.[8]

The War with Mexico redefined the borders of U.S. territory. Despite initial public enthusiasm, the war and its veterans were quickly forgotten, overwhelmed by a bloodier and far more divisive conflict. Indian Wars and the War with Mexico shaped westward progress. Frontiersmen were hard-bitten settlers for whom every day was a fight just to survive, immigrants who struggled to make a place for themselves, whether volunteers or regulars the existence for all was tough. Like their fathers, they did not shy from a hard life; they wanted land to homestead, raise cattle, farm, build communities, mine, a place to own and defend if necessary. They fell under the same old age and disability program as veterans of the Revolutionary War and the War of 1812, and the same promise of land. Land was the best reward the country could offer since it represented opportunity. They accepted it, built on it, and used their opportunity to make the country great.

SAMUEL DOWNING

Civil War ripped through the country during Samuel Downing's life; it divided the original thirteen states he helped form into two armed camps. Reverend E.B. Hillard realized only seven Revolutionary War veterans were still living in 1864, and by visiting them he began a veteran's oral history project. Samuel Downing from Edinburg, New York, was one of those living veterans. Everyone in Edinburg knew Old Father Downing and spoke of him with respect and affection. Downing had just celebrated his one-hundredth birthday when Hillard caught up with him. The day was a hot one, but the Reverend was told Downing had just made the two and a half mile walk into town to have his boots tapped, then walked home again.

Hillard found the old man's vision failing but he was strong, hearty, enthusiastic, and his mind clear. Downing invited his visitor in and recounted his memories of the Revolution. He described how he was enticed to leave his parents' home at a very young age to work in a factory on the promise of education, clothes, and a toolbox to practice a trade. He worked there for 6 years until the war began, when he ran away and enlisted in the Second New Hampshire Regiment in July 1780 to fight for 3 years under General Matthew Arnold in the Mohawk Valley. "When peace was declared," Downing recalled, "we burnt thirteen candles in every hut, one for each state."

Back at home in the wilderness of upper New York, he carved a farm from the forests where he lived and worked it for 70 years. His homestead was close to his old battlegrounds within sight of the Catskills and the Mohawk Valley. His war pension increased from $80 a year to 180 over the years. On his one-hundredth birthday, a thousand people came to his farm to celebrate. Downing cut down a hemlock tree five feet in circumference and then a wild cherry. The trunks were sold for timber and their branches given away as canes to the attendees. Downing said he would do it all over again—cut the trees *and* fight in the war for independence.

Hillard thought about his meeting with Downing as he rode away. As he looked over the peaceful valley, he realized he had met someone who had defended it from Indians and the British, tamed an unbroken wilderness, and transformed it into one of peacefulness even as a war between the states threatened to tear the country apart. Downing died on February 19, 1867, surrounded by his family, content that he had faithfully done his duty.[9]

Joseph Plumb Martin reflected on his life in his diary: "Never will (anyone) accuse me of any failure in my duty to my country...I always fulfilled my engagements to her, however she failed in fulfilling hers with me . . . . But I forgive her and hope she will do better in the future."[10]

3

Old Dixie Down

Maurice Simons was born in Halifax, Nova Scotia, in 1824 and moved with his family at the age of ten to Santa Anna, Texas. He grew up fast and hard in the southwest. It was no surprise to his family when he and his brother Thomas were among the first to respond to Zachary Taylor's call for troops to fight the Mexican Santa Anna. But Thomas never returned to Texas; smallpox killed him when Santa Anna couldn't. Maurice caught the disease too, and nearly died; then he sustained a deadly leg wound. His unit surgeon amputated the leg to save his life, using Simons' Bowie knife for a scalpel.

Simons returned home disabled to find the name of his hometown had been changed from Santa Anna to Texana; that suited him. He was determined to settle there and make a go of it, despite loss of his leg. He qualified for a federal disability pension but stayed active in the Texana Guard, his home militia. Then he met and married the love of his life, Elizabeth Hatcher. Their first child was stillborn, but they soon had another, a daughter, named Elizabeth after his wife. It almost seemed Simons' bad luck had ended, until war erupted in again in 1861; this time it was Civil War.[1]

THE WAR OF NORTHERN AGGRESSION

Disputes over the sovereign rights of states and individuals versus strong federal control continued unabated even after the Revolution. By 1860, a tangle of constitutional, economic, and moral disagreements heated emotions north and south of the Mason–Dixon Line. States were only united loosely and contentious issues such as states' rights and slaveholding weakened the linkages more. Southern states demanded the right to decide those and other matters for themselves while northerners demanded slavery be abolished and strict federal control over states.

When Lincoln was elected, South Carolina seceded from the union, followed swiftly by six other states. Together they formed a confederation of states while the federals prepared to use military force to preserve the union at all cost. Soldiers and civilians alike had to choose sides; most aligned their loyalties with their states, their families, and their heritage.

In 1860 the United States Army numbered just over 16,000 men, scattered across the country in western frontier outposts. State militias had over three million to protect settlers from Indians and Mexicans skirmishing for local control. Aging generals clung to their command billets since there were no provisions for retirement or disability. Armies historically prepare to fight the last war better, unable to imagine how the first battle of the next one will unfold. So when civil war erupted the army was organized and prepared for frontier patrolling, not their first modern war.

Texas aligned with the Confederacy, leaving 16 percent of the federal army stationed there within enemy territory. So, when hostilities erupted at Fort Sumpter on April 12, 1861, half of federal troops in Texas were immediately made prisoners. Other federal troops outside Texas were fighting Indians from scattered outposts in the mid- and far-west states and territories. Lincoln needed the militia while the army was being reassembled, but 350,000 of them belonged to the first seven seceding rebel states. Yankees hurriedly recruited more soldiers to impose national unity on the rebels.

Maurice Simons

Maurice Simons, the aging Mexican War veteran, traveled with other volunteers from Jackson County to Houston, intending to enlist in the Confederate Army. But the recruiter rejected the one-legged infantryman. The men of his platoon refused to take the oath unless the recruiter accepted Simons, as well. Thus, Company K of the Second Texas Infantry Regiment marched to war with a legless first lieutenant leading the way. Simons subsequently fought alongside his men at Shiloh and did well enough to be promoted to brigade quartermaster with the rank of major.

Back at home in Texana, Elizabeth Simons struggled to raise their only daughter Lizzie while keeping up with her regular chores and those her husband usually handled. On the rare occasion when she was not working, she wrote in her diary about her longing for Maurice's letters and fearing hers might never reach him. She had made him promise to keep a journal as well, which he dedicated to her:

> Should the fortunes of war ever deprive me of this book, I hope the person whose hands it may fall into will forward it to my wife. Her address is Mrs. Lizzie Simons, Texana, Texas. I will try and keep this diary for her, for the satisfaction of my wife and at her request.[2]

FROM MANASSAS TO APPOMATTOX

The Confederate States, like the colonies a hundred years before, rebelled before they had an army. The southern congress immediately authorized President Jefferson Davis to activate state militias for a period of 6 months and recruit an additional 100,000 one-year volunteers. Moreover, the inauspicious Confederates were all volunteers and were expected to bring their own uniforms, horses, weapons, ammunition, and food with them.

Over a quarter of the federal officers followed their hearts and their states into the Confederacy, including 184 West Pointers, so they shared common military heritage, education, and experiences with former friends and classmates, their new enemies. The larger Federal army would attack south to restore the union while a smaller Confederate army would defend its newly declared independence. The proximity of their capitals, Washington and Richmond, guaranteed northern Virginia would become the central battleground.

General Winfield Scott ringed Washington with General Irvin McDowell's troops. Southerners were spread from the Smokey Mountains to the Atlantic coast under Generals P.G.T. Beauregard and Joseph Johnston and the center of their lines touched the northern Virginia railroad village of Manassas Junction. Beauregard selected terrain just forward of the railroad junction near Bull Run, whose creek banks offered strong positions. But the shallow stream afforded crossing points for McDowell's troops approaching from the north. Southerners adjusted their lines, but nothing went according to plan. The outcome was tenuous for both sides when the battle began and remained in doubt until southern reinforcements arrived from Richmond. The fresh troops repulsed the Yanks but not before heavy losses were sustained all around. The first battle of Bull Run marked the beginning of years of bitter fighting turning the earth red as northern and southern blood intermingled on farmlands, in streams, and on city streets.

Four years later and a few miles west of Bull Run, the war ended near Appomattox Courthouse on April 9, 1865, Palm Sunday. Generals Grant and Lee agreed to treaty terms at the home of Wilmer McLean, a man who had lived within the danger zone of the first battle at Manassas and tried to move away from the path of the war. Grant allowed southern officers to keep their side arms, personal baggage, and personally owned horses and mules, but not their pride. Confederate veterans stacked their firearms in towering piles, while Yankees watched warily, wondering if it was really over. For Billy Yank, life had just improved, but for Johnny Reb the worst lay ahead: the bitter work of reconstruction, and adjusting to a cause forever lost.

DIXIE DEFEATED

War has always thrown the economy into turmoil, but nothing compared to the devastation the Civil War brought down on Dixie. The tenacity shown by

Confederate soldiers in battle was only a foreshadowing of what was required in their fight to survive after the war. As they dropped their rifles, they gave up the cause and their hopes for the future, their dreams became nightmares. They had lost the fight and were forced into submission, a stunning blow to southern pride.

On the long walk home, despair settled in with the realization that everything was lost. Sons of the South set out in sorrow but what they discovered there was more agonizing. Instead of the cheering crowds that sent them off, streets were empty, formerly vibrant towns were burned-out shells, crops destroyed, livestock dead or missing, and the faces they met were dark and sullen. Cocky southern pride was forfeited somewhere between Manassas Junction and Appomattox courthouse. The fight for their heritage appeared to be ended, spirits dead.

Sherman had set out to crush the spirit of the Confederacy and he succeeded well enough. Few southern cities escaped unscathed, homes and farmlands were damaged or completely destroyed, family treasures looted by Yanks or marauders, and key infrastructures such as bridges, factories, and railroads were dismantled or destroyed. Once proud Divisions and Regiments were not ceremoniously deactivated, but simply dismissed. Officers told their men to just leave, to go home. No transportation was available, no pay, no citations or speeches, so they wandered off in the rags they wore. Empty warehouses, deserted plantations, and a broken economic engine warned Confederates soldiers what to expect at home.

Federal militia had been already dispatched to enforce federal laws and preserve the union, and already occupied many southern towns. Confederate veterans' social and legal status was lower then that of former-slaves. Ironically, few soldiers had owned slaves but they shared the same guilt of association by birthright. Farmers, who before had barely subsisted with slave labor, were crippled by high payroll costs for field hands. Families that had lost their able-bodied sons and heads of households to the war needed their sweat to plant and gather crops. Proud generals who had once led divisions and corps plowed their own fields while freed slaves idled away their new freedom in clap board shacks. Appointed federal authorities replaced local elected officials. Southern veterans had no real means to subsist or the legal rights of common citizens in a country they had rebelled against.

Bitter veterans grumbled about moving west or leaving the country altogether. But the census of 1890 revealed that only 7 percent actually did move away from their native states. Those who migrated tried to lose themselves in expanses of new lands, seeking fresh opportunities. Most who moved west headed for the wide-open spaces of Texas, where some of the more disgruntled became marauders or outlaws or sought revenge for perceived injustices. Finding a paying job in a wrecked hometown was most difficult for the 200,000 wounded veterans. For amputees work was impossible and no medical care or rehabilitation was available to them. For the most part, veterans were apathetic; spirits sagged and they faced starting all over without support from an unforgiving United States and their former Yankee friends.[3]

R.J. LIGHTSEY AND THE JASPER BLUES

Ada Christine Lightsey dutifully recorded her father's story as he told it to her. R.J. Lightsey had fought his way through the war and returned home one of the defeated and discouraged Confederate veterans. Many southern ladies, such as Ada, were determined to restore and preserve the lost pride of their men and their states and did it in different ways. Ada recorded and published her father's account.

Lightsey had been caught up in the exhilaration sweeping through Mississippi as his state seceded from the union. So he volunteered with his friends and neighbors to fight. The local outfit from Jasper County was Company F of the 16th Mississippi Regiment, nicknamed the "Jasper Blues." They were not as interested in the broader issues as caught up in the excitement of the grand adventure. Lightsey owned no slaves and didn't know anyone who did; slave-owners were the wealthier planters. The almighty Union meant nothing to him either but he was ready to fight with his friends for their town, their state, their way of life, and especially their right to decide for themselves what they would do. They were the defenders of southern pride and heritage and they took that personally.

A group of Lightsey's friends enlisted on May 21, 1861. Families gathered in Desoto, Mississippi, in Clarke County, to see them off. This was their departure point because Desoto stood astride the Mobile and Ohio Railroad. Children frolicked nearby and underfoot, oblivious to the heightened nervous tensions evident to adults. A potluck dinner was spread over long tables for a final meal, and the men ate heartily despite unease about the unknown that lay ahead, and the rigors of preparing for war. Volunteers and civilians shared in the excitement but understood the risk of failure. Old men checked their pocket watches; mothers and wives listened for the dreaded whistle of the train coming to take their boys away.

The unwelcome moment arrived. A conductor shouted, "All aboard!" and new soldiers climbed the steps, hanging from open windows as families on the platform stared vacantly and waved. The whistle blew again and a dark cloud of smoke belched overhead as the engine first jerked the passenger cars in the direction of Corinth, then began to roll along easily on iron tracks.

Ahead of the arriving troops, quartermasters had scrambled to find housing for them in Corinth. Accommodations were scarce, so town leaders decided to billet them in the nearly unoccupied county jail where empty beds were plentiful and a roof sheltered from frequent summer rains. The Blue's company commander took one look at the bars and refused to put his boys in the jail. His firm stance created a small crisis but army leaders and town officials looked for another place before the Blues turned around and marched back home.

The argument about what to do grew more heated until they found a nearby church and the tired men stretched out on pews to sleep. They stowed their gear under the benches and out of the way of Sunday worshipers. The Blues trained with rigorous daily drills in Corinth for 3 months. As soon as they were deemed sufficiently prepared, they would plug a gap in the Confederate line.

The Jasper Blues reached Manassas and joined Ewell's division as the first battle ended, but in time to bury the dead. Although they missed that battle they wouldn't miss much fighting during the long war. Lightsey saw action at Harper's Ferry, Mechanicsville, Cold Harbor, the second battle of Manassas, and at Sharpsburg, Fredericksburg, Chancellorsville, Seminary Ridge, and the final days at Petersburg.

Ada's father told her he prayed on Palm Sunday, thankful that he was still alive when Generals Lee and Grant shook hands at Appomattox ending the war. After the surrender, Southerners were compelled to take an oath they would not use arms against the United States again. General Lee and his officers left; lower-echelon leaders drifted away, unsure how to lead their men in what followed. The stalwart commander of the Jasper Blues' gathered his men and told them the war was over, they should go back home. His barren words depicted them as unwanted chaff from a defeated army, an army from a lost confederation with no resources. Their country had been dissolved and any expectations of fair treatment from the victorious North were null. The Mississippians had no transportation, rations, or pay; the Confederate money in their pockets was worthless. They set out with small groups of friends, in tattered clothing, and with heavy hearts. The war lost, there was nothing left but to face facts. So they trudged south and west in small groups of twos and threes.

Lightsey and three Mississippians backtracked through Virginia over routes made familiar by marches to the front. As they walked, they spoke of Jasper and their farewell feast and the train to Corinth, the jail, training, fighting, dying, all in the past; and they spoke of the future. As they walked, they steered clear of communities looted and parched by Sheridan's cavalry; there was nothing to eat there. They walked until they found a Virginia farm near Danville that had been missed. The poor farm family had barely enough for themselves but shared what they had with the poor men. The family even suggested a route to skirt the destruction to find more food. They invited the Confederate veterans to stay longer and rest more before continuing; they all declined as they were anxious to reach their Mississippi homes.

Their new route took them through a border area of North Carolina, spared by the Yankees because sympathizers inhabited the region. A kind farmer's wife offered them food anyway, but her father chided them for losing the war. Tempers flared before she stepped in and calmed them all down, insisting her father let the bloody war end there. The Mississippi boys shared the last of their army coffee with them, the first the tar heels had tasted in years. And they all slept well that night.

The veterans continued south into Georgia but found conditions there worse than in battleground Virginia. Virtually everything had been destroyed, including crops, stocks, and stores; people were hungry everywhere. Sherman's troops had ravaged anything they couldn't haul north. Civilians were destitute, Atlanta was in ashes, and the railroads leading out of the path of destruction had been cut. They had intended to catch a train going west, but since there was none they resigned themselves to trudging westward into Alabama.

In Selma, they found a single rail line running west so they climbed aboard the next train bound for Meridian, Mississippi. Their spirits rose with the easy ride for a while, but when they entered Meridian, every house but one had been burned. A greeting party of three tired old men waited at the station to meet arriving soldiers and help them on their way. One recognized Lightsey and saw he was barefoot. He had walked completely through the soles of his shoes and tossed them away. His neighbor would not allow him to go home shoeless and pulled a spare pair from his bag.

Lightsey bid farewell to his friends and rode the train to Shabuto, Mississippi, reaching the dark and deserted stationhouse at 2:30 A.M. He stepped off in borrowed shoes to walk four hours, arriving home at daybreak. We assume there was no homecoming celebration since he didn't mention one in his accounting to Ada. We do know he started over with pockets empty, exhausted from 4 years of war and the long trip home, discouraged, and with only a single pair of shoes to his name.[4]

ELIZA ANDREWS AT WASHINGTON JUNCTION

Eliza Andrews lived near Atlanta when the war ended, in the small southeast town of Washington, Georgia. She described in her wartime journal how the defeated veterans such as R.J. Lightsey, the shattered vestiges of Lee's great army, had streamed through on their way home. Eliza and other ladies cooked what they could find near the railroad junction while the discouraged veterans sheltered from the hot sun under nearby trees. They asked for nothing, expected less, and were quietly appreciative of what they were offered. Citizens of Washington felt compelled to give whatever they had left. They lived in the moment, unable to worry about the next day; the moment was all they had left.

But trouble arrived when a hungry, rowdy Texas regiment looted stores for food and supplies. Eliza was distressed by their conduct, and worried others coming later would have nothing; a seemingly endless stream of dejected men kept coming. She watched her former neighbors straggle past without speaking and that saddened her. Her friend recognized a rich man from New Orleans, a gentleman, scuffling through town without shirt, shoes, or money for food. They all stared blankly into space, oblivious to their surroundings, seemingly unaware they were at home. She noticed they were filthy and guessed they didn't want to be seen that way, clinging to their pride when all else was gone.

They mumbled as they stumbled past; Eliza overheard rumors that Yankees were on the way to occupy Washington. Confederate leaders had already heard the reports and some continued west toward Texas, or all the way to Mexico or Cuba. Eliza cried at the condition of fellow Southerners: disheveled, disbanded, disoriented, and starved, heads hanging low. She fed them as she could; it was all she could do but they said little in return, and spoke only of going home.[5]

The proud First Brigade of Kentucky Infantry was prepared to fight the Yankees at Camden, South Carolina, when word of Lee's surrender came through. The men hardly believed it at first, but capitulated and marched away from the fight toward Columbia. They boarded a train there going west to Washington junction, where Eliza Andrews waited for them with some food. They surrendered their arms on May 6, 1865, and started walking back to Kentucky, no longer a disciplined brigade, but a dwindling collection of men who peeled off as they came close to their homes. Twenty-seven years later, the "Orphan Brigade" gathered in a reunion; those still alive reminisced about the old days. Colonel W.L. Clarke reminded them in 1892:

> More than a quarter of a century has passed since we sheathed our swords and laid down our arms. . . . Lost fortunes had to be recuperated and prospects, all blasted, re-established. This was hard, indeed, but remembering our loved ones, we brought . . . the same energy of will and the same redoubtable spirit that characterized us in days of horrid war—never forgetting for a moment that the sacrifices . . . demanded this labor of love that the brave only can truly appreciate.[6]

Over 174,000 Confederate soldiers surrendered and were paroled, more than 63,000 were sent home from federal prisons. All contracts with their government were null and void since the government was no more. Officers with social standing found only menial work: harnessing horses for the occupying enemy, or toiling as clerks or mechanics for the government they had fought against. Some sold tea and molasses to their former slaves.

General Pendleton harnessed his warhorse at his South Carolina farm near Lexington to plow the long neglected soil. His clothes were so frayed and tattered his friends and fellow soldiers didn't recognize him. General Elliott waded into the waters near Fort Sumter's battery at Charleston for fish and oysters to peddle on the streets he'd defended. His wife stood loyally beside him, displaying home baked apple pies.

The University of Georgia finally reopened in Athens, but students found the library had been ransacked by Sherman's troops and buildings badly defaced by occupiers. Teachers were missing, killed, maimed, or had moved on. General Lee, the Confederacy's inspirational leader, was resigned to teaching at a college in Lexington, Virginia, a school that would later append his name to that of the father of our country—Washington and Lee University.[7]

Their prestige had been blown away with defeat, gone with the winds of war. All that mattered anymore was survival. When it seemed the situation couldn't be any worse, a crop failure in 1866 devastated the overworked land. The southern veterans had been humbled, deprived of any authority over local governments, allowed only bitterness for their losses. But the Union had to be reconstructed; the process was harshly imposed and lasted for a decade.

COPING, A SOUTHERN TRADITION

Insurrectionists were allocated no federal benefits. Crippled veterans had only families to rely on, no organizations were set up for assistance and many turned to charity. Ladies' and Confederate soldier associations helped some with innovations such as shoe exchanges, where one-legged men could swap unnecessary shoes, or receive cash for the useless one. Veterans were discouraged and slow to organize; the United Confederate Veterans (UCV) did not emerge until 1889. The UCV was a byproduct of the old South, its culture and the romanticism of southern women who nurtured the idea. The UCV was more poetic than political, holding a nostalgic aura that looked backwards to better times. The energy of members was applied to making speeches, building memorials, and planning ceremonies instead of lobbying for aid that would never come. Their efforts are still evident in lasting shrines, gravestones, and well-tended battlefields. Southern pride required coping, not begging for relief from the treacherous federal government.[8]

Years after the war, hogs and other wild animals dug up grisly reminders, rooting human bodies from shallow graves near battlefields. In Maryland and Virginia, crops ripened over decaying flesh and bones and in areas where the fighting had been heaviest, unsanitary conditions reached dangerous levels. Not until 1898 and the outbreak of war with Spain did the federal government finally accept responsibility for the proper disposal of Confederate war dead.

In the romantic southland, special observances commemorated Confederates killed in the war on Decoration Day beginning as early as 1866. But when the ladies attempted to place flowers on Confederate graves at Arlington Heights Churchyard, a contingent of U.S. Marines prevented them, declaring that honoring rebels desecrated the true Americans.

Southerners resisted the heavy-handed occupation and political reconstruction. In December 1865, in Pulaski, Tennessee, radical reconstruction prompted six veterans to organize themselves to protect the weak, innocent, and defenseless from unlawful seizures of property. The initial small group evolved into a more sinister Ku Klux Klan.

The plight of aging Confederate veterans saddened those who witnessed them, yet the veterans did not ask for or expect pity. Compassion prompted a few southern states to establish soldiers' pensions, since federal assistance went only to Yankees. Confederate States' meager pensions averaged less than $40 a year compared to the federal payments of over $160 per year. Fewer than 10 percent of Confederate veterans and widows even received that small amount. The situation for Confederate veterans was hard, but hands and hearts were toughened in a fight for honor and would persevere to rebuild Dixie.

DANVILLE BLUES AND GRAYS

The Civil War touched everyone in Dixie. The town of Danville, Virginia, sent its best and brightest to fight; some returned, some did not. Although Virginia was scarred with some of the worst battles of the war, the town of Danville was not destroyed, but was visited by devastation of lives and fortunes.

In 1869, Danville was the largest town in Pittsylvania County. It nestled in the foothills of the Blue Ridge Mountains near the Dan River, which separated Virginia from North Carolina. Tobacco roads connected farms to the town. Tobacco was the growth engine that doubled the town's population in one decade before the war. The town of 32,000 was 53 percent white, most of the rest were black slave families working in tobacco fields on small farms. The relative status between poor black and poor white families was close, as opposed to the few upper class white families.

Danville gave the Confederacy's 18th Virginia Infantry several companies of it sons. Men joined with their relatives, friends, and neighbors they had known all their lives to follow the colors of their regiment. The Blues and Grays paraded through town on the Saturday they formed up and accepted a Succession Flag sewn by young ladies from Danville's Female College. The whole town turned out to see them off—sweethearts, loving wives with bawling children, stooped parents, admiring younger brothers; hands of well-wishers reached out to touch them in parting.

They tried to stay in touch through correspondence. Letters from home were more valuable than anything but food, and soldiers dreamed of food, especially on holidays. William Dame and his companions sat around their campfire and entertained themselves by ordering fantasy meals from an imaginary waiter. Some ordered elegantly, some simply, but all requested large portions. When they slept, they dreamed of eating every morsel.

George Jones wrote his wife Sarah that the happiest hour of his life would be when he reached home again. Rebecca Martin consoled her brother, Rawley that no one appreciates home until they leave. Homesickness, anxiety, separation angst, and dreams for the future spilled out of letters between soldiers a field and loved ones at home. Jed Carter's wife was 8 months pregnant when he wrote that he dreamed they had a daughter. When he heard it was true, he was so excited he would have given up his horse to go home to see his wife and little girl.

But there wasn't always time to dream of home; Danville's infantrymen fought at Gettysburg and suffered 362 casualties in Pickett's charge of Seminary Ridge. Casualties hit the entire south hard; 61 percent of southern white men of fighting age were sent to war. While the north lost a higher number, the percentage loss in the south was much higher: 18 percent versus 8 percent. Wounds and diseases plagued survivors for the rest of their lives.

Union troops never occupied Danville until after the war. So, at the end, the town appeared to be unscathed. But the ravages of waste ran below the surface;

damaged economic, psychological, and community structures of the town, and the veterans and those who waited for them. Families that struggled to get by during the war were worse off afterward. Tobacco remained the economic mainstay but culling a living on a small tobacco farm with a healthy master and a few slaves was tough before war. Afterwards, survival seemed impossible when slaves were freed, heads of households came home injured or sick, and no one had any money but the useless Confederate scrip.

Families that formed a support base before hung together, but the means of support was gone. Once-proud and independent people turned reluctantly to outside sources for help. The Baptist Churches of Pittsylvania County increased membership as people prayed for help. Some even turned to the local wealthy landowners and bankers. The Pittsylvania Ladies' Soldiers Aid Society had furnished soldiers and needy families with clothing and underwear during the war, as well as hospital supplies, and they continued to the best of their abilities. But families also needed food and money. Some assistance eventually came from the state of Virginia, but not until years later.

The censuses of 1860 and 1870 showed the value of real estate and personal wealth for veterans' families had fallen 82 percent. Twelve percent of veterans' families lost their land altogether, this in an area physically untrampled by the war. David Watson was one who was unable to pay his debts; the judgments against him came to $50.42, more than his total net worth.

Rebuilding lives was a difficult process and physical separation during the war added to the burdens, but Danville residents were determined to reestablish family ties despite the hard-scrabble times. George and Sarah Jones married shortly before war and spent most of the war separated; he lost 2 years as a prisoner. George wanted desperately to get reacquainted with his two young children but worried he would be a stranger to them. Jedediah and Susan Caters also married just prior to the war and wrote about their dreams of the future. Jedediah worried his unseen daughter Mollie would not love him and he asked Susan in every letter to kiss her for him. Typically, letters stopped with the end of the war, leaving us to wonder if they succeeded with the turbulence and life-changing experiences.

All the former rebels lived in the shadow of defeat, in a darkness that crossed tobacco and cotton roads from Appomattox to Danville, from Atlanta to Texana. Some never left the battlefields, except in the minds of comrades who never forgot them. Younger sister Bettie Penick wrote to her brother, Rawley Martin, that the family always kept an empty seat at the table for him. Communities grieved over losses of sons, while veterans grieved for lost comrades. Rawley's best friend and brother-in-law, Syd Pennick, was recovering from his wounds at home. Rawley wrote to him about the death of their friend, Thomas Tredway. A sister wrote back that when Syd read the letter he cried again, as he often did. Rawley took the death of his friend personally because when he was wounded at Seminary Ridge, Thomas had rushed to his side. But as he got to him, he was shot, falling over him.

Rawley lay with his friend on the battlefield until he was taken away. They never met again.

Survival guilt affected many of them during and after the war; the Western State Lunatic Asylum became home for many. The case file of William White reported his episodes of the "blue devils" were increasing. Another, William Herndon, held regular conversations with the dead. Ham Chamberlayne, a Richmond lawyer, served as a captain in the Confederate artillery. After 8 months in prison, he went home penniless, prohibited from practicing the only thing he knew—the law. He tried farming for 18 months and failed at that. Unable to support himself, his mother and his brother, he broke down emotionally and was admitted to Western State. His physician declared him hopelessly tied to the lost cause. He remained in the hospital for more than a year—the darkest of his life.

Families in Danville pooled their resources to survive, to rebuild lives with emotional ties to family, friends, and neighbors. But the depression that ravaged postwar Dixie forced two-thirds of veteran families to combine households into extended family units by 1870. Although family units were the main sources of support, churches took the most desperate under wing. Some needed money for food, or to pay debts, or a business opportunity to be self-supporting. When they needed money, they turned to the most prominent person in Danville, William T. Sutherlin, the last bastion of hope.

William Sutherlin was fortunate. He owned several tobacco farms in the region and manufactured and sold tobacco products grown on them before and after the war. He was also president of Danville's bank, mayor of the town, and had been a delegate to the state's secession convention. Sutherlin had opposed secession, but once the decision was made he aspired to be a field general. Instead, he was commissioned a major and assigned as quartermaster, keeping supplies moving from Danville to the troops. His position enabled him to oversee his property and manage his assets while others were losing theirs. After the war he prospered in his business and kept a solid political standing in the community.

When you needed help in Danville, Sutherlin was the person to go to. He had money, power, and as much political influence as any former Confederate was allowed. His disadvantaged neighbors made many requests, usually through letters or by personal pleas to the person of last resort when families and churches could do no more. Sometimes he did help, but even his money and kindness couldn't save everyone.

Danville veterans took many routes to sustain themselves. John Logan had lived with his parents before war, but when they died he moved in with his employer and worked for him as a farmhand. Young, single veterans often married quickly for economic as well as emotional reasons. John Gatewood had been penniless before the war, shuttling between jobs and relatives. During the war, he became seriously ill and returned invalid, his future darker than ever. But his life changed in 1870 when he married the wealthy Ella White and became an instant landowner with valuable real estate, a generous wife, and a home to call his own.

Some, like Dr. Robert Withers, changed career directions completely. He had been seriously wounded and could not continue his practice. So he became a newspaper editor, using a pen instead of a scalpel. Some discovered profound faith in battle and chose the ministry. Others moved away; according to the 1870 census only 61 percent of Danville's veteran families stayed through Reconstruction. Those who toughed out the sick economy confronted other demons such as alcohol dependency, opiate addiction, domestic violence, and lost social status. Even those who prospered missed the antebellum society of the old South.

Southern women were instrumental in restoring lost pride to men virtually emasculated by their defeat. Women willingly submitted to male dominance at home, worked in organizations, such as the United Daughters of the Confederacy, memorialized the South, and even valorized defeat.

The Virginia General Assembly eventually helped disabled veterans, and families who had lost men, with a pension in 1888. However, it was only for the most severely disabled and war widows. Eligibility required proof of income less than $300 a year and personal property less than $1,000. The poorest drew $60 a year for loss of two limbs or eyes. Widows could apply for $30 a year provided they did not remarry or move from Virginia.

Joseph Miller had lost his leg at Gettysburg and was imprisoned until 1864 when he returned to Pittsylvania. In 1871 he accepted an artificial leg from the state and used it for 13 years. He was given $40 more in 1880 for repairs, and an additional $60 in 1884. In 1887, Miller began an annual pension of $50. The state he had fought and sacrificed his leg for showed its appreciation as well as possible with nearly empty coffers. One-fourth of Pittsylvania County boys died during the war, half wounded, diseased, or imprisoned. All suffered extraordinary financial losses. Yet the survivors were determined to rebuild their lives despite the odds against them.[9]

THE SOUTH WILL RISE AGAIN

The Revolution had been the gravest possible test of a country until the Civil War tested the union more severely. The war literally ripped the nation apart; putting the country and shattered lives back together were more than just difficult. Both the Revolution and Civil Wars were rebellions against central authority. Northerners and Southerners would never see the Civil War the same way, but history is always written from the victor's perspective. Many Southerners never accepted that version. Reestablishing the Union may have been easier had Lincoln lived, but a southerner's bullet ended those hopes in a tragic irony.

Before 1860 few people had any contact with the federal government except through the postal service, but after 1863 federalism prevailed. The War Department increased control over state militias, direct taxes were imposed on individuals for the first time, and a national banking system was established to print and control federal currency. Federalism was stamped on the south with martial law by 20,000 federal troops, many of them former slaves. Four million blacks drifted throughout the south, no longer slaves, but not full citizens either.

When union army commander Ulysses Grant was elected President, Virginia, Texas, Mississippi, and Georgia were still outside the Union and not readmitted until 1869. Freed slaves, carpetbaggers, and scalawags were allowed to vote in the South, but not Confederates veterans. The Civil War ended with the Yankees on the seat of righteousness, rebels mired in malaise.

Some never accepted Dixie's fading starlight. Edmund Ruffin claimed to have fired the first shot in anger at Fort Sumter, and finished his life near his native Charleston, South Carolina. The 67–year-old man remained as defiant after the war as on the day it began. With his home, his cause, and his country in ruins, he scribbled a note: "I here repeat . . . my unmitigated hatred to Yankee rule . . ." Then he blew his brains out.[10]

Only 6 weeks before his death, Lincoln approved the creation of the National Asylum for Disabled Volunteer Soldiers and Sailors; it was later renamed the National Home for Disabled Volunteer Soldiers, a direct antecedent to the Veterans Administration. Confederates were ineligible for national shelters, but the ladies behind the United Confederate Veterans and United Daughters of the Confederacy hyped public consciousness and raised funds for Confederate soldiers' homes in sixteen southern states. Confederate soldiers' homes became the final refuge for the sons of the fallen state; they were also living museums, military camps, artificial cities, and shrines, all dedicated to preserving the Lost Cause.[11]

Confederate soldier's homes preserved southern heritage and served notice that reconstruction would not erase tradition. Granite monuments were dedicated by blaring bands and muted crowds, picnics spread over long churchyard tables and grassy lawns, and the marble stood strong against ravages of weather and time as unblemished regimental histories, largely unrecorded except for words, names, and dates chiseled there. Confederate veterans eventually gathered for reunions with their old comrades, some even with those they battled on sacred ground.[12]

Maurice Simons, the one-legged Texas infantryman, served as brigade quartermaster through the decisive Battle of Vicksburg. When the city fell, Simons was imprisoned and not allowed to leave until 2 months after the surrender at Appomattox. He and Elizabeth were finally reunited in Texana in September 1863. His mercantile business was in worse shape than Texas' economy, so he went back into business with his brother George. He and Elizabeth had seemingly survived the worst years of their lives.

But the next year, in September 1864, their youngest son, William, came down with yellow fever and died. It was almost too much to bear. Three years later Maurice caught typhoid. Elizabeth struggled to pull him through but buried him under her tears on the banks of the Navidad River.

Elizabeth lived on Simons' Mexican War pension and his land grant from the Texas Revolution; she never remarried and never moved away from his grave. Little Lizzie and Thomas grew up, married, had children of their own, and scattered throughout the southwestern United States. Maurice and Elizabeth's life was too hard to imagine, their long awaited happiness cut short after only 3 years. The legacy of Maurice and Elizabeth lives on in their strong line, as the legacy of the last Confederate veteran lives in Dixie.[13]

4

Yankees and the Union

Jonathan was husking corn with his father when William Cory arrived with the news that rebels had fired on Fort Sumter. His father turned pale. They returned to the barn together but his father left him to unload the corn and put away the team, walking slowly to the house alone. When Jonathan finished and went inside his mother asked what was wrong. He told her what had happened. She went to her husband and after a time they came out together for dinner. "Father looked ten years older," Jonathan said, and his grandmother noticed it. When she heard Civil War had started she cried for her children still in the south, dismissing a suggestion they come to stay on the northern farm. "No, they will not do that," she cried. "There is their home. There they will stay. Oh, to think that I should have lived to see the day when Brother should rise against Brother!"[1]

BILLY YANK COMES HOME

Brother against brother, cousin against cousin; the war dragged on until that Palm Sunday at Appomattox when General Lee surrendered to his cohort from the Mexican War, General Grant. As Confederates began the long journey through reconstruction, Federal troops quickly basked in the victory as they marched home to a very different reception from their rebellious and defeated southern brothers. Northern homes, businesses, and infrastructures were spared the devastation of a war fought mostly on southern soil, spared occupation and punitive reconstruction. Their honor was intact. While they were away, some were concerned about reports of ambivalent civilian attitudes at home and a lack of compassion for their sacrifices. But in the end they were happy it was over, happy to be going home, looking for the idealist visions they detailed in dairies and letters. Some would find a semblance of it, others not.

William Hodgkins first stopped to clean up before going to find his beloved Gussie. "I walked up Salem Street and there sitting in her window was my Darling, reading. She looked up just in time to see me. In another moment I was folded where poets love to sing of and this meeting and occupation paid me for many anxious waiting days." After their passionate personal reunion, they took a streetcar to Winter Hill to surprise the old folks of the family. "This coming home to stay is the best part of a soldier's life I think."[2]

John Williams of Fair Haven was single, twenty-two, a slate-maker by trade, and a Welsh immigrant. He had boarded with a co-worker until he enlisted in the Union Army in August 1862. After 11 months service he was discharged and returned home where young women waited giddily for the men to return. Williams celebrated for 6 days before returning to his old job in the slate quarry. It was as if he had never left. Similarly, Isaac Watts enlisted in Peacham, Vermont, and served for 2 years. Like John Williams, he folded easily back into his old routine. Knowing their communities were untouched by the war made coming home smoother for them. Watts wrote, "Everything is the same." It was as if he had been gone only 2 weeks, not 2 years.[3]

Hodgkins, Watts, and Williams were lucky; not everyone found getting back so easy. Katherine Wormeley was a nurse who accepted the wounded soldiers she treated in a Virginia hospital as a heavy personal burden that she found hard to release later. But while she was away, she tried to isolate their misery from her memories of home. She wrote in a letter to her mother. "I think of you . . . on Sundays, with the sound of church-bells in your ears, with a strange, distant feeling."[4] Letters between soldiers and their families carried such memories, dreams, and hopes, with feeling. They also worried about one another's safety, jobs, finances, coping with separation, and how it would be afterwards, and about how much everything had changed.

Many never found out what had changed because they didn't make it to the end of the war; battle casualties were high. At Shiloh alone, the Union Army lost over 20 percent of its men, 13,000 of 63,000 fell in battle. At Sharpsburg, 11,500 of 70,000, about 16 percent, were lost. Grant lost 12,000 of his 90,000 men at Cold Harbor in only 30 minutes. As early as the summer of 1862, remains of dead soldiers in blue and gray rotted in the woods and fields where they still lay intertwined.

Clara Barton volunteered at her own expense to nurse Union soldiers wounded at Antietam. She looked out from her covered wagon before the battle, surveyed the encamped army and realized what she would soon face. "I was faint, but I could not eat; weary, but could not sleep; depressed, but could not weep."[5] All she could do was pray for strength to face her approaching duties, obligations she could not avoid.

In battle after battle, casualties mounted and many dead were left unburied. Congress authorized the President to acquire land for national cemeteries and fourteen were quickly established. One of the first was opened near Sharpsburg, Maryland, where 4,476 Union soldiers had died in a single day. The battle was at Antietam, where Clara Barton had nervously waited. By 1870, nearly 300,000 Union dead were buried in seventy-three national cemeteries, nearly half unidentified. Veterans, like Joseph Martin from the Revolutionary War, had longed for a place to lay his bones when he died; in 1873 Congress finally authorized all honorably discharged federal veterans a burial plot. That promise was kept over the years, the number of cemeteries increased, and responsibility eventually passed to the VA's National Cemetery Administration. The army still maintains the National Cemetery at Arlington and another at the Old Soldier's Home; national battlefield cemeteries in parks are administered by the Department of Interior.[6]

DISCOMFORTS OF WAR

The war had been tough on people but life in the 1860s was hard already. Draftees were prepared somewhat for the trials of service life by their daily existence. Soldiers were accustomed to foraging for food as their forefathers had done during the Revolution, the War of 1812, and on the western frontiers. They cooked by squads and alternated responsibilities unless one person had a special talent for making a limited diet palatable. Sailors had more dietary problems due to the limited variety of food available to them, inadequate preservation, and scarcity of fresh vegetables and fruit. Ships rarely had any refrigeration. So dried products were common and scurvy was widespread.

Soldiers' uniforms were also crude, uncomfortable, and poorly tailored, and they sheltered in cotton pup tents, log-walled squad tents, log houses, or huts in winter. Sailors lived aboard ship, even in port. Unregulated sutlers used concession carts or bumboats to peddle their goods around camps and docks. Soldiers and sailors enhanced their diets or replaced worn-out clothing from supplies of the sutlers.

Soldiers and sailors were anxious to go home for short breaks but there were no established policies for taking leave. Meritorious service sometimes earned permission to go home and the navy allowed regular liberty in ports; surgeons could grant special sick leave when wounds or illness warranted. Furloughs might be granted for men to go home to vote in elections, but as infrequent as vacation was any respite from the war was appreciated, especially the opportunity to go home.

Soldiers have always been underpaid for what was asked of them. In massed formations they became cannon fodder for the big guns. There were never enough volunteers for that, so they were drafted, conscripted, impressed, paid bounties and bonuses as enticements for dangerous duty. State militias sometimes paid more than federal bounties, so recruits bargained for the best deal; some volunteers collected as much as $1,500. Prosperous draftees sometimes hired substitutes or bribed recruiters to by-pass them. But recruiting was made even more difficult by low morale from heavy losses. Military pay was low even for entry-level manual labor, despite the dangers and severe living conditions.[7]

Early drafts selected names by lottery, but conscripts found many ways to get around serving if their number was drawn. Draftees could find a substitute or pay the government $300 to draft someone else. Liberal exemptions were granted for family dependency, doubtful citizenship, marriage, and age over thirty-five. Felons, drunks, Quakers, Indians, and rebel deserters were also exempted, but physical or mental disability waivers were rare; a one-eyed man needed only one eye to aim a rifle. Dependency deferments were lenient for only sons, the last in a line, fathers of young children, or sole family providers.

In July 1863, 300,000 names were drawn in the national lottery but 40,000 failed to report, 500 were dismissed, and 26,000 paid a commutation. Despite the lenient physical standards, over 81,000 were physically exempted and 25,000 were given family deferments. Half the draftees avoided service. The navy depended on volunteers avoiding the army's draft, but that did not produce enough crews to man ships. One of every seven drafted found a way to avoid serving.[8]

COMING HOME

War ended as abruptly for the large Union Army as it had for the beleaguered Confederates but the north was no better prepared. War planners had concentrated on supporting the war with little thought to disbanding over a million federal troops. Neither government nor businesses had prepared to assimilate so many into communities, factories, or farms. A plan for demobilization was concocted on the march as troops tramped homeward after that Palm Sunday at Appomattox.

While Confederates ambled back to destroyed homes, the Union Army assembled for a Grand Review in Washington. The Army of the Potomac made the first victory march down Pennsylvania Avenue on May 23, 1865, followed by the Army of the West the next day; consecutive parades of 200,000 men. Troops in the Army of the Potomac were primarily from northeastern states and arrived first from shorter distances. They had time to rehearse, and officers inspected their uniforms before the parade. New England-discipline was on display as they marched with precision to begin the big celebration.

Sherman's troops made the grueling march north from Georgia and arrived barely in time for the second day's parade. The rough and tumble raiders came mostly from western states and had been involved in the last mopping up in the south. They had little interest in parade-ground discipline. Haggard western frontiersmen and cowboys in ragged and dirty uniforms were a sharp contrast to the New Englanders. It seemed appropriate that when Sherman's troops marched by the reviewing stand they would be out of step. President Andrew Johnson reviewed both armies as they marched past a sign over the capital: "The only national debt we can never pay is the debt we owe the victorious Union soldiers."[9] Many veterans learned the full meaning of those words only after the celebrations had ended.

Through 19 months from 1865 to 1866, more than a million northern soldiers and sailors mustered out. Some were not so eager to leave a life they had grown accustomed to, especially those not so fortunate as John Williams and Isaac Watts who returned to their old jobs. Many found their personal situations had changed. The men they had fought beside had become their new families, brothers who understood the unspoken thoughts they could never explain to civilians. But they had to move on as entire units were demobilized. As they exited, volunteer officers below brigadier were issued 3 months pay if they served until the end of the war. Regular soldiers were paid between $100 and $300 on mustering out. Sailors were issued any prize money owed them and any other pay due. It was a reasonable sum if they could keep it from swindlers. By mid-November 1865, over $270 million was paid to 800,000 soldiers, $337 each on average. Travel home was assured through a cash allowance or rides arranged by the federal government. The process of demobilization was simple: corps remained under regular commanders as units were collected from throughout the southern and border states into nine rendezvous points. After the Grand Review, they waited in the camps until their time to be dismissed. Entire units were shipped back to the original states where they had formed and were released close to home.[10]

Local camps were a venue for warm reunions with comrades they had lost contact with during war. When they found friends and neighbors still alive, they celebrated life together. War was over and they were going home. So they rejoiced with their friends to have survived, for their bright future prospects. They lay awake after the bugler's haunting rendition of *Taps* or gathered around campfires and sang "Oh Happy Day." The euphoria of winning, of being alive, made sleeping difficult. They cleaned and returned their gear, processing step by step through a structured demobilization that gradually reverted them back into civilians.

Two months of planning culminated with the release of 233,000 men, 12,000 horses, and 4 million pounds of baggage, surging north and west. The quartermaster general arranged drinking and bath water on trains for their comfort and sanitation. Some troop trains were not very luxurious as men were packed so tightly in cattle cars they could only stand shoulder-to-shoulder and belly-to-back. The more fortunate on these found room on the roofs of the boxcars where they stretched out to enjoy fresh air and sunshine.

The trains made preplanned rest stops and crowds gathered along the railroad tracks, cheering, singing, and waving flags as they approached. Local communities prepared hot coffee and lemonade, bread and butter, meat, and fruit to serve at the stopovers. Restless younger men lumbered off the trains for exercise playing leapfrog or baseball, or just flirting with local young women serving the refreshments. Older ladies boarded the cars with soap and water to bathe the invalids and serve them food and drink. The local politicians bored them all with pompous speeches. When the engineer's whistle signaled their imminent departure they were urged to fill their pockets with cakes and fruit to tide them over until the next stop, and to remember the hospitality bestowed on them in whichever town they were in. Eventually they reached their own hometowns and found victory arches with signs: "Welcome Home, Our Soldier Boys!" Celebrations in the north stretched through the summer with barbeques, hayrides, picnics, and potluck church dinners.

Most receptions were warm but not everyone was welcomed so well. The white 15th New York Artillery was among the first to get home and marched down lower Broadway to the Bowery and a wild celebration at the Liberty Gardens. But men of the all-black 52nd Pennsylvania Regiment were shunted aside when they arrived in New York. They had fought for the freedom of their brothers in Dixie but in New York they were banned from the Grand Review. They were blocked again at home in Philadelphia. But while black units were denied parades in northern cities, many were sent back to the south to assist the Freedman's Bureau in protecting the rights of former slaves. Some white officers commanding those units resembled their former slave masters. A cruel realization settled in among the black soldiers: they had won the battle for freedom but not the one for equality.[11]

NO JOBS AND OTHER PROBLEMS

The federal government was able to receive their veterans with more dignity than the defunct Confederacy, but even the victorious Yankees had to adjust to changes. Their long-held aspirations often did not materialize and the peace they had prayed for brought only disappointment; long separations turned lovers into strangers. After the parades and parties were forgotten the joys of homecoming quickly faded. Between 1865 and 1866, Ohio recorded a 72 percent increase in divorces with as many new marriages; Vermont reported a 60 percent increase.[12]

Postwar accommodations strained personal relationships and added stress to other after-war adjustments. Personal problems were no longer a concern of the government; leaders no longer told them what to do or how to do it. They had to take control of their lives and it was a difficult transition for many, especially in a postwar economy. Severance pay helped in the short-term but was not enough to subsist on forever and bought little time to start building for the future.

The skills they had learned during the war were not much help in finding civilian jobs. The army's infantry, cavalry, and artillerymen and the navy's gunners required skills unique to the business of killing. Most administration and supply positions had been contracted to civilians. So when the fighting ended, the fighters were proficient in skills useless to civilian employers.

Three hundred thousand unskilled men per month spilled into hometown streets seeking jobs. By January 1866, nearly a million had drawn their final military pay-checks and were looking for their next one, but jobs were practically nonexistent. Those discharged last found others who came before had snapped up the few jobs available. Veterans stood on street corners in Philadelphia, Boston, and New York, wearing campaign uniforms, holding tin cups for gratuities. Black veterans experienced worse than the whites. Four times as many blacks veterans were chronically unemployed in Rhode Island and they were five times more likely to be unemployed than black civilians. In August of 1865, 250 veterans of all colors marched through New York with a banner that read: "Looking for Bread and Work."[13]

Scarcity of jobs hit veterans hard with the callous realization they were no longer needed. They became restless in the valleys, having reached the highs of surviving and preserving the union followed by bitter disappointment of being relegated to the outskirts of life. They had time on their hands, time to consider their experiences, time to ponder unanswered questions, and time for personal introspection. Those too proud to accept sympathy, without work, or unwilling to beg, headed for the frontiers along with the disgruntled rebels.

Sailors were more fortunate as a thriving merchant marine needed manpower and quickly absorbed seamen willing to stay at sea. Women north and south of the Mason–Dixon Line had tackled many of the essential jobs during the war and hung on to them afterwards; northern women in the dark factories, southern women wearing their bonnets in sunny cotton fields. Women also filled vacancies in the professions; female physicians were a curiosity before the war but by the end more than 300 women practiced medicine.[14]

When men enlisted, they were asked about their occupations. Over half had been farmers, a quarter mechanics, and the rest came from commercial, professional, printing, manual labor, and miscellaneous other trades. The greatest postwar need was on badly neglected farms. Some skilled laborers returned to their old jobs but found others had mastered them while they were away, so they had to compete for their old jobs. They remembered those who had paid $300 to avoid serving, an amount equal to their separation pay. The price of a prosperous future before the war, only bought food for a few months afterwards.[15]

School enrollment surged after the war. More than 10,000 union soldiers under age 18 had enlisted, many without even rudimentary education. With jobs hard to find and time on their hands they turned to education to fill the gaps and improve their opportunities for the future.[16]

President Lincoln anticipated the job shortage before the war ended and penned a letter to Postmaster General Montgomery Blair suggesting preferences for federal jobs should be given to veterans, their widows, and orphans. He believed they should have the highest priority, especially those who were disabled and their surviving family members. Veterans distressed by the peacetime economy made no special demands for themselves, but when the dust settled they wanted more than rhetoric and beer; they wanted an opportunity, and good jobs topped their list.

Factories in the northeast had mobilized to produce enough war material to win and had invented new products in the process. Union soldiers and sailors discovered some of the modern products while in the service. On long forced marches through the devastated southern states they were issued canned food and beer and they liked it. While rebels wore hand-stitched uniforms, the Yanks wore machine-made clothing. After the war, they demanded more of those innovations. Continuing demand encouraged business investments and created jobs as new industries evolved around war-inspired products and services.[17]

Jobs weren't the only challenges that confronted Billy Yanks as they marched home. War had magnified or distorted reality for many and reinforced natural tendencies in unexpected ways. Those who went to war with dependency impulses already used crutches to satisfy unfulfilled needs, to replace something or someone lost. Alcohol supported some, drugs for others, even gambling, thrill seeking, sex, or fighting. Some depended on the army to provide everything, to make their decisions, to replace mother and they became adopted children of the service. When their obligation ended they still depended on that support. Those with lingering dependencies had to control them or learn to live with them. But many others were strong before the war and became stronger and more disciplined under the ordeal.[18]

Civilians had worked extended days, 10 to 12 hours was common, but they rested and slept at home at night. They worked for a foreman who gave orders but who were limited in their authority to giving or withholding raises and promotions, and hiring and firing. But civilian supervisors had only a fraction of the power of the captain of a ship or an infantry corporal. The differences were starkly apparent to veterans when they returned to the factories. Toughened men who had worked hard all their lives needed more stamina on the battlefields than in cornfields or factory floors. A soldier's day stretched from dawn to dusk under grueling conditions and the constant threat of death. After fighting or marching all day they might be ordered to stand guard through the night and begin all over again before the sun rose. Going home after an honest day's work was only a dream for them. Though finding work was serious business and the first priority for them, civilian employers frequently told them they were fools to have served. The population viewed them askance since they had killed and might be dangerous. Those who looted the south and tried it in their own communities earned a bad reputation or hard time in jail. Those with undesirable dependencies soon crammed prison cells.

SOLDIER'S DISEASE AND THE SANITARY COMMISSION

Medical care had been rudimentary at the front and postwar care was no better. A slight wound could kill or incapacitate if not treated properly and promptly; gangrene, tetanus, and traumatic amputations were marks of approaching death or disability. Hypodermic syringes were introduced to medicine as early as 1856 and were used to inject morphine into wounded soldiers when it was available. Union doctors dispensed over ten thousand pills and two million ounces of other opiates during the war. Forty-five thousand veterans survived their wounds only to become addicts. By the turn of the century, over a quarter of a million Americans were addicted. "Soldier's disease" was not so well documented in the south, but it may have been even worse as depression over losing the war, unsympathetic reconstruction, penury, loss of property, and respect weighed on them.[19]

In the rush to mass an army, physical examinations were perfunctory and standards set low. Tradition held that if you could raise your hand to be sworn in, you passed. After being inducted, there were no hospitals for injured soldiers or veterans. The U.S. Sanitary Commission (officially The Commission of Inquiry and Advice in Respect to the Sanitary Interests of the U.S. Forces) filled the void. The Sanitary Commission, a private agency, strived to improve the health of combat troops during war by raising funds to advance hygiene in the field and sanitation in hospitals. It provided a badly needed service but reinforced the belief that government was not obligated to care for war wounded, leaving the responsibility to others.

Henry Bellows had established the Sanitary Commission in 1861 as a private philanthropy. Bellows was a stalwart companion to Union soldiers and tolerated by the War Department. The Commission fed, transported, and nursed sick and wounded soldiers and tended needy families at home; it also recognized the linkage between good health and good jobs, so employment became a principle concern for the commission after the war.[20]

The Sanitary Commission believed meaningful work helped veterans recover, so they set up a separate Bureau of Information and Employment to match workers with vacant jobs. Work was not easily found since jobs were scarce in the populated northeast but plentiful in uninhabited western states and territories. The Cleveland bureau made a list of 170 employers seeking veterans to work in Ohio and received 258 applicants classified as able-bodied, 153 as disabled. Two hundred sixteen were assigned to manual labor but eighty did not return for the second day. Although they had no other skills they were convinced they had sweated enough in the military and deserved a better job than what was offered.[21]

The University of Wisconsin studied county records for another 275 veterans in New York and Wisconsin and found many changed professions after the war. One hundred sixty-eight returned to their former trades but 107 turned elsewhere for a fresh start. Twenty-two were too young to have learned a trade when they enlisted. The longer they stayed away from their original jobs the more likely they were to try something new. Seventeen percent of physicians and 28 percent of lawyers gave up their practices after war, most for politics. But in Iowa, 92 percent of farmers returned to the only jobs available, on the farms.[22]

Disabled veterans had even more difficulty finding jobs, such as the one-armed man who learned to drive nails by holding them between his toes. Doing common tasks in such a dramatically different way was too challenging and most soon gave up. The Sanitary Commission wanted to help but held to three guiding principles: First was not to interfere in the course of nature; they believed even dying veterans should be allowed to retain their dignity. Next, disabled veterans should rely on their own families for support instead of turning to institutions or government.

And finally, they encouraged society to absorb handicapped veterans into jobs to the fullest extent possible.[23]

While the Sanitary Commission worked to improve quality of life, the federal government made compensatory payments to disabled Union veterans. Although it was impossible to replace lost opportunities, the money helped. A lost leg was priced at $75, an arm at $50; or in lieu of money, new artificial limbs were issued every 3 years. Most accepted the money and the responsibility.[24]

Congress joined the popular appeal for permanent homes for needy veterans, approving the National Home for Disabled Volunteer Soldiers in March 1865; by the end of 1870, branches had opened in Maine, Ohio, Wisconsin, and Virginia for domicile, hospital, and medical care of 3,200 disabled and needy veterans. Marine hospitals had performed physical examinations for veterans since 1798 but the Public Health Service took that responsibility. The Sanitary Commission, local governments, and charities all opened additional shelters for the most in need.

The number still exceeded the capacity of the homes to absorb them and some states opened state homes in the 1880s. Residents frequented the libraries and the more able worked in gardens, laundries, or blacksmith shops to defray costs. Soldier's homes were generally run in disciplined military tradition with a regimen of reveille formations, drills, and mess tables. Rule infractions were punished by withholding pensions or even dishonorable discharges, and rewards included furloughs, passes, and visitation permits. Some residents enjoyed the conformity, but others stomped out in disgust.

In 1865 the *Army and Navy Journal* offered sound advice to discharged soldiers: keep up appearances, maintain good posture, and choose a suitable craft. They were advised to learn a trade quickly, then work hard at it and serve an apprenticeship at low wages if necessary, before their separation pay was spent. The handicapped were encouraged to learn to use other muscles. If they had lost a limb, they should compensate with energy, decisiveness, and their wits.

The Civil War had interrupted America's westward expansion, including building the intercontinental railroad between the east and west coasts. Before the war started, it appeared the railroad would take a southern route but when the south lost the war it also lost the route. The railroad meant jobs, and General Grenville Dodge, chief engineer of the Union Pacific, promised work to hardy veterans. Veterans and new immigrants eagerly accepted. Other industries got involved in building the railroad, including iron and coal mining, manufacture of rails and engines, and all the activity created more employment.

Knute Nelson wrote home from Baton Rouge during the war: "The careless, reckless, wild boy that left home a year ago . . . has learnt that the world is not the school house nor the narrow limits of the little farm. . . . " Though out of school, Nelson continued learning and used what he had learned before his twenty-first birthday during 3 years of war in the 4th Wisconsin when he came home. He left the little farm that was his world before the war, to become the governor of

Minnesota and a U.S. Senator. Yankee veterans found opportunities where they could.[25]

THE GRAND ARMY OF THE REPUBLIC

Doctor Benjamin Stephenson was the 14th Illinois Infantry Regiment's surgeon until he mustered out in 1864. He returned to practice medicine in Decatur, Illinois, but soon grew restless, like so many other veterans. After treating traumatic wounds on the front lines, wiping runny noses seemed insignificant and uninspiring. He reconnected with veterans who shared his war experiences to fill that void. Stephenson saw them being shoved aside, denied the respect they had earned, and he was stirred by that to do something. He held strongly that those who defended their country deserved a stake in its future. His tent-mate during their service with the 14th Illinois was the regiment's chaplain, Reverend William Rutledge, who shared Stephenson's concerns. They considered a national organization for veterans and looked to other groups, such as the Third Army Corps Union, the Society of the Army of Tennessee, and the Military Order of the Loyal Legion of the United States, as models.

As the organization evolved it adopted the same penchant for secrecy as the Masons and the Ku Klux Klan, using special handshakes, secret passwords, and clandestine inductions. National indifference toward veterans compelled them to find enough power for respect through techniques of collective bargaining; with enough veterans they could send shockwaves through Washington. The message resonated with veterans and they prepared to use their political strength for the first time. Unlike the benevolent associations from the Revolution or the Mexican War, this was an army: the Grand Army of the Republic.

Their first national meeting convened in Indiana on November 20, 1866, and captured the attention of veterans and politicians alike. Their key principle was to bring veterans' concerns to the national agenda, not by lobbying, but by electing chosen advocates and directly influencing them. The founders were well aware of the immediate needs of veterans and were determined to help. The Soldiers and Sailors National Union League, Boys in Blue, and the Republican Veterans Union followed, but none were as influential as the Grand Army of the Republic (GAR).

The GAR organized as an army and became a driving political force. They planned as they had learned in the military, and acted decisively and in coordination. They understood the political battlefield and organized along political boundaries. Their posts aligned with voting precincts and departments with states, so collective pressures could be most effectively applied within specific political districts. The GAR chose its first battle carefully—a federal Memorial Day—and they claimed an easy victory in 1869. It was their first win but not their last.

Civilians had viewed the veterans as relics of a by-gone era and in trying to put the war behind, trod on those who had saved the union. Veterans knew how intellectuals disparaged them because they read their editorials in the newspapers.

Businessmen scorned them when they turned them down for jobs. Politicians made pompous speeches, waved the bloody shirt, basked in their glory and valor, but never passed any meaningful legislation on their behalf. The GAR would change that.

When General Grant was elected President many disgruntled northern veterans were encouraged at first but the view that soldiers had fought only for patriotic reasons prevailed; many considered that to be reward enough. Although businesses had profited from the war, wealthy businessmen argued that money would only tarnish veterans' high ideals. Politicians argued that paying veterans' benefits would bankrupt the nation. The GAR had heard all the arguments before and was not dissuaded; none of those arguments satisfied their hunger or tended their wounds. They strengthened their voice, making clear the political risk of ignoring united and politically active veterans. Time for the big fight had come. GAR chapters demanded enlistment bounties be paid as promised, but since the bonuses had increased as recruiting became harder, the amounts should be equalized for everyone. They also wanted pay in arrears for disabilities even if the 5-year cutoff for claims had lapsed. It was a tall order.

Senator John Ingalls from Kansas calculated that paying the arrears would cost $18–20 million. Secretary of Treasury John Sherman projected the cost as much higher at $150 million. But both of them were only guessing how many veterans would stake claims. The bill passed and President Rutherford B. Hayes signed it despite uncertainties about the cost. Before the bill was signed in 1878, fewer than 26,000 disability claims had been filed, but in the first year claims nearly doubled. Lawyers, previously allowed to charge only $10 in cases against the government, were released from that restriction and the next year they pushed claims up to 138,000.[26]

The Dependent Pension Bill included all disabled veterans, even those not service-connected, and it was expensive. Pensions consumed nearly 20 percent of the national budget. By the end of 1893, 1 million survivors (from the 2.2 million who had served in the Union army) had drawn $150 million in pensions. The GAR proved their point: veterans were politically powerful. In proving it they gained the gratitude of veterans, the fear of politicians, but lost respect among average citizens.[27]

Nevertheless, their ranks grew steadily after the huge success with the pension laws. By 1885, the original organization of only 61,000—4 percent of 1.5 million surviving union veterans—swelled to 270,000 members. By 1890, three hundred posts had been opened in the South for Union veterans living there. The *National Tribune* trumpeted their achievements and it was not lost on Republican political circles. The membership list of the GAR represented votes, and it was well understood that veterans who never officially joined the GAR still supported their positions.

President Grover Cleveland approved nearly 1,500 individual exceptions to the pension rules, more than all other presidents combined. But his benevolence didn't save him from the ire of the GAR when he vetoed benefits for non-service-connected disabilities. Infuriated veterans defeated him in favor of another veteran, Benjamin Harrison.

Even though pensions were the single largest item in the federal budget at 18 percent, tampering with them was political suicide. Harrison enjoyed veterans' support but wanted a shield from their future influence, so he appointed James Tanner to head the Pension Bureau. Tanner was a corporal in the Union Army and had lost both legs at Bull Run. He fought for veteran pensions for everyone, even Confederates, making him a liability to Harrison. Tanner resigned after 6 months, but not before locking in pensions for one million Union veterans. Only a paltry million dollars was paid to widows and orphans in southern states. Pensions were contentious but they would end soon since 30 years after the war veterans were fast dying.[28]

Membership in the GAR reached 409,000 by 1890 but started declining as they also died or became inactive. But six of the first seven Presidents after the Civil War were ranking members of the GAR: Republicans Grant, Hayes, Garfield, Arthur, Harrison, and McKinley. Cleveland was the only Democrat and only nonmember and was targeted for defeat. Solidarity within the GAR provided the power to lay a foundation for veterans' rights. The powerful GAR was also the censor of Civil War history. Union veterans reviewed books and articles, ensuring they represented the politically correct version of the war from their point of view; Civil War history was thereby preserved from the vantage point of northern veterans.[29]

By the 1890s, war politics had softened but memories of fraternal relationships were still vivid to the aging veterans. Commemorations in the north became more focused on the veterans than the causes and effects of the war, as they had always been in the south. With old resentments set aside, northern and southern veterans came together on battlefields for anniversaries and to remember their fallen comrades. When they came together there were few dry eyes among them, few sharp words heard between former enemies. Lives lost and spared in battles of brother against brother in the American Civil War was still strong in the special bond that unites soldiers everywhere.

5

Brass Buttons and Foreign Excursions

The troubling 1800s that gave us Civil War yielded to the boisterous 1900s; the new century brought a new spirit to the country, north and south of the Mason–Dixon Line. Reconstruction of the Union was complete; new industries, intercontinental transportation, and westward expansion raised a sense of good fortune and world power as the country extended its reach beyond its borders. A mood for great expansion took hold with unshakable optimism and unbridled nationalism. Explorers had already left tracks everywhere in the country; people wanted new places to explore, an international identity.

The industrial age brought railroads to move an army from coast to coast and steam power replaced fickle winds to move the fleet. Locomotives and stage-coaches barreled across untamed western territories and connected isolated plains settlements, the densely populated Atlantic seaboard, and the sparsely settled Pacific coast. New inventions amazed; over 600,000 patents were issued between 1865 and 1900. The scope of new ideas seemed limitless as builders used wood produced by sawmills, farmers turned fields with modern plows, and pistols fired six rounds without reloading. Paper clips, lead pencils, affordable watches, and easy-strike matches made simple tasks easier; mass-produced automobiles and airplanes were easily imaginable. Anything was possible. Americans were buoyantly optimistic and the re-United States was staged to create the future to its liking.

WAR WITH SPAIN

Thirty years after the Civil War old veterans of that bloody conflict told their stories of glory and struck a martial chord with a younger generation yearning for adventure. In 1895, only 90 miles off the tip of Florida in Cuba, the Spanish empire struggled with a growing revolt. American mercenaries, such as Frederick Funston, actively supported the rebels while President Grover Cleveland suspended warship port calls to work diplomatic solutions. When William McKinley was elected, he sent the battleships *Texas* and *Maine* and the heavy cruiser *New York* to flex their broad shoulders in drills off Key West. There they were better positioned to reach Cuba quickly if mobs threatened American lives or property in Havana. The *Maine*, with a full load of highly combustible bituminous coal to fuel its modern steam boilers, was at the beckoning call of Consul General Fitzhugh Lee.

The atmosphere in Havana became precarious by January 1898. Spanish officers prodded the mobs to raid newspapers advocating Cuban autonomy. Consul General Lee cabled for help and McKinley notified Madrid the *Maine* would stand by in Havana Bay in support of American interests. The ship steamed in and anchored peacefully until early evening on February 15; an explosion literally blew the sleeping crew into the water. Two hundred sixty-six of 350 sailors were killed in the blast.

"Remember the *Maine*" and Manila

Bodies of American boys were brought home for burials in Arlington National Cemetery, riveting attention on the growing trouble in Cuba. The public ignored theories about the real causes of the explosion; minds were already set to avenge the *Maine*. McKinley ordered an investigation of the explosion, but newspapers and constituents wanted action. An excited Congress accommodated them.

Pulitzer and Hearst newspapers rolled off the presses demanding action, and the Grand Army of the Republic waved the flag of patriotism. Shouts of "Remember the *Maine!*" drowned out the official report of Captain Sampson's ordnance board and the *Maine's* commander, Captain Charles Sigsbee, that the explosion was accidental. The Spanish were blamed, despite evidence to the contrary. War was inevitable.

President McKinley was the last Civil War veteran to serve as president and he did not want war, but there would be no peace in the Caribbean while Spain plundered their colonies. The Spanish also held the Philippines where naval captains and commercial shippers wanted a forward naval and commercial operating base. Spain blocked American expansion in both the Pacific and the Caribbean. Theodore Roosevelt, as Assistant Secretary of the Navy, considered sea power the natural extension of American influence, the seas the new frontiers.

Congress declared war on Spain on April 21, 1898, to avenge the *Maine* and to end Spanish dominance over Cuba and Puerto Rico. The small regular army was still fighting Indians in the western territories but thousands were needed for a war against a European power. The President immediately called for 125,000 volunteers. With emotions running high about the *Maine*, thousands had clamored to sign on even before war was declared; a multitude swarmed recruiting stations afterwards.

The navy had burgeoned with modern weapons and power trains after 1860, but the army still used frontier tactics, equipment, doctrine, and training. They were also out-manned with 28,000 Indian fighters against 155,000 Spaniards accustomed to the tropics and equipped with modern arms. The army quickly swelled to 61,000 and President McKinley called for 200,000 more. By the end of November 1898, more than 223,000 volunteers, from cowboys to cartoonists, clamored to enlist.

Military recruiters swore in federal volunteers while militia regimental recruiters filled vacancies in state units. Militia units like the Rough Riders were bound for Cuba, the 1st Colorado Volunteer Infantry to the Philippine Islands. But applicants had to meet more exacting physical standards than in the Civil War. Charles Post bragged he passed the jumping test, the coughing test that proved he was not ruptured, and the eyesight test by explaining he was a pool shark and had once run thirty-five balls. "Thus I became a soldier, with bed, board . . . and thirteen dollars a month."[1] Post was a cartoonist and humorous writer by trade; he claimed the Army failed on part of its contract, but never reduced his pay for being undernourished in the trenches.

Men stood on long lines to sign up. Charles Post joined the 71st New York Volunteers. The 25-year-old employee with Hearst's *New York Journal* wanted adventure, ideas to fill his sketchbook and his imagination, and the fancy of young women. "Everywhere the young girls were sewing red flannel bellybands," he recalled. His were wrapped as Christmas packages by two young maidens chaperoned by his aunt. "Each package held a red flannel bellyband with three black tapes at each end with which to lash it to my person. Thereupon, I was to be secure from all forms of pestilence and intestinal fevers."[2]

Medical treatment and experience in handling mass casualties and traumatic wounds had progressed in the 35 years after the Civil War, but major unanticipated medical challenges loomed. Basic training in first aid and sanitation had not changed from the Civil War and no one was prepared for the greatest challenges of Cuba and the Philippines—tropical diseases. Red flannel bellybands did little against contaminated water, typhoid, or malaria.

In April 1898, Secretary of War Russell Alger planned to recruit several regiments already immune to tropical diseases. He looked for them in the Deep South, especially in the Gulf States. The regiments were popularly called "Immunes" and it was hoped they could withstand tropical diseases, or at least be accustomed to the heat and humidity. Four Immune Regiments were to be made up of "persons of color," the 7th through 10th U.S. Volunteer Infantry.

Four Immune Regiments were actually deployed, but only one was composed of black volunteers. The 9th Regiment marched from Camp Corbin at the New Orleans fairgrounds to board the *Berlin* amid cheers of proud black Louisianans. They arrived in Cuba 4 days later and were assigned to guard Spanish prisoners on San Juan Hill. But fevers quickly flushed through their ranks, killing thirty-one of them and dashing all ideas of inherent immunity.[3]

Preparations were rushed, especially for army troops. Volunteer militias were federalized and assembled for brief refresher training at local camps. Navy apprentices received 5–6 months training in seamanship and gunnery at the training station in Newport, RI, where many encountered their first instruction in reading, writing, and arithmetic. Most training was done on-the-job and limited to pure military skills; technical specialists were drawn fully trained from civilian professions. But modern weapons systems, communications, intelligence, mechanics, all needed technical skills not commonly found within the general population; selections of men for those were made intuitively by their leaders.

Joseph Deburgh

"A lot of water has passed under the old bridge since that fateful Sunday morning ... when our late President McKinley ... gave our country one if its greatest thrills," recalled Joseph Deburgh after the war. He was still in his teens having a traditional Sunday morning breakfast with his large family when the news arrived. The newsboy slid the paper under the door and one of the children handed it to his father, who read the news aloud. His father was clearly affected, and laying down his glasses, he said: "My sons, you all know that I fought for the South all through the Civil War. I would like to see one of you enlist for this war."

The brothers argued all day about who would go, but Joseph had seen in the newspaper a picture of a lovely Spanish girl lying in a hammock strung between coconut trees in old Manila; he was determined to be the one to find her. He talked his brothers down, finally gained his mother's consent, and joined the 2nd Oregon Volunteer Infantry bound for the Philippines.

Deburgh never left the Philippines; when his unit returned after the war he stayed on to make a life in Manila. He died there in Saint Paul's Hospital in 1939. "Personally, my only regret is that I never was able to locate that beautiful Spanish girl that was swinging in the hammock."[4]

Brass Buttons

With a declaration of war against Spain, Admiral Dewey had steamed with six ships from Hong Kong toward the Spanish fleet in the Philippine Islands. Spanish Admiral Montojo's 7-ship fleet waited in Manila Bay. Before breakfast Dewey sunk the entire Spanish fleet in a victory that cost only American one dead, from heat stroke.

An excited populace greeted Dewey's victory with wild enthusiasm and more volunteers lined up. Old Civil War enemies stood together; bands played, women cried and offered flowers, and men showed off the brass buttons on their tunics. "If there is any time in a man's life when he gets a real kick," recalled Joseph Deburgh from Portland, "it is when he puts on a uniform with brass buttons for the first time.... The fair sex has a weakness for brass buttons that I am afraid they will never be able to overcome."[5] Charles Post found it much the same in New York. "It was a wonder that there was a button left on a uniform," he said. "Girls ... looked longingly at the brass buttons ... and would trade a safety pin for a button. . . . A campaign hat insignia with its crossed rifles could bring a kiss. It was a gay time. War—war itself, was on."[6]

Tents covered the grassy lawns of state capitals, filled with mobilized local militias. Assistant Secretary of the Navy Theodore Roosevelt had engineered Dewey's move on Manila but he also wanted a more direct part in the excitement. Roosevelt resigned his cabinet post and joined the volunteer cavalry, the Rough Riders bound for Cuba.

In Cuba, General Shafter pressed troops toward Santiago while the Navy chased Spanish ships off shore and shelled their forts. After one day of heavy fighting, General Shafter met General Jose Toral on July 17 to accept his surrender. The Spanish flag that had waved over Cuba for 382 years came down, but sporadic fighting continued until General Miles accepted Spain's final surrender in Puerto Rico on August 12.

On the same day the war ended in the Caribbean, the Spanish garrison in Manila surrendered to Colonel Irving Hale and the 1st Colorado Regiment. But Dewey's appeasement of Spain, by excluding Filipinos from the liberation of Manila, riled the Filipino guerrillas against the Americans. The guerilla army's insurrection against Spain was redirected toward American troops, now seen as the new occupiers. Even as war with Spain officially ended, more serious problems began; the splendid little war was over, a dirty little war started. Trouble didn't end in Cuba either; it followed the troops home. They returned with life-threatening diseases and were treated so cruelly it became an un-cleansed stain on history, not the first nor last, but an ugly one.

Skeleton Corps

Charles Post was happy the war in Cuba was over, but with the tension gone, he felt the full weight of what he had been through. "We were weaker and sicker than we knew," he wrote without characteristic humor. There was no bugle for sick call that day because the bugler was also sick. Anyone well enough to report to sick call was well enough for detail. If he fell or died, they would call for another. Sickness spread and one city was burned to stop the spread of yellow fever. "Each morning . . . we would hear the bugles blowing *Taps* very shortly after reveille." *Taps* and salute volleys became more frequent as days passed. Then one morning there were no more *Taps*, but the files of men with shovels continued by, covered stretchers followed by a chaplain. When the last bugler became ill, there was no more reveille and everything was done in silence—guard mount, lowering the flag at sundown, funerals. The army tells time by bugle calls. "It was as if all the watches stopped. . . . "[7]

Then one bugler recovered enough for two men to help him up the hill for retreat and lowering of the flag. His notes were weak, quavering, missing some and hissing others, but it was recognizable. They clapped when he finished. Other regiments recovered enough for the bugles to sound again in the same way, "but each seemed the ghastly echo of a thinning and dying army corps."[8]

Sailing Home

Demobilization of the Cuban expeditionary force was simple next to the massive draw down after the Civil War. Mainly only the troops from Cuba were involved, since the Philippines remained mired in insurrection. From August 1898 through June 1899, nearly 200,000 army troops were dismissed as whole units were inactivated. The Marine Corps released individuals, reducing the size of units, and the navy decommissioned vessels closest to American ports and released sailors there.

The black 9th Immunes sailed from Santiago, minus seventy-six who died from disease in Cuba and were buried there. Their voyage took them through quarantine on Staten Island, then to Camp Meade in Pennsylvania to muster out. They made it home without incident. Other black regiments that had not deployed from southern states were not so fortunate. Racially inspired shootings and harassment were commonplace. Black regiments were criticized as undisciplined; the white populace was still resentful 30 years after the Civil War.[9]

Few Americans died in battle in Cuba but death stalked them home. Healthy units were celebrated with parades and parties that spilled into the streets of New York, but the sick were quarantined and ignored. The war over, veterans were quickly forgotten. Teddy Roosevelt warned his Rough Riders the world would be kind to them for 10 days, but after that they would be considered tainted just for having gone. Reality sunk in quickly as they were mustered out far from home and had to make their own way. Many arrived penniless and their veteran status did not help land them a job.

Dying Camps

Virtually everyone sent to Cuba contracted malaria; as many as 25 percent were incapacitated at one time. Diseased soldiers overcrowded facilities and overtaxed surgical staff. More than 2,000 men died of diseases, five times more than from combat wounds. Soldiers with tropical diseases such as yellow fever, malaria, dysentery, and typhoid fever were not treated properly because commanders and doctors didn't know how to, nor had the facilities, supplies, and medical staff. Surgeon General Sternberg even forbade Red Cross nurses from going ashore to help. Commanders, incapable of treating their men, planned to get them home as quickly as possible where the army or their families could. The hasty plan was simple: quarantine them until they recovered enough to be released, or died and were buried. Sick troops in Cuba, sweating under heat, humidity, and high fevers, were loaded aboard ships bound for Long Island. Infirmed were put to sea in ships without sufficient medical supplies, sanitation, nurses, food, fresh water, refrigeration, disinfectant, mattresses, or clean clothes.

Each day at sea their conditions worsened. A few nautical miles from New York nurses were brought on board to do what they could, but many of them contracted their patients' diseases. The War Department hastily established quarantine camps: Camp Wikoff at the tip of New York's Montauk Point, and Camp Alger in northern Virginia. Surgeon General Sternberg, the man most responsible for the health and welfare of the troops, had misjudged the situation in Cuba, as he did in the camps.

But for the troops, it was time to go home. Charles Post sipped his coffee, looking over the rim of his tin mess cup for the first glimpse of what remained of his regiment. Then he spotted them; the men he had known in New York came into view: lean, tanned, gaunt with hard cheekbones, glistening eyes, and ragged beards with emaciated teeth showing through. "There was Gus Pitou, a corporal now; there was Ben Payne, a new sergeant; between them they were bracing up Arthur Pendleton—a skin-tight, shrunken wreck—to help him make the transport and home!"[10]

They boarded the *Grande Duchesse* and the regimental band broke into "Home, Sweet Home." Men crawled up to the ship's rail and cheered as it slipped away from Cuba. "Sickly men and a sickly cheer. There were men who choked as they cheered, and many lips trembled to hold back their emotion. Some cried with silent tears."[11]

The early morning air was cool as the *Grande Duchesse* approached Coney Island. As names were called they lined up to drop rifles and haversacks and load a steamboat shuttle to land. Four sailors helped them shuffle along the gangplank. "The feel of American board under our feet, of American sand to press upon, and the sandy sedge grass beyond was wonderful. Men walked, helping each other."[12]

Major General "Fighting Joe" Wheeler had been the colorful commander of the Confederate Cavalry during the Civil War. President McKinley had urged him out of retirement to command the cavalry in Cuba. At the end of the Cuban campaign he was assigned the onerous duty of commanding the quarantined Camp Wikoff. His daughter served as head nurse in the officer's ward. "In the space of less than three weeks," the general wrote, "twenty thousand soldiers, fully half of whom were suffering from diseases contracted in Cuba, were landed upon the barren fields of Montauk Point." One hundred and twenty-six died there.

Dr. William Wallace accompanied sick and wounded men of the 1st Illinois Infantry to Montauk Point. "Right here, in 100 miles of New York, I cannot get medicines for typhoid fever, or chlorinated soda to wash out the bowels in typhoid fever and dysentery cases. . . . There is gross mismanagement somewhere and it is costing many lives." Unable to deal with the problems, he wrote a letter begging to be reassigned back to his own regiment.[13]

Charles Post was in New York's own volunteer regiment, the 71st. When he arrived in his home state the air felt cool after the heat of the tropics. Everyone had chills but few had blankets. A medical officer approached his group and shouted: "All those who can walk had best get to their regiment—it's about a mile off. You'll get more there than we have here. It's for your own good, so if you can make it, walk!" None were fit to walk a mile, so they stayed where they were.

That night an elderly volunteer nurse came to their tent with food in an iron pail. It was "greasy water, lukewarm and filled with ragged morsels of mutton and gristle and sinew...." On the second or third day a second-year medical student, a contract surgeon, examined them. He gave a delirious man a bandage for his head, Post received quinine pills, but the man with broken bones was told to be quiet until some bandages were found.[14]

Dying men isolated at Montauk Point were fed stale hardtack biscuits infested with worms and canned meat that was already spoiled. Those who retained a sense of humor called the meat embalmed. The most able-bodied survivors of New York's 71st Regiment marched down Broadway, a pathetic, emaciated, hollow-eyed, and feeble remnant of an army. Dr. Nicholas Senn, Chief Surgeon of the United States Volunteers, observed that the Cuban War veterans, "returned mere shadows...many are wrecks for life, others are candidates for a premature grave and hundreds will require most careful attention and treatment...." Despite his warning, there were no government programs and even the most severely disabled were denied hospital care and medicine.[15]

Camps Wikoff and Alger became the dying fields of the Spanish-American War—more men died there than in the Battles of San Juan Hill and Manila Bay combined. Regular troops paid the highest toll to diseases, since they depended solely on an inadequate federal health system. Volunteer militias were assisted by relief organizations from their home communities, well stocked with food and medicinal supplies by state and private sources.

The War Department denied there was a problem until it was too obvious to ignore. Disturbing reports of maltreatment reached President McKinley and he ordered the War Department to investigate, but Secretary Alger ensured blame did not reach the War Department or Surgeon General Sternberg. Someone had to be responsible, so they blamed the victims for getting sick. The official policy of shifting blame to them was more than just avoiding embarrassment; Alger had learned the price of undocumented pension claims after the Civil War and did not intend to repeat that mistake. The War Department still paid all disability claims out of the defense budget and he didn't want that liability to increase. Alger required strict physicals of every man before they were separated, not to identify and treat service-connected physical problems, but to establish a basis for denying future claims.[16]

"It is difficult to realize the utter emptiness of time in those days," said Charles Post of his time at Camp Wikoff. "We measured time in food; in the time between chills... we measured it in dysentery, and in latrines." Then a storm raked Camp Wikoff, a blessing in disguise when tents were knocked down. The next day a detail appeared washing everything and serving food in advance of the visit of

Secretary Alger. After his inspection, those able to walk were given clean uniforms and passes. Post hid his two sketchbooks under his uniform and caught a ride with a Red Cross worker to the Long Island railroad. When the overloaded train arrived in New York City, Post was hauled to Roosevelt Hospital. "Everybody stared at me. I was the first man back from San Juan Hill and the trenches." He was unable to keep up with time for 4 days, but in the end he was lucky—at least he survived.[17]

After their rush to sign on for America's quest for destiny, veterans were bitter at the mistreatment and neglect. The federal treasury had a surplus of $46 million but they were offered only 2 months separation pay after serving overseas, 1 month for duty in the United States. Some soldiers were provided transportation or a travel allowance to get home; sailors were released at the nearest port. Some were simply told to make their own way, like defeated Confederates. This had been the first foreign excursion; there was no visible damage to the cities and no favorable sentiment towards veterans after the boisterous victory celebrations ended.

Politicians were not alone in deserving blame for neglecting the veterans; the Grand Army of the Republic and United Confederate Veterans also ignored Spanish War veterans and closed their doors to them. Although they were shorted by the government, shunned by veterans' organizations, and ignored by the populace, there were no detectable outcries from them. Without an organization, Spanish War veterans were alone in their fight for recognition.

VETERANS OF FOREIGN WARS

Among the first American troops to return from the Cuban campaign was the 17th Infantry Regiment after seeing action in the capture of Santiago City and at El Caney Hill. The 17th went to Columbus Barracks in Ohio to replace men and equipment for redeployment to the ongoing insurgency in the Philippines. Sick and wounded men could not deploy with the regiment; they were of no further use to the army, so they were paid for 2 months and discharged. No hospitals and no medicine were available to them, so they were expected to fend for themselves. There was no official transportation home either, so they either made their own way or became wards of the city of Columbus.

Among those discharged with the disabled were thirteen men ending short-term enlistments. Privates Bill Putnam and James Romanis had served with some of the disabled and were exasperated to see them cast aside. Putnam believed his comrades were entitled to more than an early grave, so he peddled his bike around town looking for others to discuss his views with. He encouraged them to join together to fight for their rights.

James Romanis worked quietly at a pharmacy near the barracks and shared Putnam's opinions about how their friends were neglected. He spoke with other veterans coming in for relief from their lingering tropical ailments and was upset by how they were abandoned. Romanis found Putnam and volunteered to run an ad in the newspaper announcing a meeting at the end of September 1899. Twelve men came to the first meeting in Francis Dubiel's clothing store; they were eager to discuss their situation and that of their friends who were too sick to come. They considered forming a regimental organization, but Bill Putnam warned that would limit them and he reminded them how the GAR had refused them membership. He envisioned an association with enduring influence. A veteran from another regiment arrived late for the meeting, proving by his interest that they should keep their doors open wide. Eventually, they included any veteran awarded a campaign medal anywhere, including Mexican War veterans.

They talked late into the night, remembering friends who wanted to come but were too sick, crippled, or destitute. Before they adjourned after midnight, they took up a collection to help the others, a tradition they continued as the organization grew. It took the government 23 years to respond, but eventually pensions were awarded for $12 a month, $30 if totally disabled. It was even less than the Revolutionary War grants in 1818, but it was something.

Bill Putnam remembered that first meeting at a later encampment in 1933. "Men clasped each other's hands and shed tears, hugged each other and pandemonium broke loose." The emotional experience was repeated often over the years. But it was at the second meeting that they adopted the name: American Veterans of Foreign Service. All members would have equal status, whatever their previous rank and they would expand by establishing local camps in other communities.

The 1st Colorado Voluntary Infantry Regiment had been formed especially for the campaign in the Philippines from two regiments of the Colorado National Guard, filled in by raw recruits of cowboys and miners. Colonel Irving Hale commanded the unit when it was federalized at Camp Davis, near Denver. They took rigorous physical exams but received almost no training before reaching the Philippines in July 1898. The regiment served a year there, seized the Spanish Fortress of San Antonio de Abad and raised the first American flag over Manila.

The Regiment expected to return home in April after a year of service, but the Philippine insurgency extended it longer. Finally, they boarded the *Warren* in Manila in July, bound for San Francisco to be mustered out in September 1899. Denver residents were so proud of their regiment's accomplishments they raised money to hire a special train to bring the boys home in style. Seventy-five thousand citizens met them in Denver, followed by parades and speeches before General Hale finally dismissed them to join their families.

Soon enough Teddy Roosevelt's warning about a short-lived hero status proved as true for them as it had for the Rough Riders. Others had taken the jobs they held before the war; those disabled by wounds or disease were left with no rehabilitation, no medical care, and no financial assistance. A national depression compounded their situation since no new opportunities were being created. Even those in good health struggled to provide for themselves and their families. Times were hard for everyone, especially for veterans.

General Hale was discharged with his men, but he quickly found a position as an engineer and general manager with a large Denver electrical company.

But he stayed in touch with the troops and was discouraged by the stories they told him. They were suffering, starving, and helpless; he helped many of the neediest from his personal funds but he knew they needed to organize to help each another. He gathered some of his officers and planned a reunion for August 1900 on the second anniversary of the capture of Manila. At the first meeting they agreed to form an association, draft a constitution, and meet again in December to approve it and elect officers to lead the new Colorado Society of the Army of the Philippines.

Hale spoke at the second gathering, described his visits with veterans in the state, detailed their deplorable conditions and inability to find jobs. He asked for suggestions. Discussions that followed included medical care, pensions for the needy, and federal hiring preferences. Hale reached outside Colorado to others, including General Funston and his boys from Iowa. Everyone he spoke with supported them.

The Coloradoans dedicated themselves to the memories of fallen comrades and assisting survivors. The Colorado Philippine veterans connected with the Ohio Cuba veterans, the American Veterans of Foreign Service. They eventually merged into an organization that would surely endure—the Veterans of Foreign Wars.[18]

PHILIPPINE INSURRECTION

War against Spain had been brief in Cuba and in the Philippines. Although Spain was defeated, the United States still paid $20 million for the Philippine archipelago of 7,000 islands. All McKinley's navy and the American shipping industry needed was a safe port at Manila, something the Filipinos would have surely granted free of charge for their independence. But just when the war could have ended, it became a quagmire.

Dewey had brought the guerilla leader Emilio Aguinaldo from exile in Hong Kong to organize resistance against the Spanish while he waited for American troops to cross the Pacific. Aguinaldo did more; he organized an independent republic. But independence was denied the Filipinos and his guerrillas turned their rusty muskets and bolos against the Americans. The United States hung onto the islands while deciding what to do with them.

Dewey was busy guarding 13,000 Spanish prisoners with his 8,500 troops, while 10,000 Filipino guerillas clamored for independence. Emotions at home swung from celebrations for victory over Spain to outrage over atrocities in the Philippine countryside, and the guerilla war worsened every day. Americans saw Filipinos as ungrateful primitives while they saw Americans as more duplicitous than the Spanish they replaced.

American troops were mostly from western states where they had been fighting Indians. They were badly outnumbered, 30,000 of them against 7 million Filipinos. When fifty-nine Americans were killed and twenty-three wounded in Samar by guerillas dressed as women, Brigadier General Jacob Smith ordered Major Waller to savage the island, taking no prisoners over the age of ten. Atrocities were common on both sides. But attempts to censor the bad news failed as soldier's letters home appeared in newspapers. The Anti-Imperialist League and Women's Christian Temperance Union exploited them against continuing the war. Mark Twain joined the antiwar dissenters and singled out Frederick Funston for the brunt of his reproach.

Arguments erupted in Congress as those wanting the islands for commercial purposes opposed bringing the troops home. A modern navy made it possible to reach further than ever before; occupying the islands made it reality. But, fighting in the mountains and jungles in extreme weather and terrain, and with the same tropical diseases as Cuba made it a hard fight.

The insurrection tapered off after General Funston infiltrated Aguinaldo's mountain hideout and captured him. But the Filipinos would not gain independence until after World War II. The protracted Philippine War was only a glimpse of a future Asian war in Vietnam where the outcome depended more on actions at home than in the field.

SMALL WARS

Soldiers and sailors had fought on foreign soil in Mexico, but campaigns in Cuba and in the Philippines were the first interventions overseas. Internationalism engaged American troops in numerous smaller wars as the United States redefined itself. Such small wars included the Boxer Uprising in China (1899–1901), the Panama Intervention (1903), Mexican border battles and skirmishes (1911–1921), Veracruz Occupation (1914), the Mexican Punitive Expedition (1916–1917), succeeding Cuban Interventions (1906–1909, 1912, 1917–1922), Nicaragua (1912–1925, 1927–1933), Haiti Occupation (1915–1934), Occupation of the Dominican Republic (1916–1924), the North Russian Intervention (1918–1919), and the Siberia campaign (1918–1920).

These engagements entangled our military as international policeman and the Marine Corps developed a *Small Wars Manuel* to provide guidance in such politically charged expeditions. Small wars were "... operations undertaken under the executive authority, wherein military force is combined with diplomatic pressure in the internal or external affairs of another state whose government is unstable, inadequate, or unsatisfactory for the preservation of life and such interests as are determined by foreign policy of our nation."[19]

Internationalist policies challenged military people charged with executing much of it. The army had to adapt to thousands of volunteers for the Spanish Wars, and the navy found new roles in operating over wide expanses of ocean. War colleges were established to educate senior officers and a general staff was formed to oversee deployment of forces over great distances, coordinate the National Guard, and improve relations between the military departments, service secretaries, and military commanders. Not much was done to help veterans of those small wars.

Even with big changes, the military in 1900 was better suited for frontier service than as an expeditionary force. Most men in uniform were trained for combat jobs. During the Civil War, over 93 percent of enlisted men served in combat roles; in the Spanish War it was still over 86 percent. The industrial revolution introduced more specialized skills to the military; still, through the turn of the century, more men would die of disease than from weapons. The Spanish War required the government to recruit, select, train, and organize large numbers for overseas deployment. It marked the beginning of a mechanism to mobilize masses for World War I and II.[20]

MOUNTING COSTS

During the period following the Spanish-American War costs of veterans' benefits surpassed all other war expenses. The cost of pensions was so high that Congress and the administration saw problems meeting future demands. The country might not be able to afford the price of war anymore.

Pensions for Spanish-American War veterans did not begin until 1920 for those over sixty-two who had served at least 90 days, or who were no longer capable of manual labor. It included veterans from the Cuban and Philippine campaigns and from the China campaigns. Widows were included in 1918 and increased for inflation in 1926 and 1930. But the entire pension system was wrecked by the economic act of 1933, which gave the President sweeping powers to revise eligibility and levels for economic reasons. He reduced pensions until they were restored in 1934 and 1935.

Congress considered re-categorizing benefits for veterans of the 1898-1902 period while the United Spanish War Veterans argued they should be treated the same as Federal Civil War veterans. After the Civil War, distinctions were drawn

Table 5.1
Costs of Wars

War	Direct cost (in dollars)	Cumulative benefits (in dollars)	Benefits as %
Revolution	75,000,000	70,000,000	48.27
War of 1812	134,000,000	46,000,000	34.32
Mexican War	166,000,000	62,000,000	44.70
Civil War	4,000,000,000	8,200,000,000	67.21
Spanish War	57,000,000	4,800,000,000	98.82

Source: U.S. President's Commission on Veteran's Pensions Report: Findings and Recommendations, 1959: 111.

between pensions for service and disability. Legislation in 1862 permitted pensions to men disabled as a result of military service that applied to Civil War veterans living in the 1898-1902 era. Spanish War veterans wanted the same.

Benefits for veterans of the Philippines were the same as for Cuba veterans until the date Spain ceded the islands and the Philippine insurrection began. The end of the Spanish-American War in the Philippines was set as July 4, 1902.

There were many exceptions, some were clear, others not. The Veterans Administration (VA) ruled in one case a naval hospital corpsman was eligible because he was subject to being called ashore, as was the widow of a civilian surgeon when her husband died of wounds in 1933. But benefits were withheld from a nurse who died of a disease contracted in the Philippines because her symptoms appeared later and she could not prove a direct connection. Veterans of Small Wars did not fare well with the Veterans Administration. When wartime pensions were requested by the families of two marine sergeants killed in mutinies in Nicaragua, the VA ruled neither death was connected to military operations because the marines were on police duty.[21]

The toughest fighting in the Philippines was during the insurgency. When peace was declared with Spain in 1902, the status of those in the islands changed. Civilian government replaced military rule except in Moro Province, but the guerilla wars continued unabated. Troops were sent to quell uprisings until late 1913, yet Philippine veterans after 1902 were ineligible for pensions unless they could prove service-connected disabilities. Only duty in Moro Province was covered until July 15, 1903.

The VA considered service in the Philippines an ordinary expedition while veterans argued the Philippine War was a continuation of the original conflict and wanted coverage to December 31, 1913. Presidents Franklin Roosevelt and Harry Truman did not want to fund the added period and backed the VA. Congress agreed with the veterans but Roosevelt vetoed the act.[22]

The executive branch based their case on international law keyed to the ending of hostilities, holding to the fiction that the war ended on July 4, 1902, only to hold off dissenters of continued occupation of the Philippines. Negotiations over self-government continued until Philippine independence on July 4, 1946, after World War II.

UNHAPPY END

The United States had become an international power. New technology, industry, and commerce raised hopes and inspired dreams. Sailors, soldiers, and marines volunteered in record numbers to participate in the quest for international identity. When they came home they were first hailed in political speeches, songs were composed about their heroism, bands played; nothing was too good for them until calculations showed the high cost. When the price of veterans care exceeded the other cost of war their aid was vetoed. Others came home to be quarantined to die of tropical diseases in remote camps in the United States while the government denied there was a problem.

Men like Charles Post were caught up in the excitement or patriotism, brass buttons, and the romance of going overseas for $13 a day. He gave up a good job, a safe one with the newspaper, to march with the 71st Volunteer Infantry into Santiago, Cuba. But he came home with yellow fever and was quarantined and almost died. He held on to his sketchbooks until after he retired from government service. His collection of eighty pieces of combat art tells the story of the Santiago campaign from the viewpoint of an ordinary soldier, but he was not ordinary. He was lucky he survived.

Joseph DeBurgh went to the Philippines with the 2nd Oregon Volunteers, also looking for adventure and in pursuit of a young Spanish beauty he had seen in the newspaper. DeBurgh never found his girl, but he found his place in Manila and stayed there for the rest of his life. Perhaps he was better off chasing his dream there than in his native country.

Men like these laid it all on the line when their country called. They were naive, but brave and strong. They asked for nothing, and hardly got that much. But it was men like them that did their duty; they were veterans, too.

6

Doughboys

"... An old soldier ... sounded high the trumpet's first call for dinner." Martin Vilas visited the National Soldiers' home and aging veterans from the Civil and Spanish-American Wars in 1914, as another war approached. Vilas stood near the mess hall as old soldiers in musty blue uniforms, a few in gray, one with a wooden leg, some with visible scars, all with injuries less evident, answered the bugle's call. He saw battles drawn in the lines of their faces, from Mexico City to New Orleans, Manassas to Gettysburg, San Juan Hill, and Manila Bay. Vilas saw their grimness; men who had felt the bigness of youth, men who had worked hard in maturity, but in old age were worn and weak. Their eyes said they only waited to "find abiding peace in yonder soldier's resting place." He thought of the brave men that suffered and died, the mothers with broken hearts, and he felt the weight of desolation that follows war.[1] But with the new century another war approached, and another line of veterans to take their place.

THE GREAT WAR

World War I began with the assassination of Archduke Franz Ferdinand in Sarajevo and erupted into a global conflict enveloping thirty nations across five continents. When Austria declared war on Serbia they sent men on horseback in flashy uniforms, brandishing sabers. Military strategy was a relic of Waterloo and Gettysburg, employing massed formations against fortifications. But machineguns and poisoned gas resulted in enormous casualties; trench lines were hammered in a war with little movement. The battlefield was strewn with human debris with ruined lungs, sightless eyes, missing limbs, and smashed perceptions.

When the Great War ended, doughboys eventually came home and their presence reminded friends and families of the cruelty of war and the government of its obligations. This was to have been the war to end all wars; no one could imagine another reaching such scope and intensity. The war changed relations between Europeans and Americans and it changed the men and women caught up in the excitement of going "over there."

DOUGHBOYS

"When he went off to the war that was to end all wars my father was twenty-nine years old...." Robert Russell prefaced his father's war diary, describing how he left the serenity and happiness of home, a loving family, the girl he planned to marry, his straw hat and banjo, and went to France. When he returned he had lost his innocence somewhere in the trenches. Sergeant Reese Melvin Russell went over there with Company E, 317th Infantry, of the 80th Division. "I looked over the top and saw what looked like a thousand Germans making for my trench ... could not count but twenty-six of us. I told my men it was a fight to the finish and we could not and would not retreat." Sergeant Russell moved about the trench shoring up defenses and encouraging the others, stepping over those lying on the bottom, too severely wounded to fight. One asked him to "do something for me, for I am killed." Sergeant Russell assured him they would all be dead soon.

"When he returned from that holocaust my father could no longer relate to the world he had left behind," Russell said of a man he hardly knew. "He was always, for the rest of his life, traveling a lonely road, out of step with his family, his friends, his surroundings." The veteran doughboy settled into his community of Cedar Bluff to raise a family, burying his lonely burden inside. "I never heard him speak of the war, not even when he and his old army buddies got together. As children we were not allowed to mention ... World War I in my father's presence...." But every year on Armistice Day, "... he put on his little envelope-style cap and his old army overcoat and marched in the parade with other veterans."

Before the war Russell had enjoyed picnics and good times and used his natural skills to build his own home. Afterwards he drifted between jobs: building for a while, then mining, trading junk, hunting and trapping, even selling herbs. Russell had been gassed in France, his lungs and nerves damaged. "But that was his battle and we knew little of it...." He drew a small bonus before he died but didn't march with the other veterans on Washington; he kept his uniforms, leggings, steel helmet, and gas mask secretly stowed in an old trunk.

"My father never slept again after he returned from the war." His wife didn't understand his condition and a breach developed between him and his children; he fought a lonely battle with alcohol until the end. "He had a military funeral and when taps sounded I felt a sense of relief. His suffering and terrible memories were over and at last he could sleep." The military detail honored the man who had earned a Silver Star 50 years before. Uniformed sergeants reverently carried his flag draped casket; a rifle squad lined the church steps, chrome helmets sparkling in the sunlight. Soldiers saluted as he passed; his wife looked at their son and whispered. "I understand now."

Reese Russell had lived his life surrounded by his family and friends, yet alone. He was a member of the American Legion and Masons, and was respected in the community despite his private demons. "We never knew the good he had done until some of the people he had helped came weeping to his funeral saying how much they loved him."[2]

GOING OVER THERE

War had thundered over Europe in the summer of 1914, but Americans hardly noticed. The public heard warnings and calls for national preparedness, but midwest and southern farmers distrusted the northern industry elites who stood to profit. Universal military service was unpopular as were increased taxes to fund it. European armies were massed across barbed wire in 1917, bogged down in a muddy, bloody stalemate. Allies pleaded with the United States to enter with manpower, weapons, and equipment, but the public remembered the Philippine stalemate; foreign quagmires should be avoided. U.S. military power was thin with divisions poorly equipped, men untrained and without experience in trench warfare. The navy ranked third behind Germany's and was deficient in quality and quantity but racing to catch up. Funding increased from 7 percent of federal spending in 1890 to 19 percent by 1914. Yet, the fleet was still unbalanced, oriented on coastal defenses and protecting commercial shipping, not fighting at sea.

Despite inadequate preparation or resolve, war was inevitable. The Naval Act of 1916 empowered the navy to cross the Atlantic to protect the home shores and authorized a naval reserve and flying service. The navy's many missions included transporting millions of soldiers with equipment and supplies, protecting convoys, blockading enemy seaports, and defeating Germany's larger navy. Congress increased the shipbuilding program to over 150 battle-worthy ships in 3 years, but half were missing crews.

The sky was a new dimension to modern battlefields but an air force was only a dream. The Wright brothers had already made their first manned flights and had convinced the Army that air power was an essential element of modern war by 1908. But in 1914 the Army had only six planes and sixteen trained military pilots. The United States spent $125,000 on aviation while Mexico spent four times as much. Congress authorized bringing the aviation section up to 320 officers and men.

Since the Civil War the Army had been mobilized and demobilized so frequently its structure and training were still unsettled. An array of diverse smaller wars, reorganizations, and shifting priorities had not prepared the Army or Marine Corps for global warfare. The 1903 Dick Act had transformed state militias into a National Guard, set common standards for federal and state service, established an army reserve, and authorized a draft. In 1916, The National Defense Act empowered the President to call the National Guard into federal service and made qualified men between 18 and 45 subject to call. The strength of the Army was doubled to 288,000 men over 5 years; the National Guard quadrupled to 425,000.

While Germany marched through Europe the threat at home was closer. Pancho Villa crossed the Mexican border into the southern United States in 1916, a personal affront to those who remembered fighting for the Rio Grande border. President Wilson ordered General John "Blackjack" Pershing into northern Mexico on a punitive expedition. More than 100,000 National Guardsmen were federalized to restore the border and punish the invaders. But the test of the new national defense organizations and procedures revealed unexpected problems. Many federalized guardsmen did not answer their calls, others reported but refused to go, some failed federal physical standards. Vigorous recruiting could not make up the shortfall. The battle drill with Mexico revealed glaring weaknesses in national preparations on the eve of a world war.[3]

Problems responding to Mexico's limited incursion were seen by Germany as a sign of weakness. While Pershing and his troops chased Poncho Villa, Kaiser Wilhelm requested Wilson support a negotiated settlement in Europe. When Wilson refused, Germany launched a U-boat offensive on American shipping, prompting Wilson to sever diplomatic relations and declare armed neutrality.

Most Americans still opposed war despite attacks on shipping, but not all. While the debate continued a few were impatient and volunteered to serve with the French flying service, the *Escadrille Lafayette,* the French Foreign Legion, or regular British line units. Others drove ambulances for the Red Cross or in the American Volunteer Motor-Ambulance Corps.

Ships harbored in safe ports while politicians argued about arming them for self-defense; that changed when a telegram from the German Foreign Secretary was intercepted and released to the press. It proposed a German-Mexican alliance against the United States. The direct threat inflamed the public and Wilson marched to Capital Hill for a special joint session of Congress. His declaration of war on Germany received thunderous approval in the chambers and across the country. It was time to get the job done. Soldiers prepared to embark with little to offer but hope, their blood, and a remarkable record of successes. They expected to gain little for themselves beyond a great adventure and excitement for the unknown, but they carried with them courage and determination to build a better future.[4]

"All is confusion and I'm part of it," Stan Lamb wrote to his parents from training. "The shaving brushes are being used as stencil brushes to mark our clothes, the tooth brushes to clean our guns, the hair brush to shine our shoes, the extra underwear and socks to wipe our guns. The comb is no good ... for our heads are clipped short." Lamb immensely enjoyed writing and receiving letters. "Write often and long," he pleaded with his girlfriend, Mary, as he embarked, "many letters will get sunk going and coming so keep up the supply."[5]

TAKING THE TRENCHES

Rudy Neumann was born in 1897 on a 40-acre farm south of Bridgeport, Michigan, the youngest of nine children of Austrian immigrants. One evening after work in November 1917, he walked to the local recruiting office and waited for the recruiter to return from dinner. The Army recruiter gave him a stack of forms to complete then escorted him to the meat market next door to be weighed. Rudy selected coastal artillery so he could stay in the United States, but after basic training he lined up with all the others to board the *Leviathan* bound for France. Rudy celebrated his twenty-first birthday having supper with 12,000 men in the crowded mess before collapsing in canvas bunks stacked four high. Throughout the night, German U-boats tried to prevent him from reaching his twenty-second birthday but British destroyers fought them off. Rudy survived and grew into quite a different man in France from the boy who had enlisted in Michigan.[6]

Most newly mobilized units going to France left from the port at New York, the men housed at the old armory on Fourth Avenue until time to board. The 71st Infantry Regiment was one of the first National Guard units to be shipped over. They marched to the armory behind their band, colors flying high, ranks held straight all the way from Grand Central Station. Their uniforms and equipment were new and they were a splendid sight. Crowds lined both sides of the avenue and gawked, cordial and proud, but completely silent.

When civilians returned to Fourth Avenue the following day, the city had been transformed. Men in khaki filled restaurants, clustered in nervous conversations on sidewalks, or stood in small groups and whistled at the passing girls. Tents lined railroad tracks connecting New York with Boston and Washington; sentries guarded tunnels, bridges, and entrances to transportation centers. These men were bound for the front and were already on guard.

Among those at the armory was one homesick veterinarian from Iowa farm country. After college he had established a small rural practice to care for his friends' and neighbors' livestock. He lived simply but supported his family well enough when his neighbors had good crops and were able to pay for his services.

A few weeks earlier, a letter postmarked from Washington, DC, had been dropped into his mailbox. Beneath an official letterhead it announced the War Department was gathering information about veterinarians and requested he complete a form with his personal and professional details. His wife told him he should be honored for Washington to be interested in him. Despite her assurances his doubts lingered, but he completed the form and mailed it. In 2 weeks a second letter arrived directing him to travel to Douglas, Arizona. He had never been out of Iowa and planned to keep the first time brief. He had patients and a family to consider so he would treat the government's animals and return promptly.

His wife ironed a spare shirt and rolled clean socks to go into his leather instrument bag. After hugs, kisses, and a few tears he grabbed his bag and left without looking back. He didn't need the extra shirt; at Douglas he was fitted for a lieutenant's uniform. As soon as he slipped it on and raised his right hand, he was in the army. In 6 days the man who had never been out of Iowa traveled to Arizona, to New York for one night in the armory then boarded a ship for France. He had expected to be home in 5 days but for him and the others, it would be much, much longer.[7]

The Selective Service Act of May 1917 required all eligible males to register for a draft. Local draft boards examined, classified, and selected by lottery those chosen for physical examinations. Technicians and professionals, such as the Iowa veterinarian, were specially selected, while clergy, conscientious objectors, and civilians with war-critical jobs were exempted. Army enlistments were generally for the duration of the war but the Navy and Marine Corps accepted volunteers for 4 years until they also were compelled to use the draft.

In 1917, Americans were privileged ivy leaguers, or immigrants and Negroes, or hard-working blue-collars and clerks; there was hardly a middle class. The evils of sin were chastised at home and in churches while elementary McGuffey Readers stressed the virtues of hard work and patriotism. Horatio Alger stories extolled good character. Few continued beyond elementary school since education was not a formula for milk, bread, meat, or heat in winter.

Induction physicals were the only evaluations of fitness until 1917 when Robert Yerkes introduced a mental assessment. The standardized tests were not measures of intelligence but of acquired knowledge. The results were shocking. The mental ages of half the whites and 90 percent of blacks were under 14 years; fully 31 percent of the population was illiterate, high school diplomas were meaningless. Yerkes postulated that education and mental acuity were as important to achievement as hard work. These uneducated men were leaving the dusty farms and factories for battlefields in Europe. After the war, they would stroll colorful sidewalks of Paris, meet foreign women, and taste French coffee and brandy. Newly awakened minds would conceive different possibilities for their lives, while those waiting at home wondered about the changes in them.

Not only do wars change perceptions, they also drive technology innovations. Rapid mass motor transports covered long distances rapidly, aerial dogfights and observation aircraft overcame geography, heavy armored vehicles showed possibilities for industrial equipment, and toxic gases demanded new protection and treatment, all opening new vistas to those exposed to them. Ironically, killing tools spawned new ideas for a machine-oriented civilization; complex battlefields changed workplaces at home and made higher education and increased levels of skills more urgent. Men with college educations were made officers; enlisted men with natural talents were selected for technical areas such as engineering, signals, intelligence, or aviation.

Nearly five million Americans served in WWI, over four million in an army made up of 70 percent draftees. The Navy depended on volunteers until the final months when it accepted 3,300 draftees and the Marines 7,000. Blacks crowded enlistment stations as they had during the Revolution and the Civil War, but the

Marines accepted none, the Navy barely 5,000; the Army took 367,000 against greater needs. Most blacks wanted combat units to prove their worth, but only 42,000 saw combat. The United States and France awarded black units valorous unit decorations, but when the allies marched victoriously through Paris, they were not included. At least they were permitted to march in the New York City parade in 1919 on Lincoln's birthday. Italian immigrants were also snubbed for being both Latin and Catholic and distrusted because they looked the same as white Protestants. The numbers of Italians serving is uncertain but was somewhere between 245,000 and 400,000. Eighty-five Italian immigrants won Distinguished Service Crosses—the second highest award for valor.

HOME FRONT

President Wilson had won reelection in 1916 by promising to keep the country out of war, but he faced the inevitable. Citizens could be persuaded to accept war but industry had to be completely retooled. Europeans already faced shortages of food and war materials so Americans at home would have to ration food, gas, and rubber to support troops at the front. They learned to waste nothing, substitute corn and spinach for meat, and to sacrifice. Mothers guarded pantries, girls planted war gardens, and boys worked fields and handled repairs for absent fathers. Herbert Hoover ran the Food Administration like a general. "Food Will Win the War," was the mantra at dinner tables on wheat-less Mondays and meat-less Tuesdays. The Red Cross, YMCA, and Girl Scouts collected peach stones to make charcoal powder for gas mask filters; neighbors reported draft dodgers and bought war savings stamps and liberty bonds. People waved the flag, chipped in, and sacrificed for the boys.

The war no one wanted became a national undertaking. One half million men between ages 21 to 30 were drafted in May 1917, and over two million in 1918, plus nearly 200,000 volunteers who signed for the Navy and Marines. Factories cranked out weapons, clothing, equipment, and fuel to meet the military's needs. By July 1918, the Navy was commissioning four new ships a day with warships constructed in 4 months; one destroyer, the *Ward*, was christened 17.5 days after the keel was laid. Production of Enfield rifles reached 45,000 a week by May 1918. The War Industries Board mobilized and disciplined more than 350 industries to supply the war machine with everything from raw metals to caskets. The Fuel Administration rationed and conserved coal and electricity, as the Food Administration conserved food.

It was a total effort and Americans were determined to win at home. Espionage, sabotage, sedition, and disloyal speech were outlawed, and controversial publications were censored. Federal troops were called to quell labor disputes believed to be socialist inspired. The entire country went to war.

The intensely managed economy increased productivity and brought social progress along. By the end of the war workers' rights to organize and bargain had been established, an 8-hour day was normal, labor conditions had improved in unsafe factories and exploitation of women and children at work had been reduced. Federal social insurance was enacted for servicemen and increased interest in public health showed real progress. Reform touched military training camps as well, and they were transformed into service communities with sing-fests, baseball games, post exchanges, and theaters to entertain the troops with wholesome activities; university extension courses were offered to bridge the education gap. Clean, off-duty activities compensated for restrictions on alcohol and prostitution. Reforms led to a belief that military service could be a positive experience for men who returned as value-added citizens.[8]

WOMEN IN THE GREAT WAR

Women made large contributions on the home front, but they also volunteered for military service and civilian organizations at home and overseas. They served as Reconstruction Aides, Women of the YMCA, in the Medical Corps, and as Red Cross and Salvation Army volunteers. When every sailor was needed to man new ships, women signed up as stenographers, draftswomen, and clerks to rescue a navy drowning in paperwork. Navy Secretary Josephus Daniels decreed Yeomanettes should receive the same pay as men, shocking the traditionally male Navy. In the first month, 200 women enlisted and by the end of 1918, 11,000 women were added to official navy rosters.

The marines balked at accepting women, but under pressure enrolled twenty-four as clerks in the Marine Corps Reserve. When the Armistice was signed the compelling need for the women reservists evaporated; they were notified they would be discharged. The Commandant of Marines and Secretary of the Navy held a final review on the White House lawn. The women were discharged with full federal veterans' benefits and some remained in their jobs as civilian employees. Former Private Alma Swope continued in the supply department for 44 years.

Navy Yeoman Daisy Pratt Erd left the service but joined a group of Boston-area women veterans in chartering the first female American Legion post with two hundred members. They worked with industry to help women veterans find jobs. Women veterans received federal benefits equal to men, but Massachusetts denied them state benefits. They fought for the same $100 bonus the men received since many of them had given up better civilian jobs to serve and they expected the same consideration as men afterwards.

High casualties in France made medical support critical and doctors and nurses responded to the need; the army shipped several thousand nurses to France in 1917, where they lived in muddy huts and wore the same lice-infested uniforms as the men. They changed bloody bandages, patched infected fractures and gaping shrapnel wounds, and faced lungs ravaged by gas, while tolerating their own pain, trauma, fatigue, and emotional collapse. They gave the best care ever before provided to an army in the field, but under terrible conditions. When the Armistice was signed, the Army Nurse Corps had nearly 21,500 nurses with more than 5,300 overseas, and the American Red Cross staffed fifty civilian hospitals to transfer to the War Department as needed.

When the war started there was no rehabilitation for seriously injured soldiers; loss of a limb had always meant lost opportunity for resuming a productive life. The Surgeon General's office established a Division of Special Hospitals and Physical Reconstruction in August 1917. Marguerite Sanderson believed occupational and physical therapy could enhance the lives of the disabled and convinced Dr. Joel Goldbraith to add those programs. Occupational therapists taught handicapped patients to weave, paint, print, bend metal, and other employable skills. The first twenty-four women trained as physiotherapists sailed for France in 1918; by the end of the year, two hundred were in twenty Allied Expeditionary Force (AEF) hospitals. By Armistice, nearly 2,000 reconstruction aides were in uniform with three hundred overseas. After the war they were allowed to resign and go home, or be reassigned to an army hospital in the states. Enough stayed for physical therapy clinics to open in forty-six stateside army hospitals, but as their patients recovered and were discharged they were also released as no longer necessary. Some transferred to the Veterans Bureau or public health facilities; others continued at military bases or treated incapacitated veterans at national soldiers' homes.

Blackjack Pershing saw another need—reliable communications to command the large Allied Expeditionary Forces. The French telephone system was unreliable even when German shells missed their mark. When the phone lines were up he was often unable to reach his commanders due to miscommunications with the French-speaking operators. Pershing demanded one hundred French-speaking American telephone operators as mission-essential. "Hello Girls" were urgently recruited for the Army Signal Corps. Recruiters received nearly 8,000 applications for the jobs and selected 150 for training and 400 more as reserves. Their pay was the same as soldiers and they were required to wear army uniforms, but they had to purchase theirs for $400. They believed they were joining the Army.

By the end of the war, 450 telephone operators had been trained and 223 deployed to France. When they were dismissed after the war, they were denied Victory Medals and honorable discharges. The Army considered them civilian contractors without a contract. Merle Egan Anderson considered this a serious injustice and was determined to set it right; she began a disappointing 60-year battle.

When reconstruction aides left the service, they found the same mistake as the signal corps girls. They had been sworn in but were still discharged as civilians, ineligible for veterans' benefits. More than fifty bills were presented to Congress to correct the injustices but each one failed. Finally in 1977, the combined support of the Women's Overseas Service League, the Veterans of World War I, National Organization for Women, and the undaunted Senator Barry Goldwater pushed a bill through. By then only eighteen of the originals were still alive to receive their discharge certificates, Victory Medals, and burial rights.[9]

A LEGION BORN

Doughboys and the girls in France were further from home than they had ever been before, but were well aware of the threats to American values at home. Reports reached them even in France that communist and socialist extremists had infiltrated factories and mills and were creating havoc there. They were disgusted to be fighting socialism in Europe while watching it develop in America.

Some junior officers decided to take action while still in France; the small group became a legion. Founders of the American Legion were not men to waste time: Theodore Roosevelt, Jr., George S. White, Eric Fisher Wood, and William J. Donovan. From AEF headquarters they planned a first assembly in St. Louis, Missouri, for May 1919. Although they were all officers, they wanted the Legion to be an organization of and for enlisted men. The young Roosevelt refused to lead and violate that important first principle.

The American Legion was similar to the original Society of Cincinnati, the Veterans of Foreign Wars, and other veteran organizations in that the founders wanted the Legion to help disadvantaged veterans; but they also stressed the importance for developing a national post-war military policy. They stood for national patriotism, but considered local communities and posts as essential to the grass roots organization. They did not intend to be as politically aggressive as the GAR but were determined to hold government to a higher standard, especially the Veterans Bureau with its reputation for incompetence and arrogance. Later, when Congress wanted veterans' opinions, the American Legion got answers by polling local posts. Their political action plan included issues important to veterans, such as land settlements, assistance with buying homes, vocational training, and compensation based on service. These were the basis for important future veterans' legislation.

ARMISTICE

Letters were lifelines for Private Stan Lamb. He depended on them, writing and reading those that made it through the erratic mail system. Letters connected him to reality as he remembered it. In July, 1918, soon after his arrival in France, he wrote to his father: "This life, like the ordinary run, is becoming more or less a grind; strange fact that this great war should become commonplace to one of its participants!" His boredom came from his inability to see where he fit into the grand plan and he complained that the contribution of any one individual was so small that he would have to wait for the history books to be written to understand where he fit into it. But, a few months later near the end of October, 1918, he told his girlfriend Mary, "If I had time to sit down for a quiet half hour and write a real letter, it might possibly be an interesting one, for . . . we are having a taste of the war as it is written about and lots of it that is only imagined." Then, on the first of November, he warned his mother not to expect any letters for a while;

he was off to the front. The next one was in mid-November: "By firelight on the fought-over ground of this stricken country I pause to rush word to you of my safety and well-being. The last 3 weeks were terrible and of them I cannot write."[10]

Irving Johnson, a mechanic from Pennsylvania, was the son of Swedish immigrants. He enlisted at twenty-four and became a Wagoner in the ammo trains in the Meuse-Argonne offensive. He recalled the end of the war in his memoirs. Rumors of the end were flying about, but then, at 9:00 A.M. on the morning of November 11, 1918, his commander made the official announcement. "The armies fought right up until eleven o'clock," he wrote. "We could hear the cannon boom for miles. At exactly eleven o'clock in the morning, the firing ceased and everything became as quiet as a graveyard at midnight. It actually made us lonesome not to hear the roar of the guns."[11]

Sergeant Joseph Gleeson kept a daily account of his squad. On the night the fighting ended: "The first night in months I couldn't hear firing of some kind. Everybody has a light burning." Two nights later, he continued, "The boys are exploring the lines. At night they build a big fire and talk of the future."[12] Gleeson and his war buddies sat around the big fire cooking spuds, and they must have dreamed of the farms, the families, the girls they left behind, and getting back into the swing of it. Hardly could they imagine how much it had changed.

When the armistice was announced over twenty million soldiers and sailors were left with time on their hands. The axis had to be disarmed and disbanded before the allies could leave, but logistics and economics were the main reason for delay. Boredom became the new enemy of doughboys in France, left with no purpose for being there, while at home their families were impatient for their return. The AEF used the time to collect equipment and supplies and update personnel records, while keeping soldiers busy with sports, leisure activities, and educational opportunities.

Back at home, production in factories and on farms exceeded military needs after the war ended. Manufacturing was curtailed but stockpiles of war material already crowded depots; workers realized they were excess. They foresaw massive lay offs and the millions of men overseas coming to take their jobs. Idle troops in France worried where they would find jobs when they got home. They were allowed to stay in uniform until they found work, but few did. A million and a quarter men were released in 1919. Had more stayed in service the job shortage might have been reduced, but they were tired of war, bored with waiting, and anxious to find their place.

HOMEWARD BOUND

Separating from old war buddies was difficult, even as they were pulled to go. Corporal Will Judy scribbled his feelings in his diary in January 1919. "We talk much of comradeship in the coming civilian life. Like mystics, we are conscious of an association that binds us into a passionate group different and superior, as we think, to all others."[13]

They bivouacked together in seaport camps to await transportation to New York. Warships, including twenty-four cruisers and battleships, were converted to transports for the 15-day round-trip. British ships ferried 300,000 Americans a month from France to New York, but every ship available was still not enough; it took a year to get them all home.

One of the first units to reach the port of New York was the 369th Infantry of the New York National Guard. The all-black regiment had reinforced the French army during the heaviest fighting and was awarded the Croix de Guerre. They docked on February 17, 1919, to a tumultuous welcome and marched proudly up Fifth Avenue. It was the greatest black celebration since emancipation. "Welcome Home!" banners were hung from windows for all the doughboys to follow. Waves of Harlem's black soldiers in overcoats and tin helmets marched in a French phalanx, the first to pass under the Victory Arch on Twenty-fifth Street. Politicians packed the reviewing stands and families spilled off sidewalks joining their boys in the street. As the 369th approached Harlem, the noise was so loud the men could not hear the drumbeat and fell out of step. Commanders gave up trying to control them when young women and children mixed with the troops. They all walked together, singing for joy.[14]

Rudy Neumann had celebrated his twenty-first birthday en route to France in 1917. Two years later, he stood in a cold rain waiting to receive his medal from General Pershing before sailing home. Before being allowed aboard ship, he was deloused and issued fresh clothing. As he boarded the ship the band broke into *Homeward Bound* and men broke into cheers. As they got underway, seasickness was replaced by dice and cards. Seven days later the ship docked at Manhattan Pier No. 60. "While we had received a touching farewell, I must mark our reception in New York harbor as the happiest day of our young lives."[15]

When transports steamed into New York men crowded the decks for a glimpse of the Statue of Liberty. Sirens and whistles blared from watercraft in the harbor and major league baseball players hurled apples and oranges to outstretched hands on the crowded decks. Huge banners proclaimed the national sentiment, "Welcome Home," and "Well Done, Our Heroes." As they disembarked, Red Cross workers served frankfurters and sauerkraut, or apple pie and ice cream.[16] When the women arrived, their ship was clearly distinguishable from the men's due to a special woman's touch. The topside deck was lavishly decorated with the only thing available: toilet paper.[17]

New York City threw six major parades; when the 27th Infantry Division passed under the Victory Arch at Madison Square on March 25th people lined the route. Confetti swirled over the doughboys all the way to 59th Street. So many parades were held in Philadelphia, Chicago, and other cities that people grew weary of them by mid-summer. But it wasn't over until the 1st Infantry Division held the grand finale in Washington, DC, on September 17. The Big Red One rolled through the capital with full military gear, a sight to behold and the end of parades.[18]

With major celebrations over, only the realities of life after the war were left to be settled. Rudy Neumann closed his diary with a recitation about slit trench latrines in France before a final statement of resignation: "This was my part in the war to end all wars. What a farce that turned out to be. Millions of men killed, and millions of dollars made by men."[19]

Corporal Lars Greenquist was still a Swedish citizen when he joined the 88th Division on the way to France. He came home behind his division because he was participating in a rifle competition. But after his farewell to France and welcome to New York, he lingered there a few days before catching a train to Des Moines and discharge at Camp Dodge. Businessmen formed a reception committee to meet the troop trains; society ladies spread a banquet over long tables while throngs of happy people filled the streets to celebrate on Grand Avenue. Within 48 hours Greenquist finished at the camp and returned to Des Moines with red chevrons sewn on his left sleeve and a lucky cloverleaf patch on his shoulder. The railroad station was packed with men waiting for trains to Minnesota, North Dakota, South Dakota, Missouri, Nebraska, and other stops throughout the Midwest. They soon scattered like leaves in the wind to hometowns across the country for much more personal homecoming celebrations.[20]

Armistice Day was a day to remember with parades, speeches, and celebrations at the exact moment the war ended—the 11th day of the 11th month, at the 11th hour. The tradition continued unchanged until the ranks of doughboy veterans were too thinned by time.

SETTLING DOWN

Settling down was not so easy for the men of the 102nd Infantry Regiment in New Haven, New York, in May of 1919. Soldiers from the Yankee Division marched past a group of Yale freshmen. "Student Slacker!" was shouted by one of the soldiers; "Boy Scouts!" was shouted back from the students. The jeering continued until the soldiers marched away. One hundred soldiers gathered that night under the dormitory windows and challenged the students to come out and settle the matter. Instead, they pelted the soldiers with books, shoes, bricks, and bottles from dormitory windows. Police broke up the scuffle.

Hostilities didn't end there. Two days later troops gathered near the village green, complaining that students had hissed at them in a movie theater. Some were ready to attack then but cooler heads prevailed. The situation calmed until a local newspaper, the *Union*, stirred up more trouble by encouraging the soldiers to stand up to the students. Another fight broke out; this time, soldiers threw rocks through dormitory windows and pulled staves from a picket fence to use as clubs. Blood was shed this time. One student was injured trying to break up the fight,

Jim Braden, captain of Yale's track team. Braden was also a doughboy veteran of the 102nd Regiment.[21]

No one had expected the war to end before 1919; the government didn't begin planning for demobilization until a month before the armistice. Between December 1918, and August 1919, over two million men arrived at home, another two million soon followed. Units were disbanded quickly, with priority to farmers, railroad workers, and coal miners. Men traveled from arrival ports to one of thirty-three demobilization centers nearest their homes, were paid $60, fitted for a civilian suit, and offered help finding a job.

The labor market strained to absorb four million men from overseas and three million others who never deployed. The first ones released found jobs if they had the right skills. Those released later or without the needed skills, found their hunt more difficult. A third of the enlisted men in the AEF had been mechanics, repairmen, craftsmen, and service workers, picking up hands-on experience with gas engines, aviation mechanics, and modern signal equipment, highly valued in a modern world. Those with skills needed in civilian jobs, or who had increased their education, found work. Others were not so fortunate.[22]

The United States had become the richest country in the world, physically untouched by the war, and united by a strong sense of nationalism. Veterans found transportation rolling, factories humming, and farmlands waiting; prohibition and women's suffrage had gained while they were away. In all, the country they discovered was changed from the one they remembered. But after the celebrations and excitement ended, inflation jumped. Commodity prices doubled between 1915 and 1920 and the dollar lost half its purchasing power. Production bonuses and overtime pay ended for workers, who went home with less in their pockets. Some regions faced sudden high levels of unemployment.

Rising immigration slapped more diversity on a society that had not yet fully accepted blacks after the Civil War. When slaves were freed, many had moved from southern farms to better paying factory jobs in northern cities. Post WWI inflation and unemployment reduced their opportunities. Expectations for equality among the black and immigrant veterans were unmet and race riots broke out as blacks and immigrants demanded better. Sixty-two lynching were recorded in 1918, fifty-eight were black men, ten were veterans, and some were still in uniform. Nationalism developed into a deadly hysteria. In 1919, a man in Hammond, Indiana, was shot and killed for shouting, "to hell with the United States!" At the killer's trail, the jury deliberated only two minutes before acquitting him. In the nation's capital, another refused to rise for the National Anthem. An angry sailor shot and killed him while the crowd applauded.[23]

With the influx of veterans and slow down in production, two million women and men added to factories were laid off. In December 1918, six hundred thousand came home and 43,000 jobs were eliminated in the same week. Help-wanted ads were replaced by situation-wanted ads by desperate jobseekers in some cities, but opportunities were unevenly spread. In March of 1919, eighty cities reported high unemployment while fifteen experienced a shortage. Congress cut appropriations for employment services when it was most needed. The Veterans Bureau still retrained veterans, but followed the principle of not training above one's earning potential. The job squeeze was tight.

A good job was the ticket to a better life for most veterans and many believed they were qualified for better than they were offered. Their horizons had been expanded overseas and they had gained experience. One bank messenger before the war was promoted to Captain in the AEF based on his leadership and organizational skills. When he returned to the bank, he was offered his old job; he knew he was qualified for more responsibility and was unhappy. Many were difficult to place because they were so selective; only 36 percent in New York accepted the jobs they were first offered compared to 56 percent of nonveterans. Civilians already had the best jobs, had moved up the pay scale, and were invaluable to their companies. The *Philadelphia Record* editorialized that soldiers should just be satisfied they had done their duty; that was compensation enough.[24]

Battle hardened veterans sometimes saw their civilian jobs as trivial and unchallenging. Merely getting back home in one piece and landing a job was not enough. One former elevator attendant went to France to fight and considered his experience there one of high principles. When he returned to his old job, he soon quit, finding no meaning in running an elevator up then down again.[25]

The AEF included 121,000 illiterates; many were immigrants who never learned English. The Army Educational Commission developed on-post schools to teach elementary subjects to 180,000 of them, and high school subjects and vocational skills to another 27,000. College classes were offered to 23,000 men at British and French universities or extension courses. Adult education opportunities were available to one and a half million men waiting to go home. When they returned with an acquired taste for knowledge, they flooded American classrooms. Veterans had connected the value of education to future opportunities.[26]

Veterans are usually affected by their experiences, sometimes changing their values or ideals. Sometimes they didn't see the changes until someone pointed them out. A letter to Private Edward Loudenbeck at the front suggested he had changed. "Don't know what change you have figured has come over me. Perhaps I'm sterner in expressing myself or maybe my association with men only for so long has made me coarser." But he admitted that keeping close ties with home had moderated the changes in him. He hinted at the reasons: "Have seen the baseness of the world and instead of destroying my faith in mankind, it leads me to prize and respect virtue more than ever."[27]

One husband's return unsettled his family. He didn't appreciate his wife's sacrifices under rationing and separation, and couldn't get beyond his own experiences. He exploded when the children called their family outings forced marches. He hated civilian clothes and made no secret that he missed his uniforms; she stayed out of the bedroom while he dressed. He longed for his lost friends and thought the neighbors were lifeless. She saw his absent look, his restlessness and impatience, his annoyance with standing in line for a bus ticket. Looking back on the wartime drudgery of her life, she found it more pleasurable while he was gone.[28]

Civilians saw changes in the doughboys, didn't understand them, and mostly left them alone. One mother complained her son wrote home often from the front with detailed descriptions of how he would spend his time, what he wanted her to cook, what he dreamed of doing with his life. But when he came back, nothing was as he imagined. His mother despaired that he wasted time, had no appetite or motivation; he had lost interest in life.[29]

Crime, gambling, bootlegging, and speakeasies accompanied the liberal 1920s. The Mafia captured headlines while down-on-their-luck veterans wasted away in county jails. Twenty percent of prisoners nation-wide were former doughboys, frequently incarcerated for situations stemming from their service: poverty, alcohol, or psychosomatic stress. Seventy percent of those in jail were there for stealing food, or money to buy it.[30]

ROBBING PETER

As jobs vanished four million workers picketed with 3,600 strikes against a system that worked for only a few. Whispers about socialism and the red menace became shouts, citizens spied on neighbors, and blacks, Italians, and Jews were routinely added to police watch lists with foreigners and felons. The American Legion encouraged patriotism but was more concerned with veterans' support issues. General Pershing cautioned all veterans' groups against becoming too political but their members strongly backed those issues. When their leaders stormed Capital Hill for improved benefits the Legion quickly signed 650,000 new members.

The Harding administration responded by piecing together the Veterans' Bureau in 1921 to administer the sick and wounded. Unfortunately, Harding named a corrupt political hack to lead. Colonel Charles R. Forbes was tasked to assemble the Veterans Bureau from multiple disparate agencies: the Bureau of Risk Insurance, the Public Health Service, and the Federal Board for Vocational Rehabilitation. But Forbes, a pardoned former deserter, was the wrong man for the job.

Congress authorized $9 million to build hospitals and rehabilitation camps for 200,000 sick, injured, or disabled veterans, then doubled it and tacked on an operating budget of $450 million. But Forbes, and 30,000 indifferent bureaucrats, robbed taxpayers and veterans by wasting the money or lining their pockets with most of it. Very little was used for the intended purpose.

The assorted components of the new Veterans Bureau had been inefficient even before they were consolidated; the combination was worse. The old Vocational Rehabilitation Bureau had always been ineffective in handling readjustment problems. For instance, 110,000 men applied for assistance but bureaucrats approved only 24,000. Long delays and incompetence forced out most of those who were enrolled, and only 217 actually completed training. Hungry veterans went to jail for stealing food while the bureau paid $319,000 in salaries to staff, only $139,000 for rehabilitation of veterans.[31]

The American Legion helped as many as possible through the rehabilitation program and followed up after training to evaluate the program's effectiveness. The Legion had fought for those courses and wanted them to work despite the problems. They encouraged veterans to finish the training and businesses to hire them, as work was an essential element of recovery. They reported 179,500 WWI veterans entered the new bureau's physical rehabilitation programs, some died before finishing, others dropped out. Nearly 128,000 men eventually completed rehabilitation at an average cost of $5,000.[32]

If retraining was bad, health care was worse. The $33 million allocated for hospital construction produced only 200 additional beds; one new hospital in Excelsior, Missouri, had no kitchen. The bureau paid $71,000 for enough floor wax to last 100 years even though thousands of gallons were already in stock. Soap costing less than 2 cents a gallon was bought for 87 cents a gallon. Forbes needed space to store the excess supplies purchased from cronies, so he emptied warehouses by selling the contents: over 67,000 quarts of bourbon, rye, and gin that should have been destroyed during prohibition. He sold 126 railcars filled with bath towels, bed sheets, and winter pajamas worth $7 million for $600,000 cash. Over $5 million of vital medicine was sold rather than delivered to hospitals. The bureau paid dentists $5.5 million for gold fillings while cavities were filled with copper, nickel, or brass. Civil servants lived lavishly while veterans paid the price.[33]

The American Legion and Disabled American Veterans realized what was happening and directed their rage at Capitol Hill. The scandal forced Forbes to resign and his assistant to commit suicide. Forbes left 200,000 claims unattended. He was convicted and fined $10,000, but served only 20 months in Leavenworth Federal Prison. When he was released in 1927, he divided his leisure time between elaborate homes in Washington and Florida.[34]

PAYING PAUL

The plight of veterans demonstrated the indifference, delays, and irresponsibility of successive administrations. Although 300,000 were injured in the war, the Veterans Bureau approved only 49,000 claims for illnesses, and 47,000 for combat injuries during Forbes' reign. Veterans' healthcare was disgraceful yet no outcry was heard from the press, the public, or even the opposition party. Only veterans' organizations stood up and demanded action.

Veterans had been paid $60 on mustering out while defense factory workers were paid bonuses as much as $14 a day for industrial mobilization. The American Legion hesitated to align itself with bonus demands, cognizant of the stigma of demanding money for service. Eventually the abject poverty of so many members drove them to it anyway. Harding argued that bonuses would bankrupt the country, and veterans were derided in newspapers and political speeches as panhandlers, unpatriotic, welfare-seekers, or accused of being on the dole. Meanwhile enormous loans were made to foreign countries and American railroads. The dichotomy was not unnoticed.

Calvin Coolidge replaced Harding but he continued the fight against the Adjusted Compensation Act, to bridge the difference between low service pay and comparable civilian pay. The adjustment was calculated at $1 for each day of stateside service and $1.25 for each day served overseas. It was to be paid as bonds averaging $1,500 in 1932, but compounded interest increased their value to $3,287 when they matured in 1945. Therein was the problem: hungry veterans had to wait thirteen more years to collect, 28 years after the war. They were hungry and their families could not wait that long. Coolidge vetoed it in 1924 but Congress over-rode the veto; it didn't matter.[35]

The stock market crashed in 1929, wiping out businesses and investors. Unemployment drove up the misery index. Estimates from the 1930 census reported between three to four and one-half million people were out of work. The American Legion disputed that figure and calculated six million instead, including 710,000 veterans. The Bureau of Labor admitted their mistake—twelve million were unemployed and the situation was growing worse. Veterans, still angry over the long delay for adjusted compensation, would wait no longer.[36]

Tight jobs made the bonus money more urgent. Congress tried a compromise, permitting them to borrow 50 percent of the face value of the bonus certificates at 4.5 percent interest. President Hoover, as Harding and Coolidge before him, vetoed it. Congress debated only 43 minutes before overriding the veto. The solution seemed reasonable on paper, but it was too late and not enough to head off trouble.

Far from the political maneuvering, Walter W. Waters struggled to support his wife and two children by working odd jobs in Portland, Oregon. Waters had been a sergeant in 1919, and nightmares from the war still haunted him. The Veterans' Bureau was no help, so when a cannery hired him at a reasonable salary, he paid for therapy from his wages. But he was laid off again in 1930, crammed his family into a small apartment, and spent all his savings on rent and food. They pawned their belongings for more money while he searched for work, finally accepting charity.

Waters read about government loans to industries and foreigners in old newspapers he pulled from the trash. He and his friends groused over government priorities while standing in unemployment and welfare lines. They were ashamed their country denied them their pittance while giving away huge sums to others. By 1932, Waters was destitute and desperate. He and his friends hopped a freight train for as far as it would take them then hitchhiked east towards Washington. They arrived after 18 days and found forty thousand veterans gathered for the same reasons. They were a bedraggled collection of poor and disabled, some with everything they owned in one small bag. Some wore old uniforms, their families in tow, nowhere else to go. They intended to stay until they were paid.

They called themselves the Bonus Expeditionary Force, or BEF. The Capital District's Police Chief, Pelham Glassford, was also a veteran and was somewhat sympathetic; he directed them to an Anacostia campsite and warned them of trouble. He contributed $120 of his own money to their kitty for food and suggested other ways to raise funds. But Secretary of War Hurley refused to issue excess tents, cots, or bedding to the former soldiers, intending to drive them away. But they had nowhere else to go, so shacks were assembled from wooden crates, cardboard boxes, oilcloth, canvas, bricks, and discarded lumber. The slum village was named Hooverville.[37]

They elected leaders to appeal to President Hoover, but he refused to hear them, meeting with Boy Scouts instead. So they marched in formation along Pennsylvania Avenue and eight hundred sat on the Capitol steps until their bonus law came to a vote. The bill was defeated. They responded the only way they knew; they stood together and sang *America, the Beautiful*.

The shabby veterans embarrassed Hoover and Congress, but gained public support each day. The White House tried to undercut them with rumors of a communist conspiracy, then Hoover decided to break it up with police and Treasury agents to chase them from the partially demolished National Guard Armory on Pennsylvania Avenue. Police used billy clubs for eviction notices. Two veterans were shot and killed and a 12-week-old baby suffocated in a cloud of tear gas. Still they stayed.

The Pentagon felt compelled to discipline the former soldiers and Chief of Staff of the Army, General Douglas MacArthur, was prepared to lead. His aide, Major Dwight D. Eisenhower, disagreed about getting involved and they argued, but MacArthur was not dissuaded. He personally led 300 infantrymen with rifles and fixed bayonets, 200 mounted cavalry with sabers, 5 tanks, and a machinegun crew as if into battle. It was a formidable force against unarmed men. Troops in combat gear and gas masks waded through tear gas to battle veterans armed only with brickbats and profanity. General George Patton led the cavalry charge and his horse knocked down Joe Angelo. Joe had met the general once before on a battlefield in Europe; there he had saved Patton's life.

Emaciated veterans closed ranks for one last stand. But instead of fighting, they sang *My Country, 'Tis of Thee*. Their families watched helplessly as flames consumed their shanties and all their belongings. Their camp completely destroyed, they gathered their families to leave, driven away with armed might by the nation they defended.

MacArthur justified his role by claiming they were insurrectionists and that only 10 percent were veterans. But the Veterans Bureau had surveyed them in camp and reported 94 percent were veterans, 67 percent had served overseas, and 20 percent had been wounded. Deep wounds from the battle of Washington were the most painful.

MacArthur's ego and Hoover's folly cost him the next election. Franklin Roosevelt signed the Economy Act in 1933, which erased veterans' small gains by cutting service-related disability pay 25 percent. Another, smaller march was organized; it seemed pointless but caught Congress' attention. They passed another bonus over Roosevelt's veto. As for Waters, MacArthur later hired him as a clerk in the War Department for $1,500 per year. The marchers were apparently forgiven, but only so they could be forgotten.

HONORED DEAD

Private Loudenbeck wrote in his diary on October 11, 1918: "Advanced into the Argonne Woods today where the 58th and 39th Infantry have been losing men. I never have seen so many dead. They are laid in sheltered places in rows. Here is where it takes willpower to go on and face death." Irving Johnson wrote: "Many times after a battle the dead men would have to be laid to one side in order to clear a road for supplies that were coming up. It was very hard for a person who had not been at the front to realize what it looked like." Sergeant Gleeson: "We bombarded for about three hours and then the marines attacked. They gained several kilos and took some woods that were loaded with machine guns.... We want the damn woods." A few days later: "This sector is hell on earth. Shrapnel, high explosive and then the damn gas. It's terrible." And in the final few days before the end of the war: "It was a bad night, rained in torrents, everything soaking wet.... The dead are still lying around.... Don't have time to bury the dead.... Night attack was terrible—Hogan blown to bits."[38]

As awful as it was, twenty thousand former AEF soldiers returned to Paris in September 1927 for an American Legion convention. They celebrated their founding and the end of the war by reenacting the grand parade on the *Champs Elysees*. They had missed the atmosphere of Paris, the sidewalk cafes, especially the bars and bistros closed in the United States under prohibition. The boys from the farms and factories had lived through the terrible war, were changed by it, but refused to forget those left behind.

The American Battle Monuments Commission was created in 1923 to erect and maintain memorials in the United States and at the eight military cemeteries overseas where troops served after April 1917. Thirty thousand doughboys left in France were mostly buried in eight military cemeteries in Europe. Time passed, but they were not forgotten. In 1930, the War Department sent out letters addressed to the next of kin of doughboys buried in Europe; nearly half were returned as undeliverable. But 6,000 Gold Star mothers accepted an invitation to sail from Hoboken, New Jersey, to visit their son's graves in France. It was a somber rendezvous. Guides at the cemeteries helped the elderly women find their loved one's graves among the tight, long rows of brilliant white headstones. Many mothers brought soil from home, or flowers from their gardens. They left timeless treasures among rows of white marble crosses and Stars of David. Raindrops fell from the darkening sky and tearful mothers were escorted back to the buses, leaving their sons alone with the only glory they were ever promised, a place to lay their bones.

The women were taken to a room at the Hotel de Ville and told a story of six unidentified bodies from six different battlefields. A sergeant had been blind-folded and walked among the caskets. Finally he dropped a white carnation on an unidentified fallen warrior. His selection: the Unknown Soldier. Only one among them was chosen to go home. The chosen one was interred with special honor at Arlington National Cemetery on the lawn of the Lee-Custis Mansion above the national capital. "Here Rests in Honored Glory an American Soldier Known But to God."[39]

HOME IS A LONELY PLACE

Mark S. Gleeson added to his father's daily account of WWI: "He enthusias-tically went to war, served, came home, put away his medals, and talked very little about what he had done or what he had seen." His father was stoic about his experiences and if he said anything, it was that he came home without a scratch. His stomach problems and loss of hearing belied that, and his chronic conditions worsened over time. Sergeant Gleeson was proud of his service but never flaunted it. He always wore his Legion pin and rose early on holidays to plant a line of flags outside his home. He attended ceremonies with his children, but when asked to speak he always declined. He regularly tended the family plot at the church cemetery, with special care to the grave of his brother, killed in the war. When Gleeson died, his simple headstone came from Veterans Affairs, inscribed only with his name, rank, and the unit he served.[40]

Corporal Lars Greenquist, the Swedish immigrant, proceeded from the crowded Des Moines train station to Evansville, Minnesota. On the first Monday after his arrival he married Emma Berglund. After a few months he became a citi-zen in a special ceremony in St Paul to honor aliens who fought for their new country.[41]

Stan Lamb was discharged in France and worked for the YMCA there and in Czechoslovakia and Greece. In 1922 he traveled to Edmonton, Alberta, and married Mary Robertson, his high school sweetheart. She returned to Europe with him until their first child was born. In 1925 he returned to the United States and continued working for the YMCA until he retired in 1953. Stan died at Gig Harbor, Washington, in 1962, spending his final days in a house he built for his mother. The first line of a letter to his father from the Voges Mountains in 1918 was a hint of his life-script. "The beauty of army life, as in every novel environment, is the uncertainty of tomorrow."[42]

Robert Russell recalled his father's problems adjusting after the war, the demons he struggled with, the sleeplessness, physical pain, alcoholism, restlessness, guilt, and alienation. Yet he remained a valued and loyal citizen, typical of so many veterans of his generation. Sergeant Russell left behind a diary his wife had never read. When his son read it, he realized, "It is only when we read other accounts, see actual pictures, and study history that we realize what my father left out." He was proud of his doughboy father. "I wish I had told him that and I wish I had understood and helped him with his guilt and loneliness."[43]

Daniel Waldo, one of the last surviving veterans of the Revolutionary War; born about 1761 and photographed in 1864 by E. B. Hillard. (Courtesy of Library of Congress)

Union veteran and GAR member carrying child piggyback at a celebration in 1914. (Courtesy of Library of Congress)

Veterans of the Blue and Gray meet once again on better terms at the Gettysburg Assembly in Pennsylvania in 1913. (Courtesy of Library of Congress)

Members of C Troop, 6th U.S. Cavalry at Camp Grant in the Arizona Territory, 1881. (Courtesy of the National Archives)

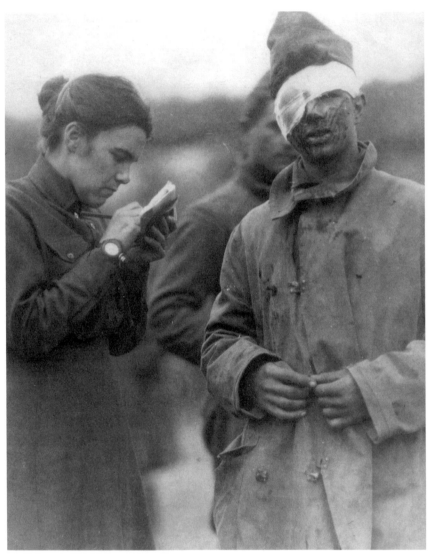

A Salvation Army worker writing a letter home for a wounded doughboy in France. War Department, 1917–1918. (Courtesy of the National Archives)

Happy soldiers mustering out of service from Camp Dix in 1918. War Department. (Courtesy of the National Archives)

A soldier with a missing foot, lighting a cigarette for his friend who has both arms missing, at Walter Reed Hospital in 1918. (Courtesy of Library of Congress)

Bonus marchers sleep on Capitol grounds as Congress debates bonuses and the national deficit in 1932. (Courtesy of Library of Congress)

Anything goes in New York's Times Square on V-J Day. Another famous kiss photo by Lt. Victor Jorgensen, U.S. Navy. (Courtesy of National Archives)

A young officer and his forlorn wife stare at a waiting aircraft carrier in San Diego, waiting for his departure for Korea in 1950. USIA. (Courtesy of National Archives)

Private First Class Dwight Exe writes home during a break in the action in Korea, 1951.
Picture by Corporal James Chancellor, U.S. Army. (Courtesy of National Archives)

Bob Hope lifts the spirits of troops in Seoul, Korea, in 1950. Picture by Captain Bloomquist, U.S. Army. (Courtesy of National Archives)

A firebase shopping mall extravaganza in Vietnam; grunts looking for something to remind them of home. (Courtesy of the 1st Cavalry Division Museum)

Care packages—they aren't heavy. (Courtesy of the 1st Cavalry Division Museum)

Troops take their first steps back in Texas after their return from Kuwait and Operation Desert Storm. (Courtesy of the 1st Cavalry Division Museum)

Families in Killeen and Fort Hood celebrate as the buses bring their guys home from the planes. (Courtesy of the 1st Cavalry Division Museum)

An army pilot with a cavalry attitude; back where he wants to be after a year on Iraqi Freedom. (Courtesy of 1st Cavalry Division Public Affairs Office)

The signs are great, but the kiss is better. Home from Iraq. (Courtesy of the 1st Cavalry Division Public Affairs Office)

The first sergeant and his girls together again. (Courtesy of the 1st Cavalry Public Affairs Office)

Buddy Bell, a Vietnam veteran, and Amy Taylor, an Iraqi Freedom veteran, at a memorial for fallen comrades in Columbus, GA. (Courtesy of Anita Bell)

7

"Home Alive in '45!"

Sidney Riches assured his parents everything was fine during a break from fighting in the Philippines: "This rest is doing all of us a world of good. Wonder how long it will last? . . . Won 70 pesos playing poker last night. . . . Listening to nice dance music from Tokyo. . . . Love, Sid." But his postscript must have worried them. "Don't know how to control my handwriting. It never was any too good but since coming down from the hills, it's gotten worse. . . . The fear of the unexpected will take some time to wear off. . . . It can't last forever, can it?[1]

When news of the Japanese surrender reached servicemen in the Pacific they cheered: "Home alive in '45!" But they worried too, about going back, how it would be, how they'd be. The generation was called America's greatest and they were great; they proved by working together the nation could mobilize enough people, industrial power, agricultural resources, military might, and national will to win a world war and transform lives in the peace that followed. A grateful nation honored them and welcomed them home. Great opportunities awaited them and they built the greatest country on earth. They were not so different but what they accomplished made them unique in history.

THE WORLD AT WAR

The Treaty of Versailles ending WWI in 1919 only postponed a worse global conflict. Germany invaded Poland in September 1939 and declarations of war by Great Britain and France failed to stop the German *blitzkrieg* from overrunning Norway, Denmark, Holland, Belgium, Luxemburg, and, eventually, France. As Europeans capitulated to the powerful German war machine, President Franklin Roosevelt signed the 1941 Lend-Lease Act, shipping allies badly needed equipment and supplies. The attack on America came from a different direction.

On December 7, Japanese aircraft and submarines struck bases at Pearl Harbor and Hickham Field in Hawaii, destroying ships and aircraft and costing lives.

Congress declared war on Japan and the European axis powers declared war on the United States. Japan followed successes in Hawaii with attacks in the Philippines and seized Manila. The United States faced powerful enemies on two fronts.

The crisis demanded strong national will. Unprecedented quantities of supplies, equipment, and manpower were needed to retaliate; virtually everything from gasoline to sugar was mass-produced and strictly conserved. Military needs on two fronts meant priorities had to be set, industries mobilized, and men drafted to fill new divisions, ships, and aircraft. Strict conservation was required at home to keep war critical supplies moving overseas for as long as necessary to win.

Americans attacked with the British and French in North Africa and fought with them across the Sahara desert; Russians repulsed the German army near Stalingrad in January 1943. Momentum shifted as Americans, British, and Canadians crawled ashore at Sicily and forced Mussolini out of power in Italy. Finally, General Eisenhower assaulted at Normandy on June 6, 1944, as the Soviets counterattacked into central Europe from the east. Hitler's capital of Berlin was in a pincer.

American and Filipino troops had clung to the island of Corregidor and the Bataan Peninsula until surrendering to the Japanese in May 1942. Guerillas in the mountains and jungles resisted until MacArthur returned with enough troops to retake the islands. As the Philippines were reoccupied, the navy defeated the Japanese fleet at sea and ground troops attacked at Guadalcanal and took Pacific islands one by one. The tide was also turned in the west.

Letters

The Second World War snatched people such as Keith Winston and altered their lives. When Japanese hit Pearl Harbor, Winston was selling insurance in Pennsylvania to support his wife and two children. He was drafted and sent to basic and advanced infantry training, then to the 100th Infantry Division to slog it out to Berlin. He valued letters from his family and wrote to stay in touch with them and his sanity. In March 1945:

> This year, with its heartaches and pain, has made a big change in our lives and when we're together again we'll appreciate life even more. Over here you see how precarious it can be from day to day. And you learn to take nothing for granted.[2]

Families saved war letters as tributes to their loved ones, never knowing if those words might be all they would have to remember them by. Robert and Jane Easton wrote faithfully, saving each letter. He was an infantryman, first in Europe and later in the Pacific, and she was a Red Cross volunteer in California. She comforted wounded men in the navy hospital, and it was much more than just killing time until he returned. She wrote from Santa Barbara: "And somehow, no matter how little I do, I feel better for having been there. . . . They know I donate my time for them, and I know what they have done for me, and it all adds up to something."[3]

Letters from the front seldom divulged the details of battles or their significance. Men at the front seldom knew where they fit into the grand plan, only prayed there was one. In 1945, the navy destroyed the Japanese fleet at Leyte Gulf, paving the way for Marines and soldiers to take Iwo Jima and Okinawa and tighten the noose around Japan. Air raids on Dresden and other German industrial cities crippled their war industries, while American, British, and Soviets troops inched closer to Berlin, exposing horrible death camps. Hitler ended his life and the war, and the Third Reich surrendered unconditionally. The war in Europe ended first. When peace seemed assured, people at home were ecstatic.

Medic Keith Winston had heard about the celebrations while he was still fighting. "The thought of folks back home making plans for V-E Day provoked me, when boys over here are still giving their blood, and plenty of it."[4]

When Germany surrendered, the V-E Day celebrations erupted, but Japanese still pressed suicide attacks on warships and fought to the death on small Pacific islands. On August 6, the *Enola Gay* dropped an atomic bomb on Hiroshima and 3 days later on Nagasaki, snuffing out war in the Pacific. Bells chimed again for V-J Day, the end of the war; the lights were finally turned on again. "Home alive in '45!"

Keith Winston still didn't feel like celebrating. "Yes, Honey, the war is over but the joy diminishes when I think of all the boys who've lost their lives in the struggle and are not here to enjoy the victory. . . . And all the boys in terrible shape languishing in hospitals. Some of them better off dead."[5]

WARTIME AT HOME

Americans at home were spared the devastation that racked European and Asian factories, railroads, mines, shops, and homes. The U.S. industrial base had doubled production to support the war machine, and the labor force kept up with industries' needs even after the draft. The aircraft industry employed 46,000 people before the war but when it ended worked fifty times that many; more than 275,000 new airplanes had flown from factory hangers. By 1945, half the world's coal and two-thirds of its crude oil were produced by the United States, and its strategic reserves held 60 percent of the worlds' gold. The U.S. merchant marine tripled Great Britain's. Over $30 billion in aid was sent to allies, yet the United States was the only country stronger at the end of the war than at the start. The war-driven boom lifted the economy from declining production and rising unemployment of the depression. The industrial base met unlimited quotas to supply, feed, arm, and transport American troops and allies, and continued after the war because the world depended on American produce and material.[6]

Americans remained steadfast for victory even through the darkest hours. The surging economy gave reason to hope for a bright future when the boys came home, but obstacles blocked the way. Deep recessions had followed the Revolution and Civil War, and the depression after World War I was still fresh. Families wanted their boys home quickly but factory workers only saw sixteen million soldiers coming for their jobs. With war production cut, the workforce of sixty million was already too large.[7]

Depression taught people to hoard, scrimp, save, and guard their property. They continued that behavior through the war years; as critical commodities were rationed they spent hard-earned cash for war bonds and savings stamps. High-paying jobs during the war were considered only temporary and anxiety increased, but the war years seemed better than the depression. The Labor Department predicted twelve to fifteen million workers would be laid off after the war, especially temporary women workers. Veterans watched from afar and knew they would have trouble finding jobs when they got home.

Anticipation

Military sociologists anticipated some postwar problems for soldiers, whether they were going home or staying on occupation duty. They knew of the problems after WWI and surveyed and observed these from WWII; their conclusions were based on history, scientific theory, and first hand knowledge. As long as there was an enemy to face, security came first; soldiers accepted the danger posed to their outfits and responded to it. But when the enemy was gone, everything changed. Their military purpose vanished and they saw their futures, hopes, and dreams far from the battlefield.[8]

Samuel Stouffer and associates made predictions from their studies. They believed initially soldiers would join the victory celebrations before they returned home. But they believed the first excitement would give way to impatience to go; the longer they waited, the more impatient they would be. When they finally got home they would be anxious over jobs, family readjustments, and misgivings about their war experiences. Some would expect someone else to carry the load, convinced they had done more than their share already; they might feel disadvantaged or nuts for even having gone. They knew some would miss their war buddies and feel isolated at home, even hostile to civilians. The predictions were well founded but not new; they were also valid after the Revolution, the Civil War, and WWI.

HOMECOMING

When war ended in Europe, GIs were anxious to go home, but fighting continued in the Pacific and more troops were needed to finish it. Soldiers prayed for a fast finish and demobilization; they added up their points based on time in service and combat records to determine who could go first. Each month of service warranted one point, another for each month overseas, more for battle stars, awards, wounds, even children under eighteen; the system was generally considered fair. Soldiers in Europe who were short points faced occupation duty or the war in the Pacific. Some griped about continued duty while their wives, girlfriends, and mothers wrote Congressmen to complain, plead, or threatened to vote against them. As the troops longed for home, coal miners and railroad workers at home went on strike.

Keith Winston was trapped in the waiting game; he wrote his wife:

> The final defeat of Germany didn't seem to make a whole lot of difference here. The boys have no way of celebrating, no place to go and they're still in the same war set up—no closer to home, and perhaps missing it a little more, especially in view of the jubilation, the celebrations back home, and knowing they're not part of it.[9]

As much as they wanted to go, many still dreaded breaking ties with their wartime buddies. Sergeant Henry Giles wrote about it in late 1945:

> What we had together was something awfully good, something I don't think we'll ever have again as long as we live. Nobody wants war, but maybe it takes a war to make men feel as close to each other as we have felt. We'll never feel toward anyone else the way we have felt toward each other, for the circumstances will never be the same again.[10]

But they were tired of orders, lines, and inspections, anxious to be civilians again. Few stayed in the military after the war, although some said they might rejoin if they were unable to find a job. Despite their eagerness to go, 79 percent expected to have problems finding work. Stouffer's studies indicated soldiers who never deployed had the same concerns as those overseas. All worried whether they could settle down after the war and get along with wives or fiancés. Based on history, they were wise to worry.[11]

Twenty-seven thousand officers and enlisted were asked in 1944 about their plans after separation. They considered their future uncertain, but over half had made definite plans: 8 percent intended to be full time students, 13 percent to start small businesses, and over 40 percent expected to work for someone else. Many counted on their old jobs; only 3 percent planned to stay in service. Almost half had no plans at all.[12]

Stouffer also questioned 800 soldiers returning to the front from medical or home leaves about their homecoming expectations. Nearly half called going home disappointing. They were ambivalent about the reasons but showed some guilt for leaving their buddies and felt alone in the stateside world. They missed their outfits, unable to find peace at home.[13]

In December 1945, the Veterans Administration (VA) found in the first months after discharge, two-thirds of veterans followed their career plans. Those who did not said the jobs they wanted were not available, or blamed financial difficulties and poor market conditions, a third were hindered by physical or mental defects, illnesses, or family issues.[14]

In overseas and stateside camps, soldiers fantasized about home. Keith Winston wrote his wife: "You know what I've been craving for? A thick slice of vanilla layer cake with vanilla icing and gobs of whipped cream. And milk, milk, milk, and more milk." He dreamed of taking a private holiday alone with her but remembered his children. ". . . First I want to be home a few days as I gotta see the kids and get to know them—not run out on them." Seventy thousand soldiers, sailors, and marines swarmed home monthly. Keith Winston landed in New York City in early December 1945. He processed out, was discharged from the army, returned home to his wife, and found his old job with the insurance company waiting. They had held it for him; he was lucky.[15]

Jane Easton described her reaction to victory in Europe as she celebrated with a family friend. She tried to comprehend its meaning but worried about the uncertainty to follow. "We drank Dubonnet and sherry together and talked of you and John coming back and the new life ahead. . . . Cars are going up and down State Street with horns blaring and the Mission bells are ringing. . . . I keep blinking my eyes trying to get used to the new meaning of life. War had threatened us ever since we met. Do you realize that? Can we love each other in peace?"

John Easton's victory ship docked in New York and he hopped a DC-3 to Fort MacArthur, California. His parents met him there. Special moments anticipated for years seldom meet expectations. "My parents seem to have shrunk. They seem not to have changed their clothes. They seem almost like strangers. I love them. I know they love me. . . . Yet I find myself resenting the fact they haven't undergone some marvelous transformation because of all that's happened to the world, to me."

He described the scenic ride between California's hills and Pacific Ocean as if he had landed in the twilight zone. "We talk in what seems incredible banalities about the weather, about gasoline being plentiful again, about old friends and neighbors who sound like inhabitants of another world. Where are the words to express the horror, the glory, the destruction. . . . ? They speak as if nothing had happened, as if everything will go on as before." He wanted to complain but couldn't. "Nothing has changed. Life is made up of banalities and trivia, and the impossibility of uttering all that has happened."

His parents dropped him at a corner near his home and he walked nervously to the front door. His wife knew he was on the way, fretted, waiting anxiously for his knock at the door. All the months before were aimed for one single moment. The door opened: "All three came pouring into my arms. Then Jane and I clung to each other, just the two of us, laughing and crying, while our little girls gazed up in wonder. It is all over—and it's all beginning." They bought a small home in Lampasas, Texas, through the GI Bill; he landed a job with the local newspaper. It was a good beginning.[16]

Sidney Riches had wondered from the Philippines if he would ever control his shaky handwriting. He returned to the aircraft plant where he had worked in San

Diego before Pearl Harbor. They welcomed him back, but with aircraft production down there were no jobs. He bunked with his parents and worked in the post office for a year. Boredom drove him to find work as a farmhand, but he was unhappy there, too. Finally, he rejoined the army as an enlisted man though he had been an officer during the war; his job was screening others for officer training.[17]

Fantasies of life after war were often distorted by time, distance, and active imaginations. Married men forgot the annoying habits of their wives, as wives forgot theirs. Memories of home were larger and nicer than reality, the picket fence whiter, grass greener, streets covered with bright orange leaves beneath strong maples; the old job was remembered as enjoyable, the boss smiling all day. Stouffer added space for free responses on his surveys: "I want to marry the girl I am engaged to and live a hundred years of happiness and peace." Or, "Settle down, get a good job, get married, and build a home, and live happily ever after."[18]

Norman Rockwell's heroic figures on the covers of *Saturday Evening Post* portrayed Americans' self-images: a grimy soldier blasting a machine gun at Jap Zeros at the front, Rosie the Riveter sweating in an airplane factory at home. After the war the scenes changed: a young soldier standing before a tenement building and his mother's arms outstretched through drying laundry, a soldier with uniform sleeves rolled up repairing an engine in the local garage. But their return threatened to displace Rosie from the factory floors, blacks on the farms, and mechanics in the garages. They were thanked for what they had done, but their presence threatened the *status quo*.[19]

Able-bodied veterans had two advantages: new skills learned in the military and opportunities from enhanced veteran benefits. The American Legion and Congress hammered out a historic veterans' program while they were still fighting. The Servicemen's Readjustment Act, the GI Bill of Rights, afforded unprecedented opportunities for education, home ownership, preference for government jobs, or assistance in finding civilian jobs. For the first time in history, their opportunities coincided with their dreams.

GI BILL

Concerns of army sociologists for combat veterans were shared by advisors, publishers, and reporters who warned the public of the impending "veteran problem" through a stream of commentary on how to handle it. The American Legion's WWI veterans understood the difficulties of readjusting and believed it possible to improve the process. Veterans' benefits had always been justified as compensation for time, wages, or health lost in service, medical care to repair them, and ceremonies, speeches, and parades to honor them. The American Legion was determined to find a better way to respect veterans than buying them off with bonuses, shuttling them to VA hospitals, making speeches, and forgetting them until Armistice Day.

Legionnaires knew that after getting home and finding their loved ones, veterans' main concerns were education, jobs, and homes; they had experienced that already and heard it repeated in Legion halls. A plan was needed to meet their needs based on the Jeffersonian idea that Americans are yeomen who will take advantage of opportunities to lift themselves by their bootstraps and succeed through innovation and hard work. With enough people lifting, the whole country would benefit. The simple concept could potentially rebuild lives, boost the national economy, and fill the national treasury at the same time. The GI Bill of Rights offered a hand up to veterans, not a hand out; it was an enlightened policy that changed the entire country.[20]

The austere measures of the Economy Act in 1933 had hit WWI veterans hardest by cutting aid to those needing it most: amputees, disabled, tubercular, shell-shocked, and the mentally unbalanced. The American Legion had advocated a 4-point program to recover: return to original levels for service-connected death and disability compensation, appeal of 30,000 rejected files, renew hospital privileges for all veterans, and support to widows and orphans.[21]

President Roosevelt and General George Marshall were determined to avoid a repeat of the bonus marches after WWI. Even before entering WWII, they prepared for the peace to follow. The Selective Service Act protected jobs of draftees but Marshall asked the Army War College to quietly study full preparations for demobilization. Roosevelt mentioned their return as early as 1943; during a fireside chat he warned about inflation and unemployment and reminded the public the armed forces had made sacrifices and were entitled to special assistance. But despite Roosevelt's public support of veterans, nothing happened. The National Resources Planning Board, the Federal Security Agency, and Congress were grid locked.[22]

WWI veterans still struggled under the Economy Act cuts when the first injured WWII veterans came in. The Legion saw new problems added to old ones and solicited examples from posts to bolster their case. Human faces caste a personal dimension in the "forgotten battalion." Their appearance disturbed the public, the Congress, and the administration. Real stories stunned people, stories of men who had lost limbs in combat and were given only their back pay, $300 for mustering out, a Purple Heart, and warned not to wear their uniforms past 90 days. The cases were intolerable to Congress and veterans' organizations; they quickly agreed to retain mustering out pay, but the Legion wanted it increased to $500. With cripples peddling pencils on street corners, a Gallop Poll showed 81 percent of Americans wanted more done for disabled veterans.[23]

American Legion Commander Atherton released additional stories from the forgotten battalion to Congress and the press, stories of men like Bill Smith; a marine unfit for service after a bomb paralyzed his left side and diminished his neurological functions. Smith was discharged from the Corps 6.5 months after he was wounded on Guadalcanal. No one helped him file a disability claim before his discharge, so all pay and his allotment to his mother ceased. His service pay was the sole support for both of them. Smith was legally entitled to disability compensation of $100 a month, free hospitalization, medication, and vocational rehabilitation, but only after his un-filed claim was approved. He was penniless, paralyzed, and forbidden to wear his uniform. Smith was not alone; thousands more were as tragic. Stories of real people with real names, faces, and families exploded like grenades on the front pages of newspapers.[24]

Disability pensions and mustering-out pay had existed since belatedly awarded to Revolutionary War veterans; VA medical care added after WWI. But the old programs were outdated, under-funded, and without vision. Veterans needed more than cash and painkillers. A better idea came in a letter from the frontlines, one that stated plainly what was missing. The American Legion's John Stelle read the letter from his son from the North African desert and understood exactly: all they wanted from their government was an opportunity.[25]

Like Rudyard Kipling's timeless *Tommy*, the boys were heroes during war but homeless, jobless, and illiterate when they returned. Stelle read the letter over and understood his son didn't expect charity, only a fair chance. Soldiers and sailors had been snatched from their jobs, left their homes and families behind, placed their lives on hold and futures in doubt when duty called. When they came home they wanted a chance at an education, training for a better job, some prospect to own a home; they only wanted the opportunity, they would do the rest.

Providing opportunity became the mantra of the American Legion. Henry Colmery gathered data from staff committees and drafted a proposal to Congress on hotel stationary in Washington. The plan ignored Roosevelt's idea of equal rights for everyone and Congressional plans for austerity, but used the momentum from the forgotten battalion to make bold assertions. The nation could not, would not, economize with disabled veterans; they could not be treated the same as others. They wanted opportunity and the GI Bill offered it. No one foresaw how much that simple idea would change America.[26]

The GI Bill awakened powerful forces. Jefferson's belief in a middle class of educated citizens, independent property owners, and self-sustaining citizens had been lost as the country became urbanized and industrialized. The GI Bill made the middle class possible again by emphasizing common values such as patriotism, community involvement, personal achievement, and offering a hand-up, not a hand-out. Self-reliance, ownership, and a fair chance counterbalanced socialism; those values were independent of big government, big unions, and big business. Such dreams were only fantasies during the war years. They hoped for a better job but doubted they could find one, a decent place to live but never imagined they could own their own homes; they thought it impossible to move from illiteracy to a college education. The GI Bill made it all possible.[27]

Millions of veterans came home to reunions with their wives or girlfriends; they married, started families, and tackled college. They went on a spending spree for houses, cars, and home appliances, all possible under the guarantees of the GI Bill. High demand for new goods and services created new industries in plastics, rubber, auto parts, and tools; shopping centers sprang up in suburbia, where new houses filled formerly empty fields. Some war-weary veterans needed time to get re-charged. They were allowed $20 for unemployment compensation for up to 52 weeks and many joined the "52/20 Club." Those who needed more cash were guaranteed approval of a $2,000 veterans' loan at a low interest rate to use for any purpose. Commonly, the cash was used for down payment on a house, a new business, or a car. The GI Bill helped them find jobs or go to school. They were guaranteed $500 a month for up to 4 years for retraining or education, and a subsistence allowance of $50 a month if single, $75 if married, while they trained or attended college.[28]

The GI Bill was more than a good program for veterans; it was enlightened national policy. Universities, junior and community colleges, and trade schools prospered with the sudden influx of new students. Illiteracy rates that had stunned the nation 30 years before, improved. In 1949, the numbers of men and women graduating with B.A. degrees tripled from 1940. The end of the war also created a baby boom, a sudden population increase that spanned 20 years and stretched prosperity into the future. Educated veterans could better support their families and send their children to college.

Veterans could buy homes with no down payment and a low-interest loan. Mortgages were less than rent, so the decision to buy was easy; a million veterans had purchased homes by 1947. The housing market and the baby boom created instant suburbia with starter families clustered in planned developments. Shopping centers and shiny cars filled new streets. Paved highways accommodated increased traffic and the daily commute to work was born.[29] The GI Bill educated a generation of professionals and businessmen, created homeowners and small-business owners, and restored a vibrant middle class; it was the driving force behind doubling average annual income from 1939 to 1949.[30] It changed the demographics of society, distributed wealth more evenly, and made the United States a land of opportunity again; veterans supplied the energy.

Les Faulk

Les Faulk graduated from high school in Turtle Creek, Pennsylvania, in 1944 with a career plan. He would caddy at the local golf course during the day and rack balls in the poolroom at night while waiting for a better job at one of the local plants. WWII disrupted his plan. After graduation he trained as an infantryman for the Seventh Army in Germany; the golf course, pool hall, and factory job would have to wait.

Faulk fought his way across Europe and came home safely after VE day. While he was overseas his father arranged a bricklayer's apprenticeship for him, a prized job before the war. Faulk took his lunch pail to work the first day but the job didn't feel right, so he quit. Instead of laying new bricks he walked into an old brick schoolhouse and used the GI Bill for college. Possibilities he couldn't imagine as a high school student were within reach. He hung bachelors' and masters' diplomas on his wall and worked 38 years as a teacher and high school principal. Faulk remembered his high school teacher's encouragement to follow his dreams, but he considered them impossible then. He joined twelve graduates from his high school class at their fiftieth reunion. Several had become engineers, one a federal judge, and another a microchip engineer and some were lawyers—all through opportunities made possible under the GI Bill.[31] Les Faulk's generation changed the direction of the country and the speed which it moved. A revolution of knowledge, industry, ownership, and wealth made the United States the unquestioned leader of the free world.

Vast Changes

The Educational Testing Service (ETS) found the grade point average of veteran students similar to civilians with one major difference: only 1 percent of veterans dropped out compared to 10 percent of civilians. Conferred degrees doubled in less than a decade. To handle the higher demand, 4-year colleges increased by 10 percent. Half of eligible veterans took educational or training courses and ETS suggested 20 percent were due directly to the GI Bill. At a cost of just over $1,800 per capita the Department of Labor estimated the federal government made a sizeable profit from education through increased earnings and taxes alone.[32]

When the war ended, half of available housing units either needed major repairs or lacked private bathrooms, a third had no refrigerators, and nearly a quarter had no gas or electricity. Worse, returning veterans found "No Vacancy" signs and over one million people lived doubled-up. One couple tried to rent a bedroom set on stage at a Broadway theater during off hours, another moved into the display window of a Manhattan department store for 2 days. GI's and their families lived in garages, coal sheds, and cellars in Chicago; the city sold 250 streetcars for homes. In San Francisco they lived in autos parked on city streets, used the public restrooms in libraries, and cooked on wood fires in the park.

The GI Bill guaranteed home loans for zero down and 20–30 years to pay, if you could find one. William Levitt understood construction, recognized an opportunity, and used his knowledge as a Navy Seabee to mass-produce them. Levitt and Sons used assembly line construction techniques to fill a barren tract of land in eastern Long Island with moderate-sized homes for veterans. Specialized teams of carpenters, masons, plumbers, electricians, painters, and landscapers moved from house to house, opening as many as thirty Cape Cod or Ranch-style homes a day through the twenty-seven step building process.

A Long Island newspaper reported on Levitt's plan as he got started and he was deluged with 6,500 applications within weeks. Demand was so high he used the military point system to determine who could buy first. Levittown suburbs sprang up all over the country. The homes sold for $90 down and $58 a month with a

VA loan; they came furnished with refrigerators, stoves, and washing machines. Bill Leavitt did not just build homes; he made dreams come true for millions of veterans and their new families.[33]

Revolutionary, Civil War and WWI veterans had gone home with empty pockets, but WWII veterans had money to spend with 52 weeks of unemployment pay, state bonuses, mustering-out pay, fully paid college tuition, cash for education expenses, and paid living expenses while in school. They enjoyed unsurpassed credit with guaranteed small business loans, home loans, and credit for $2,000 for any purpose. They made the postwar economy hum while adding value to their lives. Noisy celebrations after victory in Europe and Japan became the sounds of hammers and saws building houses, pages turning in classrooms, people driving cars and going about the business of living, the hard work of making dreams reality. Noises of industry and prosperity replaced the silence of depression and desperation. The great generation became the best educated. The GI Bill laid the foundation for a knowledge-based society and a high technology revolution. The 4-point veterans program was a Marshall Plan for America; instead of rebuilding on an old foundation it made a brand-new start.[34]

Challenges

Progress brought new challenges. Factories on a wartime production footing had to retool to meet demands for new product lines. Then, inflation followed heavy consumption. The federal budget had tripled during the war years and government had increased to control the wartime economy. Labor unions had also doubled their membership and strained relations between labor and management. In 1946, 750,000 steelworkers and 200,000 factory workers struck, and 240,000 unionized female telephone-workers demanded equal pay. Strikes by 350,000 coal miners in 1948 were followed by strikes of 500,000 steelworkers the next year. Labor problems sent wages and production costs higher with inflation. Unemployment had been under 2 percent in 1945 and stayed under 4 percent through 1947, but inflation drove it to almost 6 percent by 1948. That came as food costs rose 15 percent and energy 39 percent. The economy fizzled as unresolved issues from the Yalta peace lurched into a cold war.[35]

When World War II ended, celebrations spread throughout cities, towns, and rural communities all over the country. After euphoria, reality took hold. Blacks were still discriminated against in the rural south and in northern cities. Full participation in the war did not reward as they hoped. Navy cook Dorie Miller won the Distinguished Service Cross for actions at Pearl Harbor and a destroyer was named after him, but he and other black heroes dropped into obscurity. Women who served with distinction in the Women's Army Auxiliary Corps and the Women's Air Service Pilots were not all entitled to veterans' benefits. Only women who joined or transferred to the regular women's branches of their services were qualified.

Three hundred thousand civilians died during the war years in accidents at factories pushing to meet demands with unskilled workers; one million were disabled. The war cost over 292,000 battle deaths, 115,000 more from nonbattle causes, and 670,000 wounded. VA hospitals were in crisis with the patient load. Brigadier General Frank Hines had replaced the corrupt Charles Forbes in 1923 and had been sole director for 20 years. President Truman was determined to modernize the VA and his first act was to name General Omar Bradley as director, 1 day after V-J Day.

Bradley had led WWII soldiers in battle, but as VA director he assumed responsibility for the care of veterans from World War I, the Spanish–American War, Philippine Insurgency, frontier service, and a few living Civil War veterans, as well as WWII veterans—twenty million in all, 43 percent of the population. Bradley wanted to change the culture within the VA and instructed his 65,000 employees that veterans were not charity cases, but had already paid with blood. They were to be treated as people instead of files. He increased his staff to 200,000 and the quality of medicine actually improved.

Veterans believed veterans' organizations were influential in supporting their causes, and 85 percent of the men in the European Theater considered joining one. Their reasons included protecting their rights, or having a voice in preventing wars, influencing foreign and domestic policy, improving government, or protecting national defense and prosperity. Despite a perception that veterans' posts and legion halls were filled with old men hanging around, drinking, and playing bingo, socializing was not a stated interest. There was too much else to accomplish.[36]

Stouffer asked them after demobilization how they were affected by the war. Thirty-seven percent said they were changed adversely and cited nervousness, restlessness, irritability, and depression. As many said their changes were both positive and negative or none at all. Twenty-two percent believed their changes were only beneficial and cited a broadened intellect, more stable or independent, or they were more ambitious.[37]

GUARDING TRADITIONS

Veterans' organizations stood watch over the integrity of veterans' programs. When national magazines such as *Cosmopolitan*, *Reader's Digest*, and *Harpers* disparaged the poor conditions at VA hospitals, General Hines turned to veterans' groups for the truth. They investigated the reports and their findings confirmed changes were needed in the administration of VA hospitals. One change affiliated VA hospitals with university medical schools, bringing state-of-the-art expertise from medical colleges into the staid bureaucracy. By August 1946, 650 university resident physicians were on duty in VA hospitals.[38]

But the affiliation program had problems. Residents were eager to practice medicine and had veterans to practice on. University research departments needed to test new technologies and the hospitals had human guinea pigs. These problems only added to the normal bureaucratic ineptitude and eroded the VA hospital system's reputation.

When Vietnam veterans turned to VA hospitals years later, old WWI and WWII soldiers warned them away. "I served my country and I served it well," said Walter Stimson, a rugged WWI veteran. "But I'll die flat on my back on this floor before I go back to that hospital." His daughter Myra, a nurse, agreed, "I never saw anything worse than the way it is there." Francine Jones described how a doctor informed her of her husband's terminal condition: leave him there and they would call her when he died. "They said they would take him off my hands," she remembered. "I went outside, put my head down on the side of the curb, and cried like my heart would break. And then I went inside and took him home."[39]

In November 1949, American Legion Commander George Craig threw a 6-mile homecoming parade in the small town of Brazil, Indiana: population 9,000. Four jets thundered overhead at 1,000 feet, followed by a second flyover of WWII-era B-29 bombers. Thirty thousand people flocked from surrounding communities and a hungry crowd consumed sandwiches from local churches, fraternal groups, and civic organizations. The small-town display of patriotism was carried across the country by continuous radio coverage and developed into a national homecoming celebration; other communities duplicated it, beginning a new national tradition.[40]

Veterans' groups marched together in homecoming parades at assemblies, on Saint Patrick's Day, Memorial Day, and Veterans Day.

ONE SMALL TOWN

Robert Havighurst of the University of Chicago was curious how veterans and their communities recovered from war-time experiences, so he chose a small, unnamed mid-western Illinois town to study. While Stouffer had looked ahead with a universal group, Havighurst looked back into one community. He called the town Midwest, Illinois, to protect the participants. Midwest had families with men who had served, some who avoided the draft by working at defense plants or farms, and others deferred by the county's selective service board.

Most upper- and middle-class draftees spent their last night as civilians with feverous all-nighters in Chicago. The less affluent opted for simple family dinners at home, with maybe a round of drinks at a local tavern. On the morning they left, they met for breakfast at a local restaurant, then marched up Liberty Street behind the American Legion color guard and a single drummer, passing through cheering relatives and curious spectators. A train pulled them apart as they began the transition from civilian to soldier.

Military life was different from all they considered normal. They had heard stories of basic training from salty old-timers but were not prepared to give up control of their actions and thoughts. But once they adapted to the military way they thought it normal and their former lives surreal; civilians became outsiders who did not understand. When they were discharged, some could hardly believe they had been in service. "When I first got home, the most amazing thing to me was the complete break-off," said one Midwest veteran. "Two weeks after I got out it seemed as if it had all happened so long ago. It even seems closer to me now than it did then. I really can't think of any other period of time that seemed to place such a complete gulf between two experiences."[41]

Havighurst believed several things made military life unique. First, it was entirely outside the scope of their prior experience. The first shock was hard but it was imposed immediately and with authority. Complete departure from their old habits brought nostalgia and a strong need to reconnect with the past. Men who had never written letters before wrote faithfully and waited sheepishly for mail call to hear from people in remote, forgotten corners of their lives.

Another surprise was the speed and transience in which they lived. High mobility was routine to military operations, unsettling at first, but the effects of constant movement lingered long after they left the service. Many could no longer remain still after the war, pacing about like caged animals, or driving their cars searching for something.

They had to learn a new language of acronyms—AWOL, DEROS, and UCMJ. Stories about mishaps are the lore of military service; soldiers call it *SNAFU*— Situation Normal, All Fouled Up. Despite *snafus*, the military machine sustained, fed, clothed, housed, transported them, and tended all their needs; the army replaced mother. Within that world they bonded with those who experienced the same, and limited what they shared with outsiders who could not understand. *Esprit de corps* carried them through tough times and they missed it later.

Young men of Midwest went through all that and some found they needed crutches to lean on. Alcohol was plentiful in the service and no one asked their age. Drinking was expected and those predisposed to it overindulged under pressure. Believing each day might be the last justified a little drinking, smoking, or carousing. But some habits were hard to break back home.

They also found class structure dominant. As civilians they could have a beer with the boss after work, spout off, and even quit their jobs. That wasn't possible in the military; class lines were not crossed. They spoke constantly of getting out, but when they did, reconversion to civilian was hard. Once indoctrinated into the military way, letting go was as difficult as accepting it had been.[42]

Nearly half the men in the study were either married before, or got married during their service. While separated, their wives changed the patterns of their lives as well. Some moved in with parents, in-laws, or friends for support or to trim costs. Some worked for extra money or to stay busy. Most were faithful, poring over letters from their husbands and realized their husbands had placed them on a pedestal. Time dims human flaws and makes people or places seem better than they are. Women raising children alone at home were forced to be practical to pay bills, keep the household running, hold a job, or skimp with meager wartime rations. Letters became touchstones for both and they imaged how wonderful homecoming would be. If they were lucky enough for furlough, they got a preview. Wives and parents described them as restless, nervous, uneasy, jittery, or jumpy. When they came to stay, they described them the same way.

By March 1946, most had come back from an average of 36 months in service and 20 months overseas. In Midwest most veterans spent their first night home with their close families, swapping stories of their experiences for news of home. As the days passed, they allowed more friends and family into the circle. Clubs organized special services and banquets; organizations threw parties and stag nights. They were obligated to go to events in their honor but many went reluctantly. They were expected to talk to people they did not remember, to recall names and faces they had forgotten, they were uncomfortable on display. They wanted a few days off but needed to find normalcy instead of being scrutinized for signs of aberrant behavior. They wanted free time, but time was a burden. They missed their war buddies, but found other veterans instead who had shared their experiences, spoke the same language, knew what they were thinking without having to say it.

One Midwest single woman complained: "They're used to having the girls ask them. They expect the girls to fix up the date.... They get moody spells." And bachelors complained about them. "It's on account of the war, I guess. They got jobs and made more money than they ever imagined they could, and they got out and got foolish with it. They got to running around, and got further away from their homes." One wife complained: "In preference to wanting to go out with me, my husband seems to want to go out with the boys. He seems to have more fun that way, and he likes it better." Another: "We'd go to bed early, and then he'd be up at five o'clock in the morning. He'd be going all over the house. He'd pull out the dresser drawers and go through them. Then he'd go through every closet in the house. He'd go uptown and come back again—just fidget around—it seemed like that was all he'd ever do."[43]

Veterans struggled with family adjustments on top of a housing shortage, a clothing shortage, an automobile shortage, even a beer shortage. They could not find that perfect job and their expectations were not met anywhere; they harped about the mess the country was in. Getting into the mainstream meant getting a job; work meant social acceptance and the way to get ahead, at least to stay afloat. But jobs available were not the good ones; hourly wages were low with few benefits. Those who stayed behind locked up the best ones. Midwest's well-to-do had the family business to turn to, or family connections; some went to college. Average Joes faced the same old factory or farm jobs they wanted to escape. Eight months after V-J Day, eleven reenlisted. In the service, they had seen the chance for higher rank based on performance, more pay for more responsibility, and a way for upward mobility. They missed that at home.

Charles Taylor

Lieutenant Charles Taylor's roots were in Florida. He married Barbara there before joining the army in 1941 and she followed him to bases around the country.

When he shipped to Europe she went home to wait with their young daughter. They stayed connected over the miles with long letters. As the end of the war approached, their letters reflected new concerns. They would soon regain control of their lives, making important decisions necessary. He wavered between accepting a regular army commission, finding a civilian job, or going back to college under the GI Bill. They considered where they would live, whether to have another child, but above all, they worried about money.

Charles was accustomed to making important decisions in the army but these were vexing. "I've come to the conclusion that I just don't know what in the world I am going to do.... I am sort of lost as to how I am going to make a living." Later he added, "Maybe I am afraid of civilian life.... One does feel secure in the army.... so much so that I know it will be hard for me when I leave it." They discussed choosing an automobile, taking trips, buying clothes, Christmas presents, insurance, mustering-out pay, war bonds, savings accounts—but always came back to money. "Money, money, that's all I seem to be talking about ... oh, well, I'll worry about it when I get home."

Unspoken concerns could be read between the lines: how they would react to each other, how much each had changed, and how that would affect their relationship. They wondered if they could last as a family. They had been in love in the past, but were strangers to the future. Relationships were especially perplexing and difficult to speak of plainly. "I guess I am in for a lot of learning how to become a good father, and a good husband, both at the same time." About their reunion: "Oh, I get so mixed up about coming home and what I'll do.... " Barbara reassured him. "It scares me when I think of it—and yet I know that as soon as I look into your eyes, and read all the lovely things that you have for me and me alone—then I know that everything will be all right."[44]

Coming home from war is not going home from a day at the office, parking the car, checking the mail, and raiding the refrigerator. Living in mud makes them crude, facing death hardens them, and fear rattles their nerves; war leaves impressions that cannot be rubbed smooth, only concealed. Those waiting are also affected by separation, the endless waiting, squeezing a nickel for the next meal, operating a greasy machine, making hard decisions, and dreading the arrival of a Western Union telegram day after day. But after the first hugs and kisses, the first flush of reunion, suppressed anxieties come in disturbing and unpredictable ways. Then the trouble begins.[45]

Charles Taylor did not want to go back to college; campuses were too slow for a quickened pulse. But he took a vacation with Barbara and his parents in Miami, to slow down. After some time, the cottage behind his parent's home in Gainesville seemed more practical. It was rent-free and that solved some money worries. He could tolerate 3 years in college as long as he was preparing for something. "This is it, here, now. The future we've been promising ourselves has already begun.... We can't afford to muff this chance."[46]

LOOKING BACK

Harold Bond had fought in Italy and his experiences at Monte Cassino haunted him for 20 years. He was consumed with starting a career and raising a family, without parallels between the old war and his new life. As time passed he seldom heard Monte Cassino mentioned and never spoke of it either. Yet he frequently woke up at night dreaming about the battle. "With experiences such as those . . . so deeply branded on my mind, I could not help wondering what they finally meant to me and to the others with whom I had shared them. Had they consisted, after all, of merely senseless suffering without meaning, or was there a significance in them that I had been unable to discover?" Bond took his family with him back to Monte Cassino 20 years later to look for answers. They searched for them together, and he was finally able to share his memories with them. There was strong meaning in that after all.[47]

Bond's doubts were common. Longing to return to the battlefield, to reunite with other veterans, to share experiences with families, comes only after enough time has passed, after the pressing matters of life are tended to, and the scars have faded.

Audie Murphy, the decorated hero of WWII, tried to relax in Cannes on the south of France at the end of the war. Alone in his room, he toyed with his service revolver, "more beautiful than a flower; more faithful than most friends." He stuffed it into his bag and went into the crowded streets, where he became irritated; he wanted to be around people, but wanted to be alone, wanted to talk to someone, but wanted solitude more. Peace had broken out in Europe, but he couldn't find it. His thoughts returned to the war, to lost friends, and to devastating scenes. He returned to his small room, but he still couldn't sleep, remembering his friends, ". . .who would go again to hell and back." He concluded, "We have been so intent on death that we have forgotten life. And now suddenly life faces us."[48]

Clarence Schutt, a Pacific Marine, was raised in poverty, his mother died early, and their house burned to the ground. His father signed the papers for him to join the Corps. He remembered Iwo Jima: "when the ramp goes down and you see the bodies of guys who were alive a minute before—it's hard to think about that." But back in the states he rode a bus for 3 days back to Tennessee. All the relatives came to the bus station to meet him, but he didn't waste any time getting out of uniform to find a job. There weren't any good ones, so he took anything to earn a buck. He finally got a low-paying job in a hardware store and joined the USMC reserves; it paid almost as much as his regular job. He married and had a daughter—then war broke out in Korea and it started all over again.[49]

John and Jane Easton thought of their war days many years later. "Hardly a day goes by that we don't think of the war. . . . But we line up on the side of hope. . . . miracles can happen; dreams, even fabulous ones, can come true; and that we humans can make a positive difference if we will."[50]

They made a difference.

8

Forgotten Wars: Korea and the Cold War

"I had a strange dream," William Dannenmaier wrote in the prologue to *We Were Innocents.* "Someone told me my father had died. . . . I cried inconsolably. Finally as people came closer, I controlled myself and began talking to them. Then I awoke. My eyes were wet. . . . My father died in 1954, more than 40 years before my dream. It was the first time I had cried."

Dannenmaier came home from Korea unknown and undecorated. He considered himself a common man, but he told his story for the tens of thousands of uncommon men who served, fought, or died in Korea, and for those who lived but were unable to talk about it, unable to cry about it. Since the war had never officially ended, the demilitarized zone remained a lasting scar across Korea and on those who fought there. The world hurried to forget Korea, those who returned, and those who never did.

Dannenmaier explained that his father had died only a few months after he returned from serving as an army scout in Korea. He hadn't cried then or at the funeral; he had seen too much death already. "During my year in Korea, life had become a transient acquaintance, death a companion." But after the passage of some time he was able to look back and unlock his grief. His raw feelings, suppressed for 40 years, were finally exposed. Dreams of being expendable woke him at night; part of him died in Korea and his dreams had become his real world.[1]

World War II ended with a rush to get home, go to work or school, marry and start a family, and buy houses and fast cars. Everyone rushed to cash in on a long-awaited peace and the prosperity that came with it, to spend the dividends of victory. The armed forces and the military–industrial complex demobilized quickly from the historic peaks of WWII, deflating to perilous levels of unpreparedness.

The Yalta agreement had left Europe divided into two spheres with the continent separated by an iron curtain, east facing west across barbed wire and gun sights. A bamboo curtain in Asia, though more porous and ill defined, was as menacing as the hardened steel and concrete in central Europe. The Second World War appeared to have been settled more decisively than the first, but it left the world ideologically divided from the Arctic's icy expanses, along covered jungle trails, between islands, over mountain ranges of Africa and South America, and in shifting lines drawn through Middle Eastern dust. Mushroom clouds over Hiroshima and Nagasaki cast a nuclear pall over the world, prompted a strategic arms race, and drove the war of ideologies into the shadows. The new political divide reduced relations between the Union of Soviet Socialist Republics and former WWII allies to brinkmanship that could lead to a strategic nuclear exchange and World War III. From beneath the cover of a shaky peace, a shadowy war of a different kind immerged, intensified around the globe for 46 years: the cold war. In Korea, the cold war turned very hot, very fast.

KOREAN WAR

National defenses were sleeping when North Koreans swept across the 38th parallel on June 25, 1950. The U.S. economy was deflating and the WWII generation was not eager for another land war in Asia so soon after V-J Day, and neither was President Truman. Nevertheless, he was compelled to respond, hoping to contain the spread of communism without full-scale mobilization.

The Great Depression and two world wars had made deep impressions on a generation still striving to capitalize on the rewards for their sacrifices. The invasion of South Korea was not a direct threat to them and the country was not ready for another war. College students rushed for deferments at the first call for volunteers; WWII veterans were busy using the GI Bill to rebuild their lives. No one wanted this.

Four Patriots

Don Adams had started forestry school, but he wasn't that interested in being a forest ranger. The world was at peace, so he joined the army. He took basic training at Fort Dix and got a weekend pass to go into New York City. He remembered how an elderly lady paid his nickel fare for his ferry ride to Staten Island. He didn't know what motivated her, but never forgot the kindness. "Everywhere we went, we were treated with great respect," he remembered. But when the Korean War started, the National Guard recalled 50- to 60-year-old men along with the youngsters. Adams remembered well the families crying as they shipped out.[2]

Bud Ball had registered as a conscientious objector working in his father's garage when his draft notice arrived; he went in anyway. After basic at Camp Pickett, he was on the first boatload of draftees to Korea, seasick all the way. "We had no idea what we were up against," he said. But the ship landed at Pusan and the men took a train to the front; on the second day he was in a truck lost behind enemy lines. Ball eventually caught up with the 1st Cavalry Division. "You go to fight for your country, but when you lose a buddy, you fight because you're mad."[3]

Sidney Riches had served in the Pacific Theater as an officer during the final days of WWII. When he was discharged at San Diego after the war, he tried several unsuccessful jobs, divorced his mentally ill wife, and finally reentered the army as an enlisted man. When war broke out on the Korean Peninsula, the army immediately commissioned him a captain and gave him command of Company K in the 1st Infantry Regiment, 6th Division, at Fort Ord, California. From there, it was just a "hop, skip, and a jump to Korea." Riches had worried about his shaky handwriting in the Philippines during WWII; now he was on his way to Korea.[4]

Clarence Schutt had come home from WWII on a Greyhound bus met by Tennessee relatives. Clarence had wasted no time shedding his Marine Corps uniform and searching for work. But the illusive job was hard to find, so he worked at whatever temporary ones he could find. When he married and his wife had a baby, he needed more money to support them, so he joined the USMC reserves and was paid almost as much for drills as he was on the part-time civilian jobs. But, when the Korean War broke, Clarence didn't have time to say goodbye to his family or prepare them for his going. When his unit reached Texas, he called home to explain where he was. His reserve outfit, which had trained together, was broken up and the men dispersed to fill the ranks of other units. Clarence had kept strong ties with members of his WWII outfit, but he didn't want to get close to anyone going to Korea. He knew what to expect. He fought from Inchon to Seoul, on to Wan Son, and at the Chosin Reservoir with men whose names he didn't know and whose faces he would soon forget. Clarence Schutt lived through his second war in Korea, went back to work, and celebrated his 50th wedding anniversary with roses and champagne at a Marine Corps reunion. It was "one of the best days of my life," he said. He and his wife were joined by six of his best friends from the 5th Marine Division in WWII, none from his old unit in Korea.[5]

The War

The military response to the North Korean invasion was called a United Nations' police action, but the heavy attack had caught the United States and the United Nations off balance. Under immense pressure, American and South Korean forces fell back in disarray. General Douglas MacArthur claimed there was no chance to save Korea without a full commitment of the United States. Truman ordered the 8th Army from Japan to Korea; Task Force Smith was first to arrive.

Lieutenant Colonel Charles Smith waited with his infantry battalion from the 24th Division near Osan, expecting an onslaught. It came; they fought a delaying action for 2 weeks until they finally gave up Taejon. The arriving 1st Cavalry Division relieved them, but miles of lost ground would have to be recovered inch-by-inch after the 8th Army gathered enough strength. Early defeats exposed the lack of national readiness and plagued fighters throughout 3 years of war.

Recruiting stations had their work cut out and were helped some when individual reservists were recalled. Some Reserve and National Guard units were federalized to fill gaps in the regular forces, but combined military strength, at less than six million, was too low. Heavy recruiting and mobilization of Reserve and National Guard units could not make up deficiencies fast enough to stop the North Koreans, and the unpopular draft was again necessary. Large emergency recruit levies overwhelmed training centers unable to keep up with demands to push more troops through training faster. Units were rushed through training and sent into combat unprepared, deemed battle-ready when they bled.

Intelligence estimates had been flawed from the beginning, and more accurate estimates later were ignored. From the onset, the thin 24th Division and weakened South Korean Army faced nine North Korean divisions equipped with tanks and artillery. Only ten U.S. Army divisions and eleven separate regiments were active around the world. Four divisions served as occupation forces in Japan and the nearest reinforcements were lone regiments in Hawaii and Okinawa. Active divisions were manned at 66 percent strength and backed by a support structure severely weakened during demobilization. The draft sent raw replacements through training, and into units bound for combat, barely trained to fire their rifles. The mighty Seventh Fleet sailed with only fourteen ships; the Far East Command had only thirteen. Fortunately, the Far East Air Force still had over 1,000 aircraft and 33,000 men that were sorely needed.

MacArthur wanted boots on the ground and air support overhead as fast as possible. As soon as they came available, he flung them piecemeal into the fray to hold the small perimeter, and buy time to organize a counterattack. Pusan, at the southern tip of the Korean peninsula, was the last toehold before the Sea of Japan, the closest port for troops to disembark. North Koreans attacked Pusan with a vengeance and MacArthur demanded more of everything.

Fighting in Korea was desperate and inbound units from Japan were not well manned, trained, or equipped for the job ahead. At home, people were surprised, dismayed, and angered by failure to stop the communists. Pictures and stories of units "bugging out" were not images they were accustomed to from WWII. Americans had always been reluctant to fight in Asia and this was especially vexing. Fighting within political boundaries and artificial limits was as difficult to handle at home as it was for MacArthur. National support for the war sagged as men were drafted and asked to suspend their lives for a war no one understood. Congress was in no better mood; when the president asked them to end their budget restrictions and add $10 billion for defense he received sullen acquiescence, higher taxes, and unpopular limits on consumer credit.[6]

Defenders in Korea desperately traded space for time at the Pusan perimeter. North Koreans hammered through Taegu and tried to push them into the sea. Beleaguered Americans tightened into a sixty-by-eighty-mile circle around Pusan until a marine brigade arrived just in time to plug a gaping hole in the line. The buildup continued until the United Nations Command numbered 180,000 men, mostly South Koreans. They finally outnumbered the North Koreans and their new Patton tanks outgunned the old Soviet T-34s. The battleship *Missouri* and carrier-based aircraft defended the 8th Army's flanks for an amphibious landing behind the lines at Inchon, which retook Seoul and pinched the North Koreans from another direction. With Kimpo Airfield secured for air operations, the 8th Army pursued the enemy northward while another amphibious operation captured Wonsan on the opposite side of the peninsula. Fears of Chinese intervention abated and shivering men talked of being home near the fireplace by Christmas. But just as peace seemed assured, a massive Chinese attack crossed the Yalu River and fighting worsened.

Morale at home suffered during the harsh winter fighting as desultory news of routs and defeats punctuated newspaper headlines. Then modern Saber Jets and a new commander, General Matthew Ridgeway, brought some relief on both fronts. The air force soon regained air supremacy over Russian MiGs but could not hold the communists out of Seoul. Ridgeway fought another retrograde while pounding North Korean and Chinese troops with airborne bombs and artillery shells. Politicians and media alike openly condemned the seesaw war, causing morale to tank in muddy foxholes and around kitchen tables. As UN troops withdrew further south and concentrated their strength, North Korean and Chinese lines became overextended, enabling a counterattack to push them back to the 38th parallel. Fighting seesawed even as negotiations for an armistice continued. Unlike the unconditional surrender of WWII, the Korean conflict ended with a stalemate. With all the uncertainty, one thing was clear: the Korean War had not ended, but the cold war had definitely begun. Communists seemed to be winning ideological conflicts around the world while the red scare grew at home; paranoia and red hunts ripped at the heart of the country.

Demobilization after Korea was another swift decompression of manpower. Separation procedures, similar to WWII, included mustering out pay, pay for unused leave, and a travel allowance. But Korean enlistments had been for specified periods, not for the duration of the conflict; therefore men with different discharge dates were phased out over an extended period.

Confusion

Don Adams, for one, was happy to be home. Sailing into San Francisco Bay and being met by movie actresses was something to remember. He remembered other things, too, such as almost killing a man in Korea, but he couldn't remember the names of any of the men he served with. He turned to teaching and tried to put the war behind, but he was restless, searching for something different. His seasonal occupation as a park ranger in the Smokey Mountains increased in importance to him until he left teaching to work full time as a park ranger and park historian.[7]

The war had confused veterans and the public, inglorious from the beginning and uncertain at the end, filled with political rancor throughout, and a freezing, muddy, bloody nightmare for the troops. Soldiers experienced none of the joyous homecoming celebrations that followed World War II, rather only silent relief.

People forgot Korea quickly, and forgot veterans almost as fast. Paul Edwards returned from Korea in 1954 and met a well-dressed man on the street; they started a polite conversation. Edwards was still in uniform, and the stranger asked where he was stationed. He said quietly that he had just returned from Korea. "Oh," said the stranger, "I didn't know we had troops there."[8]

After the generous WWII GI Bill, rewards for Korean War veterans were relatively lackluster. Some took advantage of the educational provisions, but most simply blended into local landscapes when they returned. The best way to forget the experience was through a good job; modernizing of warfare had provided Korean War veterans with some added technical skills. WWII was the first modern war in which military occupational skills were similar to many in the civilian labor force. A Congressional study showed further advancements in civilian-related skills in Korea from WWII. Veterans able to master civilian skills during their term of service reaped the benefits of that experience when they reentered the job market. Technical skills in the navy and air force had increased about 4 percent from WWII to Korea, and mechanical skills increased similarly in the army. All the services had more demands for administrative talent. The need for skills with relevance only to combat had decreased slightly in all the uniformed services.[9]

PRISONERS OF WAR

In Korea, men were frequently separated from their units under fluid battlefield conditions with battle lines moving up and down the Korean peninsula. "Bug-out" was a term that described men falling back from one defensive position to the next under heavy attack as units withdrew under enemy pressure. Ground troops and downed aviators were frequently separated from friendly units; both sides took many prisoners in the confusion and fog of battle. When a cease-fire was eventually implemented, the United Nations command held 31,000 communist prisoners. One-third did not want to be repatriated, but the swap for American prisoners included sending the Communists back to North Korea.

North Korean and Chinese soldiers had brutally abused their prisoners, sometimes killed them or used them for propaganda purposes. Captured Americans were forced on long marches, and many were left to die if they fell. Living conditions in captivity were abominable: dysentery was untreated, food was insufficient and without nourishment, heat was inadequate for the harsh winters, and latrines were unsanitary. Prisoners were beaten and bayoneted, wounds and frostbite untended, and they were subjected to brainwashing attempts in the camps. But the final humiliation awaited them when they came home. Prisoners were scorned, accused of collaboration, suspected of having turned communist, or were simply ignored.

When Donald Griffith landed at Inchon and made his way through a minefield, he came face to face with Bob Hope. His 3 years as a North Korean prisoner, however, was no laughing matter. He was thrown into a pigpen for 30 days, where a buddy went insane and died. He saw another's frozen feet actually come off with his boots. Griffith was temporarily blinded by medical experiments conducted on him by his captors. He managed to survive only through tough marine training and strength of character. He remembered fondly his repatriation and being given tomato juice, ice cream, cooked meat, and a new Marine Corps cap. Looking back, Griffith believed we often take too much for granted in life. For him, "Every day is a bonus day."[10]

North Korea began releasing our 4,000 mistreated prisoners in 1953 after almost 3,000 had died in captivity. Veterans were quietly blamed for everything wrong about the unpopular war; for former prisoners the accusations were a direct affront. The federal government made no provisions to protect their privacy or reputations from reporters or the public. A scapegoat was needed to blame for the failures of an unprepared nation, and silent veterans became the most visible symbols. A Congress that had criticized the war and constrained it financially was even less generous with the Korean-era GI Bill. Basic provisions were retained from the original bill, but funded at lower levels. Korean veterans were not very enthused about the opportunities it offered.

Korean veterans were obscure, kept low profiles, and were slow to organize. Former POWs were especially distrusted, considered stained by captivity, or contaminated with communist ideology. Even veterans' organizations combed their rolls for potential communists infiltrating their posts. The army issued less than honorable discharges to anyone accused of leaning to the left, even if their records were clean, and sent a suspect list of former prisoners to the Federal Bureau of Investigation. The VA rescinded benefits of anyone on the FBI suspect lists, denying help to those most in need.[11]

The army assigned one of its own psychiatrists, Major William Mayer, to prepare a report on the loyalty of former prisoners. He reviewed secret Pentagon records and concluded that one-third of POWs had been brainwashed in captivity. He blamed the prisoners for their atrocious conditions in prisons and alleged those who died had simply failed to take care of themselves. Mayer's findings raised some serious questions about national character, education, and military training, but his report disregarded the abusive behavior of the enemy and the fact that they were sent to Korea largely unprepared for what they would encounter.[12]

Mayer's prejudicial conclusions made former POW's appear seditious, and sullied the honorable service of other Korean veterans with his sweeping allegations. But in the final analysis, only nine of nearly 4,500 former prisoners were ever reprimanded, restricted, or tried for misconduct. Another study reported that only 5 percent of prisoners actively resisted efforts at brainwashing as they tried to survive the ordeal, yet only twenty-one refused repatriation and stayed in North Korea. Seventy-five were found to have actually agreed to spy on the United States.[13]

Eventually the Defense Department made a feeble effort to clear former prisoners from the institutional bias. They were paid the grand sum of $2.50 for each day they had been incarcerated, but before receiving any money they were re-quired to swear they were not collaborators. Any evidence against them was kept secret while they prepared their statements. Nearly all were officially cleared of malfeasance, but it was too late; they were already branded, the damage done.

Dr. Albert Biderman, an air force sociologist and WWII veteran, later reexam-ined the same records Mayer had used for his original findings. Biderman came to a quite different conclusion, but his analysis was too late to alter embedded perceptions. The army had already begun tests to evaluate how much pain, torture, or brainwashing troops could withstand without breaking. Some were even tested with hallucinogens and other drugs without their knowledge, others were exposed to radiation, but when they came down with cancer their claims were denied.[14]

MOVING ON

When the Korean War closed, Alvin King wanted to move on and recognize veterans from Emporia, Kansas, even though he had not served in the military. Armistice Day still honored doughboys from WWI, but other veterans stood in the shadows without a comparable V-E or V-J Day, and certainly not a V-K Day. WWII and Korea had cost Lyon County the lives of over one hundred of their sons, who should not be forgotten. King organized a parade for November 11, 1953, Armistice Day, intending to expand it somehow to recognize all veterans. A Marine Corps color guard and the American Legion bugle corps stepped off first, leading troops from the 137th Infantry down the street, followed by a naval reserve unit, recruiters, high school bands, mothers, scouts, baton twirlers, surviving veterans of WWI, WWII, and Korea. It was a noisy salute with fighter jets roaring overhead, sirens and whistles shrieking as many decibels as spectators could withstand. The noise stopped abruptly at 11:11 A.M. for a moment of silent prayer. Then free food was served at the civic auditorium while spectators cheered on a wheelchair basketball game, free movies, a boxing smoker, and an evening of dancing. The event was so popular the Kansas Governor encouraged every town in America to replicate it. A similar proposal was passed in the U.S. Senate, and President Eisenhower made Veterans Day a legal holiday on October 8, 1954.[15]

COLD WAR

The ceasefire in Korea had been perplexing in the usual sense of winning or losing, with endless dialogue instead the finality of victory or defeat. There were some positive results from the Korean War: United Nations forces had defended South Korea from annexation, the United States had shown communists regimes in North Korea and China that incursions would not go unchallenged in Japan or Taiwan, strains between China and the Soviet Union were exposed, and collective security was proven a viable concept. Yet, the world remained dangerously un-settled. Even as fighting in Korea ended, the global struggle between democracy

and socialism escalated. Korea was the most evident barrage in a continuing con-
frontation waged mostly on city streets, jungle trails, mountains, and deserts from
September 2, 1945, to September 26, 1991.[16]

The Korean conflict emerged somehow out of the confusion of unresolved
issues between the superpowers after WWII, fear of a nuclear war, and expansion
of competing ideologies through surrogates. Lack of clarity in ending the conflict
in Korea obscured the prospects for peaceful coexistence around the world. At
home, the Korean War had been unpopular and was quickly forgotten, but the cold
war just wouldn't go away in Asia, the Middle East, Latin America, or Europe.
WWII had left groups of nations banded in collective alliances. European allies,
minus the Soviets, formed the North Atlantic Treaty Alliance (NATO) to protect
Western Europe, while the Soviets pulled Eastern European countries into the
Warsaw Pact (WP). The most dangerous place was right in the center, in Berlin.

After WWII ended, occupation forces remained in Europe on both sides of
the iron curtain in Italy, Yugoslavia, Poland, Czechoslovakia, Albania, Greece,
Austria, Hungary, East and West Germany. Berlin stood as the epicenter of the
cold war, a divided city filled with spies from everywhere. The Soviets had tried
to seal the German capital as early as 1948, but American and British flights kept
it on life support. Thirty-three USAF pilots and crew died in the Berlin Airlift. In
1961, East Germans constructed a wall to keep their own citizens from leaving
East Berlin for the west. The cold war escalated.

The nuclear arms race between the Soviet Union and United States hung over a
divided Europe. Weapons of mass destruction threatened a nuclear holocaust too
horrific to contemplate, so small wars between surrogates broke out in unlikely
places: Angola and the Congo, Grenada, El Salvador, Nicaragua, Honduras and
Panama, Chili, Peru, Bolivia, and Columbia to name only a few. Standoffs at
the Fulda Gap, at the Berlin Wall, and along the Korean DMZ continued as the
superpowers tested each other in the air, on the surface and under the seas, and
over polar ice caps. In Korea the test that had become a limited war had almost
spun out of control into a nuclear exchange. Limited war doctrine would be tested
again in Vietnam.

REMEMBERING THE FORGOTTEN

The myth that the cold war was business as usual came from misunderstanding
the details of a global conflict over 45 years in isolated pockets around the world.
The cold war was a real war where real people died, and veterans served honorably
under stressful conditions and with little recognition. Between pilots Phil Brewer
and Sid Coulson, who died in Yugoslavia in November 1945, and David Hilemon
who died on the Korean DMZ in December 1994, at least 382 service members
fell in cold war clashes at trouble spots all over the world. Their names are not well
known, except to their loved ones, but they served, made the ultimate sacrifice,
and should never be forgotten. The Berlin Wall crashed down with more than a

collective sigh of relief; it fell under the collective weight of 45 years of sacrifice by cold war veterans.[17]

There were few celebrations as the boys came home from Korea and healing came slowly for them. The national moodiness that sent them to war clouded their return from a conflict that remained unfinished. The lingering standoff along the demilitarized line at the 38th parallel seemed disrespectful of their sacrifices in doing what they were called to do, especially for the more than 33,000 killed, 103,000 wounded, and 4,500 prisoners of war. The Korea experience was the wrong way to send soldiers to war and a worse way to bring them home, but the lessons were not learned; the mistakes would be repeated.

The enduring Korean stalemate did not fit the pattern of general sacrifice and shared victory. Life had continued as usual during the 3 years of war; no unusual demands were made at home and the war was not allowed to intrude on their lives, except those with gold or blue stars in their windows. Korean veterans returned confused, frustrated, resentful, realizing the public cared little for the war or those who fought. Their war was shrugged off as a police action or a conflict, something short of a real war. Military bands met some of the first ships returning to San Francisco, a few enjoyed community picnics, but those were few and quickly fell to simple family gatherings.

Korean veterans did not generally share official views of low troop morale, but they did resent failure of the nation to commit to winning; they noticed the lack of support for them when they returned. They had risked their lives for a negotiated peace and doubted even that had been reached in good faith. Veterans of the forgotten war were left uncertain of their place in history. Don Adams gave up teaching after the war to become a full-time park ranger. He looked back and realized he did his duty by going over, and he and his buddies took the brunt of the fighting and accepted the slights when they returned. But Adams saw it as much more than a police action; they did something important, they saved a country. "We did the right thing."[18]

The Chosin Few and the Korean War Veterans' Association did not start work to commemorate those who served and died in the Korean War until the 1980s. President Reagan approved legislation for a memorial in 1986, but it was not dedicated for eleven more years. The ghastly specter of nineteen combat soldiers on patrol at different stages of the war haunts Washington's Mall. They are dispersed over a grassy plain, each an individual within a group, carrying a heavy burden, wearing winter clothes, and searching in different directions. Their eyes seem anxious, alert for the enemy even at home. Each stands alone although they are bound together. Their figures are poignant, heroic, speaking to us of something we want to understand but cannot quite. They appear to be still unsettled, uncertain, but not wanting to be forgotten.[19]

Bud Ball, the conscientious objector who fought as an infantryman, remembered listening to a sermon by a chaplain who had fought at St. Lo in WWII. "That's when I was saved," he said, "going up that hill saying the 23d Psalm." But when he came home, he fell silent. "People didn't care if we were over there dying for them. . . . We did a good job, just like the Vietnam troops. We should have stood up for our troops against the protesters."[20]

William Dannenmaier, the Korean scout who could not grieve for his father's death, recalled a thunderstorm at sea on his voyage home. He wondered if Korea had been without thunder until he realized he had considered every noise as artillery or air strikes, forgetting God and nature. Only when the ship passed beneath the Golden Gate Bridge did he finally realize that he was actually going home. In San Francisco, they were instructed to stack duffle bags, enjoy a hot meal, and when they returned their orders would be ready. All were sent to Fort Carson, Colorado. Those with less than 3 months remaining in service were discharged from Colorado; those with more time to serve went home for 30 days. A medical examination was offered before they left, but no one wanted to delay going home. Too impatient to wait for public transportation, Dannenmaier stood in the snow and hitchhiked, beating the warm bus to St. Louis. But after charging home, he hesitated. Instead of going to his parent's house, he walked first to his old college to visit former professors. Home could wait a little longer.

When he eventually walked in, his father said he was temperamental, with a quick temper; his mother called him unstable, unsettled. His friends thought his year in Korea wasted, one to be forgotten. At first, Dannenmaier believed the only changes in him were ruined teeth and lost hearing, but gradually he realized his every-night headaches would not stop. He had wild mood swings; thought life was meaningless and flew into rages. Ideas others considered immensely important seemed trivial to him. He was detached from his surroundings for a long time, but gradually reengaged life.

Dannenmaier returned to Washington University in St. Louis and earned masters and doctorate degrees. He taught classes and worked in administration until returning to the army as a civilian. Thirty years after he left Korea, he returned as a psychologist and found Korea very different than he remembered. He visited the DMZ and saw North Korean soldiers on duty. He realized he still hated them; that much hadn't changed. Near the end of his term of duty, he learned of a plan to honor Korean veterans at a special dinner. He telephoned for reservations to attend, but was told it was for veteran's children currently serving: "We're not interested in Korean veterans." It was an ugly end to the Korea saga—just not interested.[21]

9

The Unforgotten War: Vietnam

Lynda Van Devanter was an army nurse in Vietnam. In *Home Before Morning* she described coming home. "We didn't ask for a parade. We didn't even ask for much of a thank you. All we wanted was some transportation to San Francisco International Airport so we could hop a connecting flight to get home to our families." She remembered how easy it had been to hitchhike in Vietnam. "Back in 'Nam, I would usually stand on the flight line in my fatigues, combat boots, jungle hat, pigtails, and a smile. Getting a ride was a cinch." But she found out just how far a uniform and a smile would take her in this country. Some drove by and gave her the finger; others shouted obscenities or even threw trash at her as they sped by.[1]

Americans had sacrificed during WWII but afterwards discovered enlightened self-interest. The GI Bill encouraged higher education, home ownership, and better jobs; they worked hard to define themselves, acquired assets, and passed those values to their children. Women began a sexual revolution, blacks a civil rights movement, and new-agers discovered long hair, bell-bottoms, and pot.

In the first 20 years after WWII, forty small wars percolated around the globe; one side was expanding its influence, the other containing. Ideologies clashed below the nuclear threshold since mutual assured destruction (MAD) made using the nuclear bomb unthinkable. But when the Soviet Union pushed the limits by moving nuclear missiles into Cuba, within easy reach of the United States, President Kennedy used air and naval blockades to defuse the crisis at the brink of holocaust. Nuclear threats influenced every major decision of the cold war.

The stalemate in Korea, MAD, and cold war encroachments were harbingers of a crisis stalking Asia. The First Indochina War left 200,000 Vietnamese and French dead between 1946 and 1954, with France mired in an un-winnable quandary without public support. Although Presidents Truman and Eisenhower streamed military and political support to a world war ally, continued ambivalence toward the Vietnam problem burdened every U.S. administration from Roosevelt through

George W. Bush. Korea was the forgotten war, Vietnam the one we can never forget.

VIETNAM

Vietnam was not the bloodiest in American history but it was the longest and seemed even longer. Conventional dogma dominated military and political strategy during the cold war, overlooking unconventional warfare. Vietnam was not a choice between conventional or unconventional war, it included both. If the public and the administration were confused by the stalemate of Korea, they were confounded by quagmire in Vietnam.

The Vietnam problem seemed a small enough irritation until a battalion of the 7th Cavalry narrowly avoided a massacre in an obscure valley of the Ia Drang River. Helicopters, artillery, and courageous young Americans won the Battle at Landing Zone X-ray, but a few days later other cavalry battalions on foot were ambushed near Landing Zone Albany and were not so fortunate. Those two battles made Vietnam America's War.

Expanding search and destroy operations required many more combatants. Troops increased steadily through 1968, until the Viet Cong (VC) and North Vietnamese Army (NVA) mounted a general offensive during the Tet holiday truce. American and South Vietnamese (SVN) counter-offensives decimated the VC and NVA, but shocking headlines and critical editorials ignored that account. College students burned draft cards, marched in the streets, and fled the country; zealots demanded peace at any price.

North Vietnam was not a powerful country, its population one-tenth that of the United States, one-sixtieth the land, and one thirty-fourth the gross national product. Nevertheless, it was pummeled with 6.8 million tons of bombs, three and one half times the number dropped on WWII Germany. With the bombs fell 12 million gallons of a chemical defoliant called Agent Orange.[2]

Lynda Van Devanter, the nurse who couldn't catch a ride to San Francisco International, never healed. Following college and army nurse training she was sent to the 71st Evacuation Hospital in Pleiku. "If our boys were being blown apart, then somebody better be over there putting them back together again." Lynda volunteered, but afterwards she could not pull herself together. She made it home but stumbled through life with posttraumatic stress and recurring nightmares about one patient, a young soldier with half his face blown away. She drank heavily, cried frequently, and landed on unemployment, food stamps, and welfare. Therapy helped, and she tried writing her way back to sanity; her book inspired the popular China Beach television series. It ended for Lynda at age 55 when she died of complications from Agent Orange.[3]

About 11,000 military women served in Vietnam, many were nurses, but the number of civilians in the Red Cross, USAID, and other agencies is not clear. Studies of women from Vietnam with post traumatic stress link their experiences to problems later in life. Some nurses compressed several patients into a single image that haunted them for years. One nurse couldn't forget a patient who was lucid and awake when he was brought in, but had lost his penis, arms, and legs. She couldn't comfort him, so she washed his hair until he died. When Vietnam nurses got home and resumed nursing they found peacetime boring, missed the bonds with those they had shared life and death. Red Cross workers gave another kind of care; they represented civilization to grunts in the field, to remind them they had to go home. One Donut Dolly remembered playing board games with a soldier; the next day he was dead. Reentry was as hard for women as for the men; they felt the same anger, rejection, hostility, and disgust from the civilized society they were suppose to represent.[4]

The average age going to Vietnam was younger, but better educated than WWII or Korea. More were needed so Department of Defense (DOD) expanded the volunteer and draft pools without calling up reserves or National Guard units. Admission and training standards were dropped to allow more from lower mental and physical groups, Project 100,000. This entitled disadvantaged youth to military training and discipline and veterans' benefits if they lived through it. Military service had become a social program for the poor and disadvantaged to meet manpower needs. Project 100,000 added more men but also more drugs and disciplinary problems.

Many people tried to ignore the unpopular war but television news pumped it into their homes. Students disregarded it until the draft made them vulnerable; many WWII baby boomers used liberal deferments to avoid going, some even fled the country. Volunteers still signed on, many for patriotic reasons, others to learn career skills, for educational benefits, or to choose their military occupations since they had no choice if drafted; some were just desperate to escape a dead end existence.[5] Most brought with them a longstanding faith in America and hoped it would all work out somehow.

The media frenzy over the 1968 Tet offensive turned a clear victory into a perceived defeat, swaying a segment of the public against the war. Fighting was heavy that year, and continuous body counts and flag-draped coffins dragged down public support. Unfortunately, antiwar sentiments were often misplaced on the boys coming home. Those going over already felt the loss of support, confusing directions from Washington, and a lack of purpose; those coming home felt the hate.

James Wallace accompanied some servicemen to Vietnam in 1968 and listened as they talked about protesters and draft dodgers. "I can't go along with those peace demonstrators. . . . They should all be drafted." A buddy disagreed, "The antiwar protesters are not wrong as long as they don't harm anybody." But they agreed they would feel different in a year. A colonel at the Long Binh reception center confirmed that. "The average man here is 19 years old, going on 42."[6]

Families watched television war scenes in their homes and were repulsed by what they saw and heard. Returning soldiers stared at television in disbelief, unable to reconcile the images there with what they had seen. Eugene Cleary said no one even asked what Vietnam was like until 10 years later. He assumed they thought they knew because of what they saw on the news. When Steven Gist arrived at Chicago's O'Hare a woman asked if they were killing civilians over there. After he watched the evening news on television he understood why she asked.[7] Distorted coverage turned the public against the war and the warriors and many veterans remain forever embittered at the media.

Despite search and destroy missions, the enemy initiated 80 percent of firefights, mostly at night; mines, booby traps, and mortars were faceless enemies during the day. Terrain was fought for then abandoned, only to be fought over again. Women and children tried to kill them, which raised a sense of futility, ambivalence, and unbalanced their expectations. Grunts fought to win their battles but winning the war was out of their hands. The day their tour of duty ended mattered more, so they managed for a year with determination, crossing off each day on short-timers calendars, praying time ran out before luck. Each step along a jungle trail was one step closer to home or death.[8]

But home disappointed. David Morrison said he carried an image of home just as it was when he left: that life would be better when he returned, no more violence; that was what kept him going. But he found the country had changed when he returned, just as he had.[9]

Troops were constantly going and coming in rotations that disrupted unit integrity, teamwork, and cohesion. Replacements broke unit solidarity and some never knew the other men in their platoons; few left with lasting friendships. Gary Garcheck remembered his infantry unit as a collection of college educated, inner-city blacks and farm boys, rich and poor, potheads and straights, all with a single purpose: to get out of Vietnam in one piece. "We were so close, yet I have not seen or heard from any of the men in my unit."[10]

When their flight home was called their heads were filled with dreams for the future. As they had come, they left on a plane filled with strangers; as danger sank behind the horizon, pulses slowed and their hearts picked up a new beat. But they found home was different, a strange place, and they were lost, lonely, and isolated. No one cared where they had been or what they had done, so they kept quiet, got out of the way, and grappled with a new life alone.

Spitting

Bob Greene had heard rumors of Vietnam veterans being spit on when they came home; he was skeptical but he mentioned it in a column for the *Chicago Tribune*. He asked for specifics. Over one thousand letters reached him. Greene knew Vietnam veterans carried some anger but he found the most prevalent emotion was hurt. Many wrote they were spit on when they came home but had never told anyone about it before. Greene figured it was not unusual for them to be ashamed, considering their youth, exhaustion, and confusion. He assumed some might even have fleeting thoughts that they might be somehow at fault. When people are made to feel that way they are reluctant to share it with others. Leonard Caldeira went over during the hard fighting in 1967–1968. But everything had changed when he came home after the Chicago Democratic Convention, riots in Detroit, assassinations of Martin Luther King and Bobby Kennedy. He confessed that he felt safer in Vietnam than at home. A stranger spit at him. "I took off my uniform later that day and never put it on again...."[11]

That no one cared was the worst thing. All they expected was a "thank you," or maybe a ride home. Instead, their character was questioned, they were feared, or called drug addicts and baby killers. Most worked through their personal adjustments alone, removing their service from their resumes. Combat had been the most profound experience of their lives, yet they had to hide it. Doug Roberson served three tours in Vietnam and was proud to have fought for their country. He decided to ride a bus home instead of taking a plane. "And I want the slowest one that goes across this country because I'm going to see what I fought for." Doug settled into his window seat for a long, unsettling ride through four rowdy antiwar protests. "I asked myself for the last twelve years why in the hell did I fight for this country? Because they don't care nothing about us anyway."[12]

Vietnam confused everyone, including Lieutenant William Calley. Some civilians shot at his men, but not the whole village his platoon massacred. Calley and his men were indicted but only he received a court-martial; was convicted and sentenced to life in prison, reduced to 20 years, then ten, and finally paroled after 3 years of house arrest. Calley deserved punishment for crimes and leadership failures, but the lowest link in the chain of command became the symbol of national irresponsibility, misunderstanding, and blame.

President Nixon was elected on a promise to end the war and national divisiveness, but by 1973 he was under siege over the Watergate affair. He brought the troops home, then vetoed a health care bill to increase the number of VA physicians and reduced veterans' education benefits. Economic concerns outweighed rehabilitation and education for unpopular veterans, so he redistributed the funds to more popular programs. But the economic slump was real and it affected veterans as they looked for work. The Watergate scandal eventually drove Nixon from office. Gerald Ford pardoned him, but when Congress restored the education cuts for veterans, he vetoed that. Congress overrode the veto in a gesture mostly symbolic, because most veterans had already given up on their government and the anemic assistance it offered.

Facing the Hate

Going home disappointed most veterans. They had gone alone and scared and returned alone, if a little less scared. Happy to be returning, they thought the worst was over, but when they reached arrival terminals they were outnumbered and surrounded by unfriendly strangers. Wrinkled uniforms and new battle ribbons made them easy prey, but sometimes they were met only by silence. "So when you first got off that airplane ... there's a sign ... 'Welcome Back Soldier. America is Proud of You.' That's incredible, that sign. Cause that's all there is—that sign.... And no steak dinner, and no amount of words written in red are going to prove anything different. Once you get back, you know that no one really cares.... That war was some isolated thing ... something that Walter Cronkite talks about for five minutes every night."[13]

Jack Coughlin met both kinds. He made his way past the protesters to the first restroom he found to change from uniforms to civilian clothes. "The sight of all those once-proud young American soldiers taking off their uniforms before traveling to their hometowns will stay with me forever...." Coughlin said he met only two types of people when he came home—those actively against them and those who said nothing. He became one who said nothing.[14]

San Francisco's airport was the worst, but most had some troublemakers and more who just looked away. Most veterans took the abuse quietly. John Leary remembered landing in San Francisco with wild cheering among the soldiers on the plane; then walking alone through the San Francisco airport to complete indifference.[15]

Megan Meadows saw her older brother go to Vietnam twice. The first time he came home in his uniform, he looked sharp, his pride on display. But the next time he came was different. Megan went to meet him and was surprised to find him in civilian clothes. She asked him why he wasn't wearing his uniform. He told her people would spit on him. "I must have been all of twelve years old at that time, but I will never forget the emptiness and sadness in my big brother's eyes. He was my hero."[16]

Blending in was difficult; they were different from veterans of other wars. Gary Wood called WWII vets the biggest obstacles to Vietnam vets making it. "They grew up in the depression, and came back to victory parades and prosperity. They saw World War II as a means of getting out of bad times. We grew up in prosperity, and we came back to no jobs, lousy bennies, and civilian contempt. We see the Vietnam War as a means of getting out of good times."[17]

VIETNAM VETERANS AGAINST THE WAR

Increasing opposition to the war troubled the stream of replacements on 1-year tours. Most faded into obscurity to put their lives together, silent and out of sight. Some gathered for rap sessions to talk about the war; a few joined the opposition. Veteran John Barry Crumb had opposed the war as early as 1967 but did not want to join the peace movement. He found a few others to organize a march on the Pentagon to demand ending the war and improving benefits. As soon as they went public they were linked with the peace activists they wanted to avoid; disgruntled veterans gave credibility to the radical college protesters and counterculture misfits. Their experiences were more than dreamy idealism, though some of alleged veterans were discovered to be frauds. Vietnam Veterans Against the War (VVAW) came to epitomize the antiwar movement. Jane Fonda quickly saw their value to her socialist agenda at home. In Hanoi the North Vietnamese watched the most decisive battle of the Vietnam War shaping up in Washington, not Saigon.

Communists, socialists, left-wingers, students, and the media pressed the administration to end the war at any price so the North Vietnamese waited it out. Protesting was fashionable in the 1960s and the antiwar movement found common ground with civil rights and women's liberation groups. Editorial pages and news clips spewed distorted views from the front, opposition at home, and a steady drum roll of body counts.

Veterans rotating home could not avoid the protests. David Parks, a wounded black veteran, could have joined antiwar protesters or civil rights marchers. Instead, he enrolled in photography classes and filmed them. He was shaken by the hate slogans shouted at soldiers and police. "I had fought for my country and was in no way ashamed of it." He saw soldiers bombarded with rocks, bottles, and profanity at the Pentagon. "I could only watch as the soldiers were overrun, and I found the experience more frightening than any I had known in Vietnam." When they reached the top of the Pentagon steps, they celebrated and screamed obscenities. "The soldiers didn't retaliate because they were sick, tired, and broken. I couldn't take any pictures. I hated what I had seen and I hated America for it."[18]

One naval officer, John Forbes Kerry, emerged as the main spokesman for veterans against the war. National attention caught up with him in late January 1971 during a staged rap session in Detroit, the Winter Soldier Investigation. The group-gripe alleged atrocities, mostly unsubstantiated rumors. Some of the speakers were imposters but they played well to an eager media. National exposure encouraged them to plan a more dramatic demonstration in Washington, DC, Dewey Canyon III. They gathered at the Capitol in mismatched uniforms for speeches, then tossed medals, ribbons, and citations at the Capitol steps as cameras rolled.

Opponents of the war turned customary symbols of patriotism to their own purpose to make the war effort ineffective; protesters usurped traditions as their own. Hippies used the two-fingered V-for-Victory as a peace sign; commuters turned on headlights for Memorial Day, not to honor the dead but to end the war at any cost. Veterans against the war joined peaceniks wearing old uniforms as antiwar symbols, called heroes criminals, and flew the flag upside down.[19]

Kerry had received an incredible number of decorations in only 4 months, surprising many of his antiwar friends from college and cohorts in the navy. He used his Purple Hearts and Silver Stars as props for his public performances.[20] Then he led others before Congress to call Vietnam veterans barbarians. Department of Defense investigated the allegations but none of the accusers substantiated any of their claims. Soldiers in Vietnam read accounts of their statements in the *Pacific Stars and Stripes* and North Vietnamese jailers ensured prisoners heard Kerry's words. Jane Fonda even traveled to Hanoi personally to harass prisoners of war and was memorialized grinning astride an antiaircraft gun.

Nixon stuck to his plan for withdrawal and by early 1972 only 65,000 troops remained in country; a Harris poll reported in May that the public was satisfied with the pace. In July, the FBI subpoenaed twenty-three members of the Vietnam Veterans Against the War as the Democratic Convention opened in Miami. They had lost momentum and tried to reenergize their movement with sit-ins or VA "hospital zaps" to highlight unsavory conditions there. But they generated no sympathy for improving benefits for men they had already caste as war criminals.[21]

Veterans against the war realized the public, especially veterans, did not much support them either. While Winter Soldier and Dewey Canyon III were staged in 1971, 156,000 troops were still in country, over 1,300 were killed and almost 9,000 more wounded. Thirty years later Jane Fonda apologized for her embarrassing public display in Hanoi but not for slandering veterans or prisoners of war. Veteran William Sydnor never forgave her; he longed for the day when he could return the favor and spit in Jane Fonda's face.[22] Another vet, Michael Smith, found an opportunity as she signed books in Kansas City in April 2005. He stood on line until close enough to spit a wad of tobacco juice into her face. "There are a lot of veterans who would love to do what I did," he told the *Kansas City Star*. Ironically, Smith was arrested and charged for disorderly conduct; Fonda was never charged with treason and no hippies were charged for spitting on veterans.

The antiwar movement had undermined popular support for the military and became a catalyst for change. Widespread draft evasion had fractured the selective service system and an all-volunteer military was envisioned to replace it. The professional military had always been small, augmented by citizen soldiers when needed. The all-volunteer concept depended on pay and benefits sufficiently high to attract enough volunteers, professionals, to meet military manpower needs; a draft would be retained only for emergencies.

The new professional military eventually became the best the world had ever seen, but professionals made service an economic decision as much as patriotic, and needed improved incentives for volunteers. Cost restrained its size and a smaller and more expensive military increased the risk of expanding in an emergency, adding more reliance on the Guard and reserves. Military structure had become more budget-driven than threat-oriented, with heavy reliance on technology.

The administration tried to spare the economy and Johnson's Great Society plans by micro-managing the war. To the government and the public it was business as usual though the war drained billions from the economy. After an especially difficult 1968, Johnson withdrew his reelection bid and Richard Nixon won on a vague promise of peace. While negotiators argued about the shape of the negotiating table in Paris, fighting continued in Vietnam. Fighting was gradually passed to the South Vietnamese, but enemy supply routes, sanctuaries, and headquarters in Cambodia were attacked to buy time. Troop withdrawals continued but the final settlement left enemy troops poised to strike. When the North Vietnamese did attack in 1975, the United States watched passively on television as our allies waited for the promised assistance. All the sacrifices, lost lives, and broken bodies were disregarded; but the scar on the national psyche may never heal and cannot ever be forgotten.

THE VETERAN PROBLEM

Pamella Petersen wrote to Bob Greene for her husband, though she wished he would. "He doesn't trust anyone—he will never allow this wall to come down." Facing war demons and antiwar critics were hard enough, but a struggling economy and public antipathy made it harder. Susan Melville wrote of a friend who owned a business and would not hire a Vietnam vet—he considered them all murderers. Peter Tiffany couldn't get hired as businesses made it clear that druggies and baby killers were not welcome. His service-connected back injury made his job hunt more difficult as companies avoided possible disability claims. Danny Kelly had several issues to contend with; he was only twenty-two and unable to get a job, a date, a place to live, or a drink with other vets.[23]

Congress asked Louis Harris to conduct a national poll to find out why the veteran problem persisted in August 1971. Sixty-two percent connected veterans directly with a bad war and half considered them dumb for going. Veterans said they believed their families and friends tried to be supportive but didn't understand how it was. Dr. Sarah Haley, a psychiatrist, held rap sessions and offered counseling to veterans. She saw their problems with readjustment, including reconnecting with children, and intimacy with their wives. She found they associated the brutality of war with children's play games; veterans had literally slid down the development scale during combat.[24]

Lisa complained in *Living with the Ice Man* that she and Allen hadn't held hands or hugged for 11 years. He hugged her and apologized when she reminded him of her birthday, again. She said he was never sentimental before, but after Vietnam he always overlooked birthdays and anniversaries; he essentially dropped out of life. Allen agreed to take her out to dinner for that anniversary as long as it wasn't to an Asian restaurant. They fought over dinner anyway. "We went home, Allen went out drinking, and I went to bed alone. This is the thanks I get for fifteen years of being a loyal wife."[25] Doug Roberson, who rode the Greyhound bus home through four demonstrations said, "My attitude toward life is zilch." He nodded at his wife and children, "I got goals, to make them a living. But as for me, hell, if I wasn't married, nobody would see me."[26]

Robert McClelland shut out memories of Vietnam for 15 years by working 12 hours a day. He thought he was safe because he refused to let it get to him, but then the tough guy started to crumble. His wife of 16 years couldn't do anything right in his eyes, and she and their three children were ready to leave. Some veteran friends told him the truth: she hadn't changed; he had. He drifted from one counselor to another, looking for help until he ended up at the Veterans Clinic where a psychiatrist told him about posttraumatic stress and depression. When he wrote Greene, he and his wife were still trying to put their lives back together.[27]

Wayne Smith, a conscientious objector, joined the 9th Infantry Division as a medic. After some tough fighting, he went home for 30 days. "It was the worst mistake I ever made. I came home and it was stranger than going to Vietnam. My value system changed. Much of what I believed in was a lie. . . . " While he was home, a neighbor threw a party for him. He delayed going and went to a bar to brace for it; when he finally went, he took a prostitute with him. His high school basketball coach was waiting for him but Wayne locked himself in the bathroom. "I couldn't wait to get back to Vietnam." He returned to finish his tour but continued melting down emotionally until he was discharged. After 3 weeks as a civilian he was convicted of manslaughter and sentenced to 10 years in prison. Inside, he completed a degree in psychology and later helped other veterans deal with their emotional residue.[28]

Bob Greene read thousands of letters after his column on spitting and was surprised how often they mentioned "emotional shutdowns" and "building walls." He concluded that suppressing the sense of isolation for years only aggravated the problem. "The cause for the hurt had much more to do with what happened in the United States than with what happened in Vietnam . . . the inability of the rest of us to see that back then must be something that stays inside so many veterans even today."[29]

UNWELCOME AT HOME

Negotiations continued in Paris as troops withdrew from Saigon until American presence there was minimal. POWs were finally released in 1973 and a red carpet was rolled out on the tarmac in Honolulu. It made good drama for television but Vietnam veterans stared at their sets with mixed emotions, relieved to see the POWs home but wondering about the welcome they never received.

New York and Chicago responded with parades for any Vietnam veterans who dared turn out. The New York parade was on a Saturday when Wall Street and most of Broadway were closed so traffic would not be interrupted. No ticker tape fell from closed second story offices. Reviews of the parades were mixed. Jerry Garchek said he came home to family, friends, and responsibilities, coped with it, and just wanted to get on with his life; no one expected a parade. Richard Davis couldn't go because he was at work, but Anthony Stanfa marched and his family loved it. He did it only for them, it was too late for him; the damage was already done. John Leary marched with fellow marines. As he walked he saw a woman standing alone and clapping. When he got close, she whispered: "Welcome home!" It was a shot to his heart and he broke down, but he admitted that it felt good, even 17 years late. He saw families holding pictures of sons or brothers, and disabled veterans reaching out to shake hands. It was an opportunity "for all of us to wipe a little spit off our hearts."[30]

The centerpiece of the Vietnam-era GI Bill was education, but Vietnam veterans avoided college campuses where so much dissent had been fomented toward them. Finding a good job was difficult, more so without education; by war's end over 250,000 young men were unable to find work. In 1971, unemployment among Vietnam veterans was 11 percent, 22 percent for young blacks. With a total of 330,000 unemployed Vietnam veterans in the spring of that year, more stood in unemployment lines than were in Vietnam.[31]

The unskilled hoped to develop a trade while in the service but found combat training did not meet business needs. The VA offered guidance counseling and unemployment assistance but it was hardly effective. Dreams of a satisfying job turned into a nightmare of unemployment lines, government runarounds, college hassles, and stares from strangers. Some fellow Vietnam veterans had even labeled them criminals, and WWII veterans shunned them at Legion halls and in job interviews. When their VA-sponsored life insurance policies expired, the cost of replacing it was too high. Life wasn't worth that much any more.

Some young men had postponed higher education to serve, while others used college to avoid going. When veterans tried to redeem their earned benefits to finish college they were confronted with barriers. College front offices tightened enrollment criteria, professors ridiculed them, fellow students harangued them, and Congress cut funding by one-third. The government that never understood the war questioned why veterans left education benefits untouched.

Ronald Trousdale knew why. He went to Palomar College near Oceanside, California, for entrance exams in the summer of 1969. A young woman and two young men approached him in the parking lot. The girl asked if he was in the Marines and he nodded, his short haircut made that evident. Then she asked if he had been to Vietnam and he nodded again. She screamed at him, calling him a baby killer; one of the guys with her spit on him. He just drove back to Camp Pendleton. Kenneth Ball also knew why. An overweight, filthy, braless girl spit on him and cursed him on the way to his mechanical engineering exam. He passed the exam but skipped college to stick with his part-time job. College campuses were too hostile.[32]

Many vets couldn't afford the education anyway. Their fathers' tuition was paid in full plus enough to subsist while in college. Vietnam veterans drew only $200 a month to cover an inflation-ridden tuition and rising living expenses. It was not enough for either. Vietnam vets did not value the skimpy benefits. A Harris poll found only 36 percent used them. Fifty-three percent considered education the most important benefit, yet only a fraction went back to college.[33] Michael Lambright determined to stick it out as a journalism student anyway. His professor asked him and another veteran to speak about the media and the war. They had barely begun when a student interrupted, accusing them of attending class on GI Bill blood money. The classroom erupted and the instructor had to clear the room.[34]

Veterans struggled with their war experiences and homecoming horrors alone. Others could switch their television sets off, but they could not stop the movies in their minds. Dave McDonald carried recurring malaria along with his battle experiences, shrapnel in his arms and the scar on his forehead to Mississippi State. He found doing routine things had become more difficult. He didn't like shopping, being in public, or even talking with friends; the smell of rain on a hot summer day took him back there. But nothing distracted him from coaching high school baseball for 26 years, accumulating 500 wins and a national coach of the year award as he sent eighty players to college and fifteen to professional baseball.

McDonald admitted he had been in love before, but could never commit. "I spent a lot of time by myself. . . . The experience over there had a lot to do with me never marrying." But as he prepared to retire, he took stock of his life. Twenty-five years after the war he discovered his nine medals meant something to him, enough to ask a Congressman to help him claim them. "I don't really know why, or what to expect," he said. "I just think I might go and see." McDonald was considering going back to the A Shau Valley to see if he could find something he lost there.[35]

VIETNAM VET'S VA

Physical and psychological injuries drove some veterans to VA hospitals but few were satisfied with their experiences there. So many complaints piled up in Washington that President Carter asked Max Cleland, a Vietnam triple amputee, to head the VA. Cleland promised to clean up the backlog in 6 months; that proved impossible to do.

Cleland had lost both legs and an arm in a grenade incident in 1967. He couldn't tell his parents the full extent of his injuries, so he dictated a letter to a Red Cross volunteer reporting he was okay and would call from Walter Reed Hospital. Difficulty facing his disability was only the beginning. His first meeting with his parents was strained, as was his first trip to a restaurant in a wheelchair, his first date, and his Georgia homecoming. He was embarrassed to go home in a wheelchair, but throngs of reporters, motorcycle escorts, and crowds were in his future to stay. When he got home, he found his old room exactly as he left it except for the award citations his mother had hung on the wall. He had her remove them.

Cleland returned to Washington with the realization that he was changed but was unprepared for how he was received at the VA hospital. He was only a claim number there, not allowed to take clothes, personal effects, food, or anything personal to his room. "I was scared. I had come here to get rehabilitated, but it felt as if I had been sentenced to an old elephant burial ground. I expected the VA to be different but not this different."[36]

Veterans considered VA hospitals the last resort for medical care. In combat, medics had risked their lives to save them and helicopters whopped in under intense enemy fire to get them out. Medical care in combat was crude, but fast, effective, and always there. But at VA hospitals they could die in a waiting room and no one would notice.

Six out of seven veterans first sought medical care outside the VA system. But as they aged or lost economic independence, they were compelled to risk treatment.[37] By the late 1970s, growing disgust with the VA was evident in letters such as that of Alex Wells to the *DAV Magazine*: "I have exhausted every remedy except civil action against the VA for severe and irreversible physical and emotional damage." Jim Dunn, a VA nurse wrote to the *Stars and Stripes*: "The patient must be submitted to a de-humanizing process that makes euthanasia look inviting."[38]

As the Vietnam War ended, the VA budget swelled to $15 billion and 240,000 employees to support surviving veterans ranging all the way back to the Civil War, but the influx of three million Vietnam-related cases would drive costs up for 40 years into the future.[39]

Max Cleland had been a fighter and he didn't stop fighting political battles and inner conflicts at the VA. He wanted to be the master of his fate and run his own life. But in trying, he was literally broken into pieces. "Shattered. . . . But through the crises and defeats I have learned that it is possible to become strong at the broken places."[40]

The VA is the largest healthcare system in the nation, but by 1979 mysterious claims piled up unresolved. The numbers and types of claims were unusual for such a young veteran population: cancer, deformed and stillborn babies, miscarriages, loss of sex drive, low sperm counts, chronic aches and weaknesses, lumps, sores, and precancerous conditions. The main suspect was a chemical used for defoliation: Agent Orange.

AGENT OF DEATH

Agent Orange had been spread over jungles and crops to kill vegetation, denying the enemy cover and food. The chemical included dioxins used in small doses to kill weeds but highly toxic to humans. As hundreds of new claims reached the VA daily, only a few were approved. Six years after the war veterans died like crabgrass, contaminated in Vietnam and just becoming aware of the poisoning.[41]

Maude deVictor, a counselor at the center in Chicago, saw patients and heard stories that disturbed her. She made hundreds of phone calls to chemical companies to find out about dioxin and prepared a memo detailing her findings. Not only did superiors ignore her report, they ordered her to stop her independent investigation. But the information she had discovered was too important to bury, so she shared it with a television reporter in Chicago. The shocking report *Agent Orange— Vietnam's Deadly Fog* aired on March 23, 1978.

Under intense pressure, the VA hired two consultants to investigate: one from Dow Chemical, the company that made and sold Agent Orange, the other from the USAF, the service that sprayed the chemical from low-flying aircraft during Operation Ranch Hand. The air force study assumed danger only to aircrews, overlooking ground troops exposed to the highest doses. Findings were slow to be released and the delays angered veterans and their families. The biased investigations fixed no responsibility, so the VA continued to blame the media and veterans. Those going to the VA for help received only denials that Agent Orange was at fault.[42]

Paul Reutershan was angry about the government's slow pace as he lost his race with cancer. The VA denied his cancer claim. Laws prevented suing the government, so he sued Dow Chemical Company for $10 million; the class action was joined by others angry about government stonewalling. When Reutershan became too sick to continue, he handed off the baton to Frank McCarthy. McCarthy needed operating funds, so he borrowed from a bank and persuaded his ex-wife to guarantee the note; two army buddies jumped in to help.[43]

Students who had protested against Dow Chemical for developing napalm to use on the enemy were silent about troops dying from Agent Orange. Dow worried about bad publicity and stock prices. The VA sweated the cost of long-term care; sick veterans were an unwelcome and unbudgeted expense so long after the unpopular war. The Environmental Protection Agency and the Federal Drug Administration remained aloof and the Department of Defense sided with the Veterans Administration. But the victims weren't dying fast enough to make the problem go away.

President Reagan offered temporary medical care to anyone suffering with dioxin poisoning, then prodded the investigation forward to get some help in time. But Reagan faced choices: funding veterans and other social programs or increased defense spending to force an end to the cold war. Star wars and the future won out over sick veterans and the past.

Robert Nimmo, as new VA administrator, announced yet another study, but when he discovered veterans' medical care would cost hundreds of millions a year for 40 years, he hesitated to release it.[44] Meanwhile, veterans' organizations had recruited Vietnam-era members to replace dwindling rolls from World War II and Korea. New members complained loudly about Agent Orange-related problems, so the veterans' associations hiked the pressure on Congress. But the Agent Orange study no one wanted was passed off again, this time to the Center for Disease Control (CDC).

Congress allocated $60 million to the CDC to complete the unwanted investigation. Lieutenant Colonel Richard Christian assembled a staff of fifty-five in the Pentagon to track troop movements and chemical spraying. They collected 40,000 boxes of material, but Christian considered the parameters of the study flawed and argued with the CDC and the White House about it. Meanwhile, the American Legion commissioned an independent study that showed an increase in tumors, acne, rashes, blisters, sensitivity to light, faintness, fatigue, depression, aches, and colds among members exposed to Agent Orange. The Legion confronted the VA with this information and they finally admitted a study that connected deaths among marine ground troops with cancer at an abnormally high rate. Dr. Richard Albanese had tracked his subjects after the original Ranch Hand study and confirmed the health problems related to Agent Orange.

After 7 years and millions of dollars a report finally appeared, but the urgency had already passed as veterans died or coped with chronic health problems alone. The death rate for veterans who served in Vietnam was 45 percent higher than those who served elsewhere during the same period. Suicides were 72 percent higher and violent deaths from homicide, accidents, and drug overdoses were above norms. Such behavioral problems were largely linked to the effects of dioxin.[45]

As the scandal became public, survivors of the atomic tests of the 1940s and 1950s reported leukemia and other problems from radiation exposure. More bad news leaked that the Army and CIA had tested hallucinogenic drugs on unwary subjects after the Korean prisoner fiasco. Sick veterans had become a serious political liability. The hapless VA ducked behind the Civil War era law limiting lawyer's compensation for veteran's claims to $10. The chemical industry, under duress, settled the Agent Orange suit for $180 million, more than Reutershan had sought but only a fraction of what it might have cost. In 12 years of combat 58,000 soldiers had been killed, but in the first 6 years afterwards, 51,000 died at home, 5,000 with cancer. Among Paul Reutershan's last words to his mother: "I got killed in Vietnam and didn't know it."[46]

MORE INDIGNITIES

On his second day in office President Carter granted full, complete, and un-conditional pardons to 9,000 convicted and 4,500 un-convicted draft-dodgers and countless others who failed to register. A case-by-case review of deserters and those with less than honorable discharges was ordered. The actions stunned veterans who had risked their lives to serve honorably despite their beliefs about the war. The new commander-in-chief then tried to eliminate veterans' preference in federal hiring; more evidence felons were preferred over those who served.[47]

The Vietnam generation deserved a GI Bill with substance, plus effective heath care. They had been sent to an unpopular war, returned alone, spit on and humiliated, poisoned with toxic substances, discriminated against in jobs and education, while those who deserted were given a pass. In 1988, the VA director was elevated to cabinet rank to give veterans better representation, but the opposite occurred. The VA, often out of touch with average veterans and their needs anyway, was moved closer to the administration and further from its clients.

When veterans stepped off planes in the "real world," they arrived at an unreal place where home seemed more foreign than the war zone. John Allan Wyscarver described how his heart was pounding with anticipation, but when he arrived he found the country had changed. He wasn't able to say exactly what it was except that he felt like an alien from another planet. He was afraid he would wake up back in Vietnam.[48]

Donald Watson joined the VFW, only to find that he was not accepted. After three visits to the post and being ignored he was finally told Vietnam vets were not welcome. May Eckhardt said her son was home on leave when a Presbyterian minister refused to shake his hand as they were leaving church because of the killing he was involved in. Needless to say, he stopped going to church. Nicolas Chesley remembers passing under San Francisco's Golden Gate Bridge on the aircraft carrier *Constellation*. Garbage, animal blood, and urine were dumped onto the sailors lined up on deck. Joyce Nicodin wrote about her husband, a Marine combat veteran. She said he didn't want to write because it just didn't matter since hippies didn't spit on him. She told of his bitter reunion with his family and hostile receptions everywhere he went. She said her husband felt for the combat veteran; and he "still feels the betrayal of the American people. We weren't there when they needed us."[49]

HEALING

Bob Greene also heard from Vietnam veterans who were warmly received, having meals or drinks paid for anonymously, being moved into first class cabins, or someone giving up a seat for them. Sergeant Glenn Endress knew how rude most travelers were, so he was surprised when a middle-aged man and a teenage boy approached him in the airport. "Merry Christmas, Sarge!" The complete stranger invited him into his home for Christmas dinner, but he declined, afraid of missing his all-important flight. He pointed out others in the terminal with longer layovers that might accept. The man said he understood and he and the boy turned to leave. Endress stopped him, asking why he wanted a stranger in his home at Christmas. The man said his son had recently died in Vietnam, and they wanted a soldier at their table for Christmas dinner. Sergeant Endress faced the snow-capped mountains and cried alone.[50]

Healing takes a long time just to begin, for many it will never be completed. Kay Schwartz was in her twenties and busy raising three small boys in the 1960s. She and her husband wanted to instill sound values in them and tried to keep out the trash coming from the drug culture, college professors, students, movies, and especially television news. When her boys asked why commentators said the soldiers were dopers, murderers, and fools, she had no answers for them, so she shut off the television and they read instead, shutting out the world and the war.

Ten years after the war, her son made a banner: *Vietnam—10 years—We Remember. To Those Who Died—Thank You. To Those Who Returned—Welcome Home.* They hung it over the garage the morning he left for college. After he had gone she sat on the front porch with her coffee. A man delivering telephone books approached, but went straight to the garage and stood under the banner. Then he went to the porch and set the telephone books down and stood there crying. "Lady, I love your sign." They cried together and she apologized because it was 10 years late. "Lady, it is never too late." Tears were still streaming down his face as he walked away. "I sat there crying for all of us."[51]

Memorializing Vietnam veterans was as controversial as everything else associated with that war. Half of Jan Scruggs' platoon had been killed or wounded in battle, and in 1979 he asked the American Legion for help in honoring the dead from the war while recognizing the living. The American Legion supported him and in 1980 Congress authorized a memorial to be built on the Washington Mall near the Lincoln Memorial. Maya Ying Lin won the design competition with a black granite memorial engraved with the names of those who died. The blackness of it depicted the nation's grieving; the Wall, people divided. Many veterans had mentioned their invisible walls but making it visible could be threatening. "I never expected it to be passionless," said Maya Lin. "A lot of people were really afraid of that emotion; it was something we had glossed over."[52]

Strong opposition to the Wall came from every corner and almost stopped it before it could be built, but the full political and fundraising power of the American Legion prevailed. On November 13, 1982, The Wall was dedicated in Washington and a year later a flagpole was added. The following year a sculpture of three servicemen stood guard and later the women's memorial was added.

Large numbers had gathered in 1892 when Union veterans assembled for a reunion, and again during the bonus marches after World War I. In 1982, veterans came together in another defining moment. One veteran sold his washer and dryer for plane fare, another walked 3,000 miles in his old combat gear; a hitchhiker fell asleep and woke up at the airport with a ticket paid for by a stranger. Veterans drifted in alone or in small groups, answering a far bugle's call.[53]

This time they were welcomed on the streets, in hotels, bars, taxis, restaurants, wherever they went. One Medal of Honor recipient wore his blue ribbon for the first time. The entire country wanted to heal. When veterans saw the Wall they needed each other more than ever; they cried, hugged, and touched the names reverently with their fingertips. Promises were kept.

"The Wall! Designed by an Asian-American woman no less," wrote Bob Moon. "Black granite etched with the names. There it is. A beginning. An end. Stand there in front of his name, look carefully at your fully erect reflection, and tell yourself how much you've suffered, how much you've lost. Try to lie to him, to yourself. Never happen."[54]

A crowd of over 150,000 at the dedication listened to Senator Warner say, "we learned a terrible lesson . . . we must never forget." The lessons are never to ask men and women to serve in a war we do not intend to win, never go to war unless it is necessary, and if we go we must support our men and women to the fullest extent of our powers. It was a war we must never forget.[55]

10

Deserts and Terror

Only four and one-half years after Saigon fell, the all-volunteer military was a still hollow shell and foreign policy was in disarray. The United States still faced the Soviet Union in the cold war in Europe, stalemate with North Korea in Asia, and small wars continued in the Middle East, Africa, in Central and South America. But as communist influence waned, Islamic radicalism seemed too remote to be of concern, more an empty threat than a holy war. That was a tragic miscalculation.

DESERT ONE

On November 4, 1979, three thousand Iranian militants stormed the American Embassy in Tehran and seized sixty-six American hostages. The crisis remained unresolved for 444 days, humiliating a powerless United States with no feasible response. With the military in shambles after Vietnam, the all-volunteer force was still an arguable idea stunted by tight budgets. The Pentagon desperately assembled a small raiding force to rescue the hostages and restore American honor. Usable intelligence for Operation Desert One was scant since human intelligence had been replaced by technology. The hostages were isolated, under heavy guard in the fortified embassy, and exhibited as propaganda. A lightning raid was the only solution, but conditions made that a high-risk option.

The plan called for a rescue team to land in the Iranian desert in C-130s, link up with helicopters at a remote staging area, refuel, and hide in the desert 50 miles from Tehran. The next night, agents would escort them in trucks to the embassy for the raid. Helicopters would recover raiders and hostages at a nearby soccer stadium and fly them out; a security force on the ground and air-cover would provide protection.

The mission began as planned but quickly ran into trouble. A civilian bus and a gas tanker drove through the secret staging area with glaring lights. A raider fired an antitank rocket that hit the tanker, which exploded in a huge fireball. Despite that problem, the aircraft with assault teams and fuel arrived on time, but rescue helicopters were delayed by sand storms; two were downed with mechanical problems. The lost helicopters meant too few remained for the mission; a decision was made to abort. But, tragedy struck when a helicopter rotor clipped a C-130 fuel tank, igniting an inferno. Eight Americans burned in the wreckage and the residue of American pride vaporized in the black smoke.

A somber President Carter announced to the world that eight had died and others were seriously injured. As he spoke, Sergeant J.J. Beyers lay unconscious and badly burned in a Texas hospital bed. He was lucky to have survived but was confined to the hospital for a year, enduring eleven operations before he was medically separated. Beyers never questioned his decision to volunteer: "We do things other people can't do. We would rather get killed than fail." Air Force Colonel James Kyle described his full range of emotions as "the most colossal episode of hope, despair, and tragedy I had ever experienced. . . ."

Urgent investigations and hearings followed the disaster. Admiral James Holloway noted in his Pentagon report that people and machines were expected to perform to perfection with no margin for error. The ad hoc nature of planning and execution made clear that changes were needed for the nation to respond to the increasing threat of terrorism. A fix was needed quickly, before the all-volunteer force could be fully ready. The Special Operations Command was organized in 1986, and the special counter-terror force was initially assigned to it; later Army Rangers, Navy Seals, and Air Force special air units were added.

The hostages were ceremoniously released when Ronald Reagan was elected President. Reagan immediately began a massive rebuilding of the military but concentrated on winning the cold war before stopping Islamic radicals. His strategy brought down the Berlin Wall, dismantled the Soviet Union, and won the cold war. Meanwhile terrorism was gathering like a sand storm in the Middle East.[1]

BEIRUT

International terrorism increased dramatically with fundamentalists hijacking airplanes and cruise ships, setting off car and suitcase bombs, and murdering innocents for press coverage. In June 1982, the Palestine Liberation Organization (PLO) fired artillery into Jewish settlements in northern Israel, and Israelis went after them with tanks. They pursued the PLO into Beirut where they fought for 6 days until a tenuous ceasefire was arranged with their sponsor, Syria.

Marines from Camp Lejeune waited on navy ships in Lebanese waters for 4 months while the situation developed. A 2,000-man international peacekeeping force with 800 American Marines went ashore in late August to evacuate Syrian and PLO fighters. Soon after, the PLO killed Lebanon's Christian president-elect and the city fell into chaos. A United Nations multi-national force tried restoring order with a contingent of more than 1,200 American Marines. By September, Marines were taking casualties from unexploded ordnance and snipers but they dug in around the airport and ran peacekeeping operations from there.

The original Marines were replaced with fresh troops in late October, and they continued vehicle and foot patrols despite increasing sniper fire. "I knew it was a bad situation," said Major Robert Jordan. "It was much more intense than what I had experienced in Vietnam. At least there we had mobility. We could strike back. In Beirut, we just sat there and took it." On October 23, 1983, a truck loaded with 6 tons of explosives plowed through concrete barriers, rammed into the building where the Marines lived, and exploded. The attack killed 241 Marines and injured more, the highest casualties after Vietnam.

Air force bombs and naval gunfire pounded Syrian positions near Beirut, but that prompted more ground attacks until the Lebanese Armed Forces totally disintegrated, leaving the airport and the Marines unprotected. Attempted peacekeeping was abruptly ended as the Marines evacuated civilians while they withdrew.

Lance Corporal Jack Anderson crawled out of the destroyed Marine barracks alive but years later still missed a best friend. He and John Blocker had planned to exchange visits during the Christmas holidays. Instead, Anderson visited Blocker's parents alone, and paid respects at his friend's grave. "I have not had the courage to face his parents again, and I spent the next 20 years running away from the memories of that day and that time in my life—indeed that time in history." The truck bomb had proven to be an effective weapon of terror. President Reagan took the heat for Beirut and withdrew the Marines, but the deaths of 266 Americans between August 1982 and February 1984 foreshadowed more vicious attacks.[2]

URGENT FURY

Marines left Beirut in October 1983, headed for home at Camp Lejeune, but urgent orders diverted them to the small Caribbean island of Grenada. Deputy Prime Minister Bernard Coard, a Marxist aligned with Fidel Castro, had used Grenada's small army to seize power in a bloody coup. Cuban soldiers and engineers were already constructing a military airfield adjacent to a medical school where American students were enrolled.

In the early morning of October 25, 1983, the Beirut Marines, Army Rangers, Navy Seals, and a task force of the 82d Airborne Division invaded Grenada against light resistance. The steady buildup of troops discouraged serious defenses and by mid-December the government was restored and the troops departed. Nineteen soldiers and Marines died there. Kennedy had blockaded Soviet nuclear missiles from Cuba in 1962 and Reagan blocked communism from Grenada 21 years later, both pivotal events in the cold war. But if Grenada was the beginning of the end of the cold war, the Beirut bombing was the end of the beginning of the war with terror.

PANAMA

During the period of American expansion overseas, Theodore Roosevelt envisioned a canal for commercial and military transit between the Atlantic and Pacific Oceans. American engineers endured extremes of weather, geography, and tropical diseases digging and blasting a ditch across the narrow isthmus. The canal operated under U.S. authority, but by the mid-1980s it had lost much of its significance to air travel and faster ships. President Carter transferred control of the canal to Panama and Manuel Noriega, a dictator, drug trafficker, arms smuggler, money launderer, and oppressor.

Noriega rigged Panamanian elections in 1984 and 1988, securing his power there. Protests by international observers only encouraged him to void the election results and install his handpicked cronies. His paramilitary squads beat protesters in Panama City and intimidated troops protecting the canal. Then in December 1989, he declared war on the United States. Panamanian defense forces killed a Marine officer at a checkpoint, arrested and beat a navy lieutenant, and sexually assaulted his wife. President Bush ordered the military to arrest Noriega on drug charges, protect lives and property, and restore Panamanian liberties. The first job was to seize Noriega, but he hid in the Vatican embassy while mobs looted Panama City and Colón. Two thousand additional troops were needed to reestablish order and nab Noriega.[3]

Twenty-three U.S. soldiers died in Panama, but Noriega was brought to Miami in handcuffs to face justice. The invasion was the first use of American forces outside the framework of the cold war, other than Korea and Vietnam, and the first large-scale use of power after Vietnam. President Reagan stayed the course to win the cold war with a major new treaty ending the military divide of Europe. The Berlin Wall cracked, Germany was finally reunited, and the Warsaw Pact and Union of Soviet Socialist Republics disintegrated. The cold war was won but peace was not found.

DESERT STORM

On August 2, 1990, while negotiators were wrapping up the cold war in Europe, Saddam Hussein invaded Kuwait with Iraqi Republican Guards hardened through trench warfare and poison gas attacks in an 8-year war with Iran. The United Nations demanded Hussein leave Kuwait while the United States gathered a coalition to ensure he did. Within a week, military troops arrived in Saudi Arabia. Hussein declared a holy war as a naval blockade ended his oil shipments; the United Nations set a deadline of January 15, but Hussein drew a line in the sand and promised the "mother of all battles" if crossed.

Desert Storm was well suited for television: short, with sweeping dimensions, dramatic, and shown in living color. Attacks began on January 17 with air and missile strikes in Baghdad. In response Hussein fired scud missiles at Israel, set fire to Kuwaiti oil fields, and contaminated the Persian Gulf with oil. The coalition continued to concentrate forces and logistics over 5 months as 697,000 soldiers deployed from the United States and Europe. Their final ultimatum went unanswered. With the buildup complete, a 39-day air war was launched ahead of a 4-day ground attack with a frontal assault and a wide left hook around the Iraqi

Republican Guards. Iraqi defenses crumbled as the coalition entered Kuwait City, though fighting continued on Medina Ridge and the Highway of Death.

Television news from the front was welcomed at home. "We had given America a clear win at low casualties in a noble cause," said General Colin Powell, "and the American people fell in love again with their armed forces."[4] The stigma surrounding the military and Vietnam had faded some and veterans, especially Vietnam vets, were rejuvenated.

The all-volunteer force had proved solid in the Gulf, but it was different from the old military, including more minorities and women, older, more married and single parents, more religious, economically stable, and better educated. Ninety-five percent were high school graduates in a nation with only 75 percent graduates. They were better trained than any previous military and relatively free of drugs and racism.[5]

Jeffrey Clark was one of the new volunteer soldiers. He joined the National Guard in Greenville, South Carolina, and found he enjoyed it, after basic training. He was encouraged by some rangers in his guard unit to go on active duty and to go airborne. "It was a blast!" After 3 years with the 82nd Airborne at Fort Bragg he left active duty for the reserves. His reserve unit was activated for Desert Storm and he landed in Saudi Arabia on Christmas morning. His job was to courier classified documents between headquarters, and he sorted regular mail from home for the rest of the troops. "We'd get tons of letters addressed to 'Any Soldier.' " He also handed out boxes of chocolate bars, sunglasses, and game boys to any soldier from organizations that sent case lots. There was also plenty of personal mail. "I got letters from people I hadn't heard from in years, ex's, pictures—'We Support Our Troops.' Makes you feel good. Too bad they couldn't do that for Vietnam vets."[6]

Cliff and Cindy Acree

On the second day of the war, Marine Lieutenant Colonel Cliff Acree was shot down behind Iraqi lines. He was captured and beaten, tortured, and starved for 48 days. Back home his wife, Cindy, organized other wives into support groups while she waited for news of her husband. Finally, Cliff came home and Cindy met him on the tarmac at Andrews Air Force Base. The responsibilities of commanding a Marine air unit occupied his days and kept him busy; his spare time was filled with parades and ceremonies. He seemed fine outwardly but stoically concealed his physical and psychological wounds—a good Marine. Most of his friends couldn't see through the tough veneer, but Cindy did. She accompanied him to many local events, ostensibly to enjoy the festivities, but mostly to keep an eye on her husband; she knew something wasn't right.

She recalled one parade with graying men marching in old jungle uniforms: "A Marine officer suddenly bolted from the crowd," she said, "and embraced the Vietnam veterans." His response brought tears to spectators and grizzled veterans alike. After the parade ended a reporter waited to interview Cliff, but since he was busy with another reporter, he asked Cindy how she thought the celebration compared to Vietnam. "Thanks to the Desert Storm victory, Vietnam veterans are finally getting the homecoming parades they deserved twenty years ago."

She had noticed her husband still flinched at unexpected noises and his eating habits had changed; a baked potato for lunch instead of the usual sandwich. He told her how he had searched for just a small portion of a potato in his prison broth, now he had whole ones. She knew it was a different hunger he was trying to satisfy. "Sometimes an object, such as the yellow plastic bowl in our cupboard, would take him back," she said. "He used a bowl like it as a prisoner, not only to eat from, but for every other conceivable purpose. The sight of one took him back, like an old song."[7]

When the deployments began, wives near Camp Lejeune, North Carolina, suddenly faced the abrupt departures of their husbands. One told how they stayed in touch while he was away. "Robert always talks with me about what he really feels and thinks." But later, she said, "Robert has been so ambivalent. . . . He acts like he wants reassurance in one moment, then in another moment he acts as though he does not want to be bothered." When he returned: "He has tried to readjust; he has just laid around and slept, like he was trying to sleep it off. . . . It's amazing to watch him going around touching everything. It's like he was getting acquainted himself again with our home, like he was trying to remember where he belongs. . . . He hasn't unpacked yet."[8]

At the End

When the war ended, coalition troops rolled into Kuwait City on February 27 to a heroes' welcome by flag-waving, cheering Kuwaitis. More parades followed that one. By mid-March thousands returned home every day to be welcomed by appreciative Americans. Fifty thousand lined up at the Norfolk Navy Base to greet them, and in Moorhead City school children were given the day off to cheer the troops on their way to Camp Lejeune. Happy days were back.[9]

Dick Goddard was a veteran of Vietnam and Grenada, so his expectations coming home from Desert Storm were not very high. The MAC flight from Kuwait landed to refuel at Bangor, Maine, in the middle of the night and soldiers streamed into the terminal for coffee. One hundred and fifty people had lined up to celebrate. Someone shouted for Vietnam veterans to go to a private alcove off the main terminal. A contingent of local Vietnam vets had waited all night. They wanted this to be a welcome none would forget: "Welcome Home, Brothers!" This time it was personal and heartfelt.[10]

Buzz Williams, a Marine reservist, was pulled from college to join his outfit en route to the desert. As they prepared to return home he had cheeseburgers and Cokes, waiting for someone to address them. The officer, a Vietnam veteran, was glad their homecoming would be better than his. "You boys are going home to the biggest . . . party you ever saw," he told them. "And you're the guest of honor. The whole goddamned country's wrapped in yellow ribbons." He encouraged them to enjoy the attention but never forget their loved ones. "When the fanfare fades, they'll be all you have left."

Williams planned to finish college in his hometown and get reconnected with his girlfriend. He expected the transition from warrior to civilian to be difficult, but he set about reversing his cycles, releasing his ego. It seemed easy letting go at first. A crowd met the busses at Camp Upshur with a standing ovation, yellow ribbons, white tents, and a band. "The air was full of the smell of women's perfume. Gina's perfume! Then I caught a glimpse of her teary face, her outstretched arms, and felt hair mashing my face. Looking on I saw Mom, wiping her eyes, waiting patiently." Williams wondered how he looked to them. "My tattoo would remain covered, like so many other things, buried until later. . . . "

Back in his room, he stretched out on his bed and scanned the mementoes around him. He saw the sports trophies on the dresser but couldn't recall when or how he had earned them, the scattered cassettes with music from another life. His found his high school diploma, a picture of Gina, and a Marine Corps poster, all insignificant. But when he closed his eyes to sleep, he only saw Kuwait and the war.

Williams returned to Towson State University to complete his teaching certificate. Other students seemed juvenile. Some professors were glad to see him, but others disliked the war and with it, veterans; they were determined to make life difficult. But despite all that, Williams made it through. He used leadership he learned in boot camp as a physical education teacher to motivate troubled teens to turn their lives around, while he continued to struggle with his.[11]

Some Things Unsettled

A traditional victory parade was thrown in New York City with ticker tape, confetti, and balloons; it was widely televised. Many Desert Storm commanders were also veterans from Vietnam and they asked others of that war to join with them in the parade. Yet it was only a taste of what had been denied when it was needed most.

The smaller all-volunteer military kept up a high operational tempo after the Gulf War, but with the cold war over and Saddam contained, their numbers were reduced again, and many were encouraged to leave the service. Captain Keith Rosenkrantz hung up his air force uniform after 21 of his 24 months service away from his family. ". . . A day doesn't go by that I'm not reminded of the experience. . . . The war stole a part of my life that can never be replaced, and left me with a burden of guilt that will remain in my heart forever."[12]

When Desert Storm ended, many matters were left unsettled. Saddam Hussein was still in power and many wondered why the job was left unfinished. The public had seen women in dangerous roles, captured, killed, wounded; the debate about roles for military women remained unresolved. Fratricide in the extreme violence and mobility of the modern battlefield absolutely had to be reduced. Yet deaths were fewer than if Hussein had employed chemical weapons, but many casualties went unnoticed until long after the victory parades ended.

Medical claims poured in from strange illnesses, and the cycle of complaints, investigations, and government dodging began all over again. Stress from the lengthy buildup and waiting for the battle to begin had taken a heavy toll on nerves. Veterans complained of strange, unnerving symptoms to military doctors or to the VA. They were turned away with denials that their symptoms were in anyway connected to service in the Gulf. Complainers were called names: National Guard malingerers, Reservists who couldn't handle stress, or spongers looking for claim money. But by early 1993, over 4,000 veterans had reported problems, and the long lines for treatment could not be ignored. First Lady Hillary Clinton became aware of the complaints and prompted a Presidential Advisory Committee, but the committee again blamed stress. Veterans were angrier than ever.[13]

One hundred forty-eight men and women had been killed in the desert war, 24 percent from friendly fire. Eleven died in an explosion of an ammunition dump, 121 in other accidents. But most of the casualties were those uncounted until over 100,000 reported for physical examinations for symptoms of the mystery illness; fully 15 percent of those serving in the Gulf came home sick.

Kimo Hollingsworth was a Marine platoon commander. He went to war as a specimen of good health, but when released a year later he had a nagging nasal drip and coughed up dark sputum. He accepted a civilian position with a Wall Street firm, but after 4 months his symptoms became worse and his health degenerated with constant headaches, muscle and joint pain, chest pains, coughing, blurred vision, memory loss, and a low-grade fever. "Despite my symptoms, the VA hospital in Washington performed a complete physical and concluded that I was in excellent health."

Hollingsworth sought a second opinion from a private physician who prescribed massive antibiotics; his health improved some. "As an American who volunteered to serve my country," he said, "I can accept bad medical news. What I cannot accept and will not tolerate are professional bureaucrats that first deny a problem exists, then minimize problems once they surface, and lastly make the problems seem more complex so endless studies can be conducted . . ." His circumstances were repeated over and over in case after case. "Young men and women of this country are a valuable resource; I am a combat veteran, not an expendable item."[14]

The various symptoms were collectively labeled Gulf War Syndrome. The most common physical ailments were fatigue, headaches, muscle and joint pains, diarrhea, skin rashes, shortness of breath, and chest pains; other problems included sleep disturbances, impaired concentration, forgetfulness, irritability, and depression. Panels from Defense, the VA and the Senate Committee on Veterans Affairs, the Presidential Advisory Committee, and the Government Accounting Office were determined to study Gulf War Syndrome into submission. Altogether they spent over $100 million investigating, practically nothing on treatment.[15] Some active duty troops also were sick, but tried to disguise it to protect their careers.

"A hell of a lot of soldiers lied about their illness," one said, "and there were some doctors who helped them cover it up because they would be out otherwise."[16]

The suspect list of possible causes included Iraqi chemical or biological weapons, pesticides, unproven vaccines, depleted uranium from ammunition, fumes from oil fires, and infectious diseases; scientific and medical examiners could not isolate a single cause. Without a clear resolution, the panels continued to blame stress. The lengthy buildup and uncertainty of waiting for fighting to begin had produced tremendous stress on those in the danger zone, but veterans could not dismiss their symptoms that easily. Most believed chemicals were involved and were distressed further by the recurring pattern of official denials.

Vietnam's Agent Orange deaths were still in the news and Pentagon and VA evasiveness about Gulf War Syndrome raised suspicions higher. Steve Robertson suffered from many of the symptoms and all the bureaucratic roadblocks, but he had no regrets about his service: "I'd go back—because I know we were right." Deputy Secretary of Defense John Deutch left the E-ring of the Pentagon to teach chemistry at Massachusetts Institute of Technology. "If ever there was a question of good intentions going badly, this was it. It's an example of how a government that wants to do right somehow cannot."[17]

Many matters from the war were unsettled at home, but a major problem of concern remained in Iraq. Despite the one-sided victory Saddam Hussein had been left in power to wreck havoc on the lives of his people, prevent UN observers from determining whether he had nuclear or chemical weapons, and fill his treasury with money from oil proceeds intended to feed starving Iraqis. His continued presence meant more trouble.

ENDURING FREEDOM

During the morning rush on September 11, 2001, terrorists hijacked four commercial jets and crashed two into the twin towers of the World Trade Center in New York City, another into the Pentagon. The fourth went down in an empty field in Pennsylvania when courageous passengers overcame the hijackers. Americans finally realized they were under terrorist attack at home as they had been by Islamic radicals for years overseas.

The attacks cost thousands of lives and made the war on terror the nation's greatest concern. The lessons of Beirut, hijackings of airliners and cruise ships, an earlier truck bomb attack on the Trade Center, strikes at navy ships, and the bombings of embassies had been clear warnings that went unheeded. Islamic terrorists used Afghanistan as an operating base and training ground to launch the attacks. President Bush acted promptly to seize known terrorist financial assets and disrupt fundraising and communications networks. Defenses were hastily and clumsily thrown up at aerial ports in an initial reaction, but much more was needed. For all Americans their world truly changed that bright morning.

Troops deployed overseas within days, and Enduring Freedom started on October 7, 2001. Strikes began against known terrorist training camps and Taliban infrastructure in Afghanistan with air and cruise missile strikes and bomb runs from land- and carrier-based bombers and fighters. Within 2 weeks, coalition forces destroyed virtually all Taliban air defenses and launched ground actions around Kabul to chase down terror leaders and return the country to legal control. Special Forces joined local militias to coordinate and support. In 20 days, provincial capitols began falling and an interim government was installed by the end of December. Rounding up terrorists in the rugged mountain ranges was more problematic.

During the buildup, Central Command tripled its numbers in the region to 60,000, with 5,000 in Afghanistan. By August 2002 the in-country number increased to 8,000 while air and naval forces supported them from offshore. During Desert Storm the military had flown 3,000 air sorties per day, but with improved efficiency, better planning and technology, only 200 sorties per day were flown in Afghanistan and the results were just as effective.[18]

"Dear Son," Marine Corps Reserve Lieutenant Colonel Tom Barna wrote to Alex. "My deployment seems a little more personal this time." When Alex was only two, Barna had left for Kuwait and Desert Storm; now his son was a teenager and his father was in Afghanistan. "As you know, it was our nation that was attacked. It was our people who died. And this fire has been brewing for quite a while. . . . This time we finish the fight."[19]

Captain Nate Self seemed fine when he came home from leading Army Rangers in Afghanistan. He had taken a leg wound in a battle where several members of his platoon died, but his calm leadership steadied the others when the situation was desperate. His men knew he was as hard as the rocky soil they fought over. As they prepared to go home, Self encouraged them. "Make sure the things that happened here aren't forgotten and that lives lost aren't wasted." But when he got home, he held his feelings inside. "It's funny, but I felt comfortable talking about the battle with everyone but the people who meant the most to me." His wife assumed he had simply moved on but when his parents commented that he was different, she asked him about it. He denied everything. "I felt like Afghanistan didn't faze me a bit." Why should it? The world was going his way; he was invited as a guest of the President to the State of the Union Address, received an award for combat valor, and was selected for advanced army training. But gradually he realized something was wrong. He gained weight, became morose, and woke up from nightmares. Academically, he was near the top of his army class but intentionally failed his final exam. "I didn't want to succeed. I wanted to be mediocre." He knew he was in trouble, though he looked fine by outward appearances. Then his unit was ordered back to combat, this time in Iraq.[20]

IRAQI FREEDOM

Saddam Hussein still controlled Iraq after his defeat in Desert Storm; he tortured and murdered citizens and dared the UN to enforce economic sanctions while he cut illegal deals under the UN oil-for-food program. Despite UN reluctance to enforce their sanctions, the United States forged a small coalition of the willing to remove him from power, bring democracy to Iraq, look for evidence of nuclear or chemical weapons programs, and break any existing ties with terrorists. Debate over the war continued within the United States and international community, but for the troops it was war; they were going in.

On March 19, 2003, the United States and United Kingdom targeted missile and air strikes at Iraqi defenses. Special operations forces, Marines, and Army units easily breached defenses and roared into Baghdad and other provincial capitals. Conventional fighting was fast and furious but ended quickly. Hussein's statue was toppled but an active insurgency exploded, run by old regime loyalists, foreign terrorists, and religious extremists. While Iraq was rebuilt and democracy established, casualties mounted and critics at home became more strident than ever.

Chief Warrant Officers Randy Weatherhead and DeWayne Browning flew into hostile territory in Iraq frequently in their Blackhawk helicopters. The army had changed since their first war; they were both grandfathers and Vietnam veterans who deployed with the National Guard's 42nd Infantry Division. The war was different, too: they had a clear mission this time, the public at home was mostly supportive, and Iraqis were friendlier except for the insurgents. Browning was able to go home for 2 weeks leave and more than a hundred people met the plane when it landed. "I can't tell you what, as a Vietnam vet, that means to me."

The professional military force was more capable than the one in Vietnam, more even than the professional force of Desert Storm. It was more technical, with more women doing jobs formerly precluded, was one-third smaller, and filled with well-educated volunteers. Chief Warrant Officer Herbert Darque flew corporate helicopters as a civilian pilot. He had a Distinguished Service Cross for fighting in Vietnam but was assigned a desk in Iraq. His daughter was a medic on her second tour and he was very proud of her.[21]

In another sector, an alert soldier manned the turret gun of the rear security vehicle in convoy. The gunner spotted a vehicle approaching too fast, violating curfew. "Don't hesitate," ordered the convoy commander. "Do what you need to do!" The gunner's .50-caliber machine gun thundered in the darkness. The errant car wheeled around and sped away. "Whoa, Williams! You go girl!" Less than 1 percent in WWI had been female, only 2.5 percent of WWII forces. There were even fewer in Korea and Vietnam; 1.2 percent of Desert Storm soldiers were women, some in combat situations for the first time. But fully 10 percent of soldiers in Iraqi Freedom were female. Williams had been working at a Speedway convenience store in Savannah when her Guard unit was called. "I had so many emotions. . . . OK, I'm going to Iraq," she said, "and I'm going as a gunner."[22]

When the war began, the new military had more than 200,000 women on the rolls. Americans had reluctantly accepted them in combat roles during Desert Storm but reports of women being wounded, killed, captured, or raped made chilling headlines. Eight nurses had died in Vietnam but more than five times that many in Iraq.[23] Army Sergeant Leigh Ann Hester, a military policewoman from the Kentucky National Guard, was awarded the Silver Star for combat action, but it hadn't come cheap; she pays a continuing price. "I think about March 20 at least a couple of times a day, every day, and I probably will for the rest of my life," she said. "It's taken a toll."[24]

Thirty years after Vietnam, its shadow crossed the political landscape during a bitter presidential election. This time it was about Iraq. John Kerry, the Vietnam veteran against his war, ran on his record as a war hero while dodging his record as a Vietnam protester. This time he protested the war in Iraq. Swift boat veterans who had served with him challenged him with *Unfit for Command*. Meanwhile CBS News attempted to smear President Bush's National Guard service with counterfeit documents from his National Guard service. Waving the bloody shirt had long been a ploy for politicians seeking veterans' votes, but these were extreme. Words hurt and divided veterans, stirred up old bitterness from Vietnam. "We were finally getting to a point where we could forget the bad stuff, and now they're dredging it all up again," said Blake Magner.[25]

Back in Iraq, Brean Hancock used a step stool to hoist her one hundred pounds into the cab of an enormous fuel tanker. She was the youngest member of the Georgia Guard's 48th Infantry, enlisting at seventeen while still a cheerleader at Dublin High School. Brean had just turned nineteen and received a birthday present from her best friend, fellow soldier Ryan Crispen. She spent her spare time thinking and talking about her future. "It's my antistress thing." She was growing up too fast.[26]

She had earned 2 weeks at home and took advantage of it. By 8:00 A.M. the morning she arrived, a small crowd had gathered at Atlanta's Hartsfield-Jackson waiting for the flight to land. Her mother stopped her for inspection but couldn't hold her long. "I want a big coffee and a shower," she insisted, "and then I want to go shopping. I need makeup. I need clothes. I want to go, go, go." Fortunately, Ryan was waiting for her at baggage claim since his half-empty duffle bag was crammed with her overflow clothes and teddy bear.

Brean's parents were moving from Dublin to Atlanta for a new job, but they kept the old house in Dublin so she could go to the home she knew. Fifteen days was a mere fragment of a lifetime but her hiatus from the war ended all too soon. She returned to the airport in desert fatigues with Ryan at her side, this time with a diamond ring on her finger. As CNN announced that five more soldiers had been killed in Iraq, a sergeant bellowed: "Get on board!"[27]

Going Home

"Home, that sounds nice, doesn't it? What does it mean? What is it about a familiar sight, a familiar smell or perhaps a sound that makes a certain area just feel right? ... Coming home ... what a welcome thing! We just don't realize what it means until we can't have it."[28]

Troops dreamed of going home from Iraq and Afghanistan as they always do but readjusting was no easier for them than for any of the others. The anticipation of going home was long lasting, but the excitement of homecoming didn't last as long. Major Patrick Ratigan warned troops of the 3d Infantry Division: "You've changed," he told them. "You don't notice it, but when you get home, your family and friends will. . . . " Families often found the one coming off the plane was not as open or understanding, more quick-tempered, more distant than the one who left. Captain Chris Carter remembered, "I felt like I would have preferred to still be in Iraq." Many had already missed a child's birth, everyone had missed an anniversary, an important birthday, a teenager's first date or first driver's license; some had missed a funeral. Each one missed some slice of a life, a hole that could not be completely patched with a picture or story, but they helped.[29]

Nate Self, the Ranger officer who attended the State of the Union Address after serving in Afghanistan, went with his unit to Iraq as a staff officer. Although in a relatively safe position, he still felt the uncertainties of combatants. The unshakable man was rattled when the brigade sergeant major was killed. When two helicopters collided, his heart raced and he broke out in a cold sweat. "It was like I lived through things I never saw." He calculated the odds of his survival and he didn't like his chances; vivid nightmares stirred him at night. When his unit finally returned to Fort Campbell, his wife saw he was distant, distracted, talked in his sleep, and was off balance. He announced he was leaving the army, changed his mind and took command of a company, changed his mind again and resigned.

Self moved his family to Texas and took a job selling medical supplies. His wife said, "I looked at him in his business suit and I thought: Who is that?" Getting out, moving back, changing suits, none of it solved his problem; his nightmares got worse. When he went to the VA, he was diagnosed with severe PTSD but they didn't offer much help. A friend introduced him to a retired army chaplain who did understand and helped him learn just to live with the bad dreams. But he couldn't go back to the way he was, he never would. "I feel like I have lost the ability to be myself."[30]

Richard Ingram came home early, never to be the same either. The 22-year-old army scout was blown from his vehicle by a roadside bomb. He lost his left arm and was evacuated with injured buddies to Walter Reed. "I'm not going home until I've got my arm and can use it well," he insisted. "The truth is I almost never miss having a second arm . . . until someone tries to help me." First, he planned to finish his degree, which had been interrupted by mobilization. Afterwards, he wanted to go back into the army as a ranger. His older sister objected to his going back in, saying he had given too much already. His mother watched while he fumbled. "He makes it very clear that if he wants your help, he'll ask for it. And he doesn't ask very often."[31]

American Legion Commander John Brieden visited a 24-year-old who stood propped on crutches, recovering from a shattered heel and loss of two toes. His only wish: to rejoin his unit in Iraq. And of another at Walter Reed who lost a leg after 17 years in service who was less concerned with his disability than the prospect of a new prosthetic. And, a young sergeant who had lost an arm; his commander died next to him. He told his visitor a million men before him had made greater sacrifices; he would do it all again.[32]

Imperfect Homecomings

People living near military bases could see how much the veterans had changed. They said they were not as courteous, more aggressive, more likely to cut them off in traffic. Veterans admitted they were less tolerant of civilians; they couldn't stand crowds, or "stupid people doing stupid things." In-service counselors warned families to expect changes, advised them to allow adjustment to children first, not argue about "who had it worse," and realize homecoming would not be perfect for either of them.

A smaller military meant repetitive deployments. Those making the rotations were older and more likely to be married than before, at least 15 percent more than in Vietnam. As they came home they spent most of the first months mourning losses, sweating out nightmares, and getting re-established with families who had managed without them. On top of everything was the chance for another deployment within a year. Divorces jumped nearly 50 percent.[33]

Signs of trouble surfaced after the second rotation between Iraq and Afghanistan. Combat was stressful, but repeated separations strained military families. An outbreak of domestic homicides erupted at Fort Bragg, North Carolina, in 2002. A noncommissioned officer shot and killed his wife and himself right after returning from deployment. As soon as that shock had settled, a senior sergeant strangled his wife, and then a junior sergeant stabbed his wife fifty times and burned her house. Another shot and killed his wife before killing himself, and in a fifth incident, a wife shot and killed her officer husband while their four children were at home. The community was stunned and the military invoked stronger preventions.[34]

Marital tensions factored into each case, intensified by rigors of military life. Normal family stresses were magnified by shortened time for reintegration, un-predictable schedules, unexpected deployments, heightened risks, austere living conditions, and compressed time between life-changing events. Careerists avoided counseling that could jeopardize promotion opportunities and tried to deal with it alone. The concentration of so many incidents so soon after coming home pointed to problems that needed to be faced. More comprehensive programs were enacted to manage stresses and reduce family abuses. At Fort Carson, commanders took returning soldiers through a 2-page checklist of family behaviors and attitudes to isolate potential problems before they occurred. They warned about what they should expect at home, and guaranteed counseling would be threat-free.

Returnees had just left urban combat where car bombs and improvised explosive devices were commonplace, and the first thing they would do at home was drive into cities. They relived situations where massive doses of adrenaline had raced through their veins, heightened their reflexes, and seared vivid memories. These new images, words, odors, and sounds triggered those old reactions again.

Never Ending

Buzz Williams, the Marine reservist from Desert Storm, had earned his master's degree and was teaching, coaching, and counseling high school students when the September 11 attacks came. Outwardly, everything about him seemed normal. Five years had passed since his last nightmare, even longer since he had opened his wartime photo album. "After all that time I had finally managed to put my combat demons to rest. Until the around-the-clock media coverage during the buildup to Operation Iraqi Freedom woke them again . . ." Simple things, like Fourth of July fireworks, sand at the beach, and especially war movies triggered memories. Gina saw how the movies bothered him and asked why he watched them. "I tell her that I want to see if Hollywood got the details right . . . or some other half-truth. The reality is that there is a part of me that needs to get back in touch with the raw emotion that those movies bring out."

He was glued to television in January 2003. "I knew it would uncover thoughts and feelings that had taken me years to forget." He tried to stop watching but was so engrossed he ignored his son asking to play, missed his daughter crying for a bottle, Gina's pleas for help with the kids or housekeeping. "I was angry that our troops had to go back to the desert to take care of business left unfinished by the war I had fought." Williams channeled his emotions into writing that gave him reason to call some loyal Marine Corps buddies. "The Marine Corps has been . . . the most influential institution in my life. . . . I still rely on the values I learned in the Marine Corps."[35]

Captain Chris Young returned to Fort Riley, Kansas, and went shopping with his family the following day. His running dialog centered on how he would never have driven over such a bridge in Iraq, or how a trash pile might conceal a roadside bomb; his wife tried to keep him talking but he broke it off. The next day, she helped unpack boxes at his office and found a shrapnel-ripped helmet cover of a soldier killed in Iraq. He couldn't bear to part with it in Iraq. "Throw it in the trash," he told her. Suddenly, he wanted it gone.

Captain Young was soon ordered back to Iraq. He drew a heart on the blackboard with "Chris + Wendy" inside. "It was so unlike Chris, I figured I'd leave it," she said. Sergeant Fairservice retreated from his family when his second deployment approached; occupied himself with long-neglected chores or lost himself in video games. His wife intervened: "The last time you were in Iraq, all you talked about was how you wanted to spend more time with the kids," she told him. "This time I don't want to hear it." A few days later she saw him holding their 6-month-old son, quietly talking about his hopes for him, and crying.[36]

Jose Hernandez was bothered by the gunshot wound in his arm when he returned to Cincinnati, but not as much as by the lock on his door. He couldn't relax until he had locked it and then double-checked it several times to ensure it was secured. "I kept thinking about the things I saw over there."[37] No lock could shut out those memories.

The military strained to meet manpower requirements for the second Iraq War and Afghanistan at reduced troop levels. The war on terror was fought with existing units, relying heavily on National Guard and reserves. Original contracts were thrown out and policies were imposed to keep soldiers from leaving, or to prevent moves at the end of a normal tour if their unit was on the list to go. The all-volunteer force was severely tested.

The 3rd Armored Cavalry Regiment had arrived in Iraq as the statue of Saddam Hussein was pulled down, their arrival delayed by logistics and politics. But those who believed the fighting was over were wrong; the race to Baghdad turned into a long and tortuous counterinsurgency. Even support troops were in the thick of it on convoys and in bases. Medics discovered the red crosses on their ambulances were targets. "A lot of these young kids don't know how good they had it back home," said Command Sergeant Major Muniz. "It was a big eye-opener for them."[38]

After a year, the cavalry packed up to go home to Fort Carson. Support Groups that had kept families informed announced their arrival plans. Nicole Schintgen got the word out by email: "Beds in the new barracks are made, snacks, balloons and ribbons were ready, banners made; each of the troopers would get a burger, fries and a cookie when they landed. They will have a big party after taking a month of block leave, a Regimental Ball, and organization day, and plenty of hugs and kisses."

The first 185 soldiers landed at Fort Carson after a long ride on a C-17 cargo plane. Most were covered in desert dust when they walked into the mountain night air at twenty-two degrees Fahrenheit. They were raring to go when they entered the gymnasium, met by rousing cheers and patriotic music. The general knew they had not come for a long speech; as soon as the Army song ended he dismissed them. Sand-colored battle uniforms blended with colorful civilian clothes, whole families reconnected in joyful reunions, but not without some tears.

Ahead lay a rough road, the one to adjusting. A sister worried about her brother: "I could not wait for him to get back; I thought he would be different, but not like this. He's so depressed. We didn't do much; he didn't like being around people. He just wanted to lie around the house and drink. He was okay around me and my dad, but didn't interact with anyone else, and when he was forced to be around others, he didn't talk to people."[39]

Emotional residue lingered. A faceless enemy had used car bombs and snipers in windows in Iraq; at home they could not avoid passing cars or open windows. Sometimes it hit them in a movie theater or watching television, in traffic, or in a crowded mall; for most it came at night when the mind dropped defenses. It came as depression, anxiety, irritability, hyper vigilance, or unexplained panic and snuck in when least expected. A Walter Reed research study named some of the reasons: over 94 percent had seen dead bodies, 92 percent had been ambushed,

82 percent knew someone killed or seriously injured, and nearly 52 percent had killed an enemy combatant.[40]

Reconnecting with the old threads at home was made harder by marital or financial problems. At work, tasks that once seemed routine became frustrating or insignificant; job performance dropped as divorces increased. Army statistics showed officer divorces rose 78 percent and enlisted by 53 percent in just 4 years. Deployment cycle support programs from initial mobilization, deployment, redeployment, and afterwards relieved the strains some, as did other special get-away-together programs. But no programs could fully overcome looming repeat deployments.

Americans care about their veterans, but binding wounds, making them whole, replacing losses is never cheap. Costs of wars are always high and the bill for veterans' aftercare comes well after the war and saps federal funds that could be used for something else. The price of veterans' medical care and benefits troubled the First Congress as it still does. Undersecretary of Defense David Chu complained the cost of veterans, retirees, and survivor benefits harmed the nation's ability to defend itself. Politicians tinkered with veterans' benefits before and they tinkered with benefits of veterans of the global war on terror; the GI Bill was marginally increased in 2001, the Jobs for Veterans Act improved states helping with jobs searches, and Small Business Development Centers helped start small businesses with education and loans. Disabled veterans were permitted set-asides and sole-source authority to compete for government contracts. National Guard careerists were allowed to retire earlier. But the changes are always marginal and never keep up with inflation. The VA hospital system is perpetually behind. By 2006 the waiting time for first-time medical exams had doubled from a year before, disability cases waiting adjudication increased by 8 percent, and but those over 6 months increased over 28 percent.[41]

A special tax on disabled veterans was a one hundred-year-old law that allowed the government to collect a dollar from veterans' pensions for every dollar paid by the VA for disability compensation. Congress finally repealed the Civil War law, but even the cost of that will have to come from other programs, most likely from veterans of Iraq and Afghanistan. Yellow ribbon magnets supporting the troops are meaningless unless the public brings them home with honor, respect, and dignity and with support as long as it is needed. That is the price of going to war and winning; losing is more costly. Signs, flags, and brass bands aren't enough. We owe our veterans everything.

Sergeant Jason Adams wrote letters home from his National Guard unit's duty in Iraq as his unit prepared to go home. "We never again will all be together doing the same things we are doing now. It is over. When we get home, we will go our separate ways. . . . I can't say I particularly like all the guys in this unit. I am sure they would say the same about me. But I do know if during the past year, the time had come to put their lives in danger to save one another of us, they would not have hesitated. . . . It is this bond then which will forever bind us, no matter where the roads of life take us. Forever more we will all look back and remember that chapter in our life when we were as one."[42]

When he got home he was thankful for the short welcoming ceremony; he wanted to go. But Adams noticed the small group of veterans from World War II, Korea, and Vietnam in a corner of the gymnasium. "I felt humbled to think these guys traveled out here in the wee hours of the morning just to welcome us home."[43]

As the bus approached Kewanee he saw the local John Deere dealer had rolled out a brand new combine with its auger extended and an American flag hanging from it. Finally he was home and looked to where the road of life would take him. "I drove past the county highway garage and turned north, up the six-mile stretch. The six-mile is long and straight and just like my future, it is wide open."[44]

For former Sergeant John Oman, the road was not as open. A midnight attack on a Baghdad highway left him with shrapnel wounds, a broken nose and shattered cheek, and third-degree burns. Only an emergency tracheotomy and four titanium implants in his face saved his life. He was evacuated through Landstuhl to Brooke Medical where his wife met him, but she was not allowed to touch him for weeks. As he began to recover, his future looked bad: he could not stay in the army and without a job he couldn't get a loan on a house, couldn't afford an apartment, and used all his money to get back home to Oregon. "After renting a truck, buying gas, paying for food and motel rooms—well, we were broke." Christmas looked worse. He had no job, no money, few civilian skills, and suffered from PTSD. Finally he asked for help from the local American Legion in Milton-Freewater. The Legion Post, along with the Oregon Veterans Motorcycle Association, Elks, Kiwanis, Lions, and other community organizations all pitched in. Oman doesn't know how they would have survived the winter without help. "It is important that local communities really support these injured young men and women when they return from military service," said Oman. "Believe me; such community support can make all the difference."[45]

Roads from Baghdad and Kabul are long and winding but they also lead to Hometown, USA, where Americans wait for them to come home. History repeats itself, sometimes in different ways, a resounding echo from the past.

11

Homeward Bound

The United States was born of Revolution and matured as a nation only because patriots were ready to leave their homes, take up arms, and risk their lives to defend the blessings of liberty for all of us. They accepted their duties despite the chance of pain or death, oblivious to all they would suffer, unprepared for its lasting effects, and uncertain of their futures. Some avoided going or hung back and criticized, but the proud and faithful marched to duty's call. Our continuing hope is that there will always be enough patriots to go and enough veterans coming home with determination and courage to lead.

From battlefields afar, warriors dream of returning, not just to a place but to a condition of safety, comfort, and happiness. Many of them take a piece of that with them: a picture, locket, letter, a verse, or some other symbol of what they value. Those connections brace them before battle and calm them after. After WWI, mothers took things from home, pictures, letters, flowers from their garden, or plain American soil to leave with their doughboys in French cemeteries. They left the simple treasures with their tears and their sons in that grassy foreign field. The Red Cross, Salvation Army, Sanitary Commission, United Services Organization, and others take the same essence of home to the troops where they are, and wait "till they all come home." Families reach out to touch them with something of themselves, something of home in socks, cookies, or precious words. The rest of us wait for the end of the war, unable to relax until the troops are home.

No nation ever cared more about their veterans than the United States. Americans want peace but will fight for freedom while pouring out their hearts and wallets for war's victims and veterans. Veterans are also victims of ravages of war, of a government anxious to forget the old war and looking to the next political fight, and of a public that blames them too easily and forgets too quickly. The same country that created amazing programs like the GI Bill of Rights, perfectly timed and aimed to give a hand up with programs that created a national economic explosion, turned a blind eye and deaf ear when the boys came home from Cuba with malaria and yellow fever, ran doughboys out of Washington and burned their shacks, shamed the tortured from North Korean prison camps, shunned the grunts poisoned in Vietnam jungles, and denied serious illnesses from the Gulf War.

Some are strengthened in the crucible of war but many are weakened; some get through without a scratch, others are crippled physically or emotionally. They dream of going home but the journey becomes treacherous, more when they are spit on or ridiculed, called names, ignored or forgotten. A simple "thank you" or "welcome home" is a strong message and sometimes all that is expected.

COMING HOME

From the frontlines of freedom they dream of going home but their long-waited advent is sometimes the beginning of a nightmare. Just getting home is an odyssey of the heart and mind, as well as the body. Battlefield visions of an idyllic haven spring partly from distorted reality imperfectly remembered and partly from glorified fantasies based on hope. Flawed perceptions become the movie played over and over again in the mind's lens, starring the returning warrior as hero with his loved ones waiting. But reality falls short of the advanced billing; home is more than a place with actors in a scene. Home is a complex concept that changes over time from where it started to where it is on that day. Extended absences separate real people who emerge from what they were before to the ones waiting in an inconceivable new drama.

Homer told of Odysseus, the veteran sailor of the Trojan Wars, an allegory of going home. The Greek hero faced nightmares in the form of Sirens and a Cyclops who obstructed his journey. When Odysseus reached home he didn't recognize the place, but discovered soon enough that several suitors pursued his wife while he was away. He boasted of his conquests to frighten them, then disguised himself to spy on them, hardened his heart against all of them, and finally just ran away. He tried to make the best of his unhappy homecoming, but the place had changed just as he had, and nothing worked.

While families prepare for the extended reunion, they must worry how much he was affected by his experiences. After all, their sons, husbands, or even neighbors were exposed to bad habits: profanity, drinking, smoking, carousing, fighting, gambling, or even worse, they were trained to kill. When they finally see them marching back home, pride shines in misty eyes behind the waving flags, banners, and yellow ribbons. Some returning veterans are uncomfortable with the ceremonies and fanfare although they need to know someone cares enough, consenting to go only in deference to fallen comrades or just to please their families. They hardly speak of their wars, keeping secret memories for private reflection later, visiting them less frequently as the years pass until memories fade and the pain eases enough.

Homecoming is an idea so intangible as to be mystifying and vaporous. Along with the loyal families, faithful pets, and yellow ribbons are surprises that land hard. They expect safety at home; a great escape from danger, combat, foreign places, and an uncertain tomorrow. But when the baggage is unpacked and the guard is let down, the illusion of safety can be shattered by battles still unsettled. They also expect unconditional acceptance from loved ones who overlooked their shortcomings before the war and forgave who they were. Now they are that way because they were touched by the war, altered or made different somehow. Instead of unreserved approval they find rejection in a crowded workforce, a sour economy, name-calling from the public they protected, and their wounds are left untreated by the government they defended. They want respect and they get it at first, but that is quickly gone as they join the amorphous crowd.

They thought home was so familiar they could step right back into it as if they had only gone to the store and come back. Altered states changed that, made home as foreign as the battlefield once was, disquieting and strange where comfortable patterns, cycles, and relationships seem to run in different directions. Homecoming veterans no longer fit into the rhythm of their old communities, their own places; the people who live there became strangers. The future they expected to share with countrymen of common purpose is elusive and hard to find. Yet they still believe something is possible; there is comfort in that, and a chance to sleep without cannon fire and with kindred folks keeping a watchful eye. Home is a warm blanket of hope.[1]

Whether the remnants of the Continental Army trudging penniless toward home, frail skeletons sailing from Cuba or shell-shocked doughboys from France, lonely outcasts flying alone from Vietnam, or a Marine on a Greyhound, the trip from frontlines to home is the easiest part of the journey. They go with hopes high but nervous despite their proven courage. They hide their doubts, fears, confusion, and hope that everything will work out. Waiting at the terminal, bus stop, or front porch are those special people looking and hoping for the best, too. From a distance they look the same but up close they are different; clues are found in the distant looks, lapses, changing moods, sullenness, heavy drinking, or silence.

In combat their survival depended on hard-learned habits: a weapon always within reach, taking it everywhere like their best friend or a guilty conscience, cleaning away every speck of dust while their clothing remained filthy and their feet wet, honing a blade, a bag ever packed and ready, never sleeping in the same place twice. Those were learned away from the sanctity of home and are out of place there. But some power transposes them to the former time, back to the old ways, to safety; keep the guards posted because peace is not to be trusted. None intended to pack the battles into their duffle but it happened anyway, less a souvenir of the war than a burden they can't put down. They fought then as part of a finely tuned machine but now join an unskilled labor pool with time on their hands and stray rounds still going off in their minds.

Shay told of one veteran who took his young wife on a picnic. He chose to spread their blanket in a shady forest but she complained it was too cold and insisted they move into a grassy field in the warming sun. Sunlight and openness made him nervous, exposed and unprotected. He passed the entire afternoon on the grass remembering snipers, mortar attacks, and ambushes, but he couldn't talk about that with her. She thought his sullenness bizarre. The romantic picnic ended with a fight.

Some escape by channeling every ounce of energy and all their thoughts into activity. Work replaces a vengeance, a mission with constant overtime, a drive to succeed at anything and everything and no tolerance for mistakes, never idleness. Incompetence must be avoided at all costs because people were killed by simple mistakes; they do all the important jobs because no one else can be trusted. Work becomes another combat run, a forced march, an all-nighter without sleep, keeping vigilance and trusting no one. Those are usually good providers, bringing home the bacon, buying grand houses to live in, sending their children to college, and saving for a retirement that never comes. They never have time to bring the paycheck home, direct deposit, they are just too busy. The money isn't important anyway; it's all about the action. If not consumed by work then fast cars, motorcycles, long weekends hunting or deep-sea fishing, alcohol binges, or sexual misadventures. Some escape into movies or television, writing memoirs, or attending reunions with other veterans, but in trying to forget they reinforce old memories. When my wife told our Vietnam veteran neighbor, who keeps a collection of M-1 rifles, that I had gone to Baghdad, his only reaction was, "Once you get it in your blood, you can't shake it." Old scars must be touched from time to time to verify them.

Readjustment is complicated, especially when obstacles are added by slandering, questioning their loyalty, denying medical care or counseling. Veterans all the way back to the Revolution, the War of 1812, the Mexican War, and WWI were refused compensation for their service or it was delayed. Veterans from Mexico and Cuba were quarantined to die from tropical diseases; Korean prisoners of war were ignored and forgotten, Vietnam grunts were sometimes spit on and discriminated against. Veterans from Vietnam, Desert Storm, and from atomic experiments were refused treatment while the government denied their illnesses even existed. The least they expect when they return is a warm welcome, not a minefield at the end of the parade.

Sometimes distant dreams of home get in the way of resettling once they are there. The image of a loving spouse dressed to kill with an adorable baby in her arms, the venerable father and aged mother in the background, hero-worshiping siblings, and a faithful dog is not likely to materialize. More likely there will be a depressed wartime economy, few good jobs, discrimination, or find their war was unpopular and they are blamed for it. People think too much of the military rubbed off on them, and maybe it did. Home is different than they remember: The yard is full of weeds, paint peals from the picket fence, the front door needs oil. The promised benefits are less than expected, dreams don't materialize, and even a decent job is hard to find. Main Street is not as wide and shady as it once was.

The blurry line between civilians and soldiers sharpens after the war. The youngster, who was never challenged before, met the demands of military training and combat, did things he never imagined, and somehow found his real strength. But the crucial need for him during the war passed. The best marksman in the company, the best pilot in the squadron, or the best naval gunner on the ship is no longer valued for what he did; he was indispensable when the stakes were high but no longer needed when the crisis ends. A young hero spends most of his life after his finest moment has become history. No simple job can ever replace that.

The first 5 years are crucial. Soon after mustering out and reentry into society, important decisions are made about where to live, where to work, whether the family stays together, and whether he can find peace with himself. During that time, the public forgets the unpleasantness of the war except for special days designated for flag-waving. Veterans never forget, not late at night when the nightmares come, not when they can't stop working and don't know why, or when they just can't settle down. When the memories sneak up, distorted by the passing years, they long again for the old weed-strewn battlefields, touch the scars on their bodies or in their minds, and shake their heads at the waste, destruction, and loss of fallen comrades.

Veterans' wrap themselves in organizations after every war like a security blanket woven from tradition; comrades help each other and their widows and orphans, lead community activities, toast the fallen, or just wave the flag like the rest. Speeches, parades, and flags preserve our heritage and soothe old wounds, but words and symbols are never enough. Understanding and opportunity are more important. Our veterans are America's treasure; we must never forget what they have done.

Maneuvers, attacks, defenses, and desperate battles are carefully preserved in history but not the truth about the cost of going to war. The total price paid is not listed in War Department records or Veterans Affairs case files, not in the Library of Congress or National Archives, but in the hearts and minds of veterans, the living relics of battles fought, won, and lost. Books, battlefields, memorials, and parades become touchstones for the rest but true understanding of the cost of liberty is only realized by understanding the veterans who stood at the front and came home. It is there we should seek the truth.

Notes

CHAPTER 1

1. Usher Parsons, "The Descendents of Peter Hill of York Co., ME," *The New England Historical and Genealogical Register* (1847–1868), April 1858, 12(2) APS Online, p. 139.

2. Judith Millidge, *Letters from the Front* (London: PRC Publishing Ltd., 2002), p. 14.

3. John Phillips Resch, *Suffering Soldiers: Revolutionary War Veterans, Moral Sentiment, and Political Culture in the Early Republic* (Amherst: University of Massachusetts Press, 1999).

4. Joseph Plumb Martin, edited by George F. Scheer, *Private Yankee Doodle* (Boston: Little, Brown and Company, 1962) (Originally published in Hallowell, Maine, in 1830), pp. i–xvii.

5. Ibid., p. 203.

6. National Magazine, "A Revolutionary Patriot," June 1858; 12 APS Online, p. 532.

7. Martin, *Private Yankee Doodle*, pp. 283–284.

8. Lloyd DeWitt Bockstruck, *Revolutionary War Bounty Land Grants Awarded by State Governments* (Baltimore: Genealogical Publishing Co., 1996), pp. v–xxvi.

9. Dixon Wecter, *When Johnny Comes Marching Home* (Cambridge, MA: Houghton Mifflin Company, 1944), p. 92.

10. Ibid., p. 95.

11. Resch, *Suffering Soldiers*, pp. 1–2.

12. Ibid., p. 9.

13. Ibid., p. 48.

14. Thomas L. Purvis, *Revolutionary America: 1763–1800* (New York: Facts On File Inc., 1995), pp. 234–242.

15. Robert C. Bray and Paul E. Bushnell, ed., *Diary of a Common Soldier in the American Revolution, 1775–1783: An Annotated Edition of the Military Journal of Jeremiah Greenman* (Dekalb, IL: Northern Illinois University Press, 1978), pp. i–xlii.

CHAPTER 2

1. John Phillips Resch, *Suffering Soldiers: Revolutionary War Veterans, Moral Sentiment, and Political Culture in the Early Republic* (Amherst: University of Massachusetts Press, 1999), pp. 90–92.

2. Ibid., p. 143.

3. Joseph Plumb Martin, edited by George F. Scheer, *Private Yankee Doodle* (Boston: Little, Brown and Company, 1962) (Originally published in Hallowell, Maine, in 1830).

4. Robert C. Bray and Paul E. Bushnell, ed., *Diary of a Common Soldier in the American Revolution, 1775–1783: An Annotated Edition of the Military Journal of Jeremiah Greenman* (Dekalb, IL: Northern Illinois University Press, 1978).

5. Thomas L. Purvis, *Revolutionary America: 1763–1800* (New York: Facts On File Inc., 1995), pp. 234–242.

6. Frederick Von Raumer (translated from German by William W. Turner), *America and the American People* (New York: J. & H. G. Langley, 1846).

7. Richard Severo and Lewis Milford, *The Wages of War: When America's Soldiers Came Home—From Valley Forge to Vietnam* (New York: Simon and Shuster, 1989) p. 117.

8. Donald S. Frazier, ed., *The United States and Mexico at War* (New York: MacMillan Reference USA, 1998), p. 315.

9. Reverend E. B. Hillard, *The Last Men of the Revolution* (Originally published in 1864 by N.A. & R.A. Moore, Hartford) (Barre, MA: Barre Publishers, 1968).

10. Martin, *Private Yankee Doodle*, p. 196.

CHAPTER 3

1. Julie Lynn Brandt, *The Civil War Diary of Elizabeth Hatcher Simons: Life and Hardship in Texana, Texas* (Texas A&M University–Kingsville, 1999); and Douglas Lee Braudaway, "A Texan Records the Civil War Siege of Vicksburg, Mississippi: The Journal of Maj. Maurice Kavanaugh Simons, 1863," *Southwestern Historical Quarterly*, The Texas State Historical Association, July 2001.

2. Ibid.

3. Larry M. Logue, *To Appomattox and Beyond: The Civil War Soldier in War and Peace* (Chicago: Ivan R. Dee The American Way Series, 1996), pp. 82–102.

4. Ada Christine Lightsey, *The Veteran's Story* (Meridian: The Meridian News, April 3, 1899).

5. Henry Steele Commanger, *The Blue and the Gray* (Indianapolis: The Bobbs-Merrill Company, Inc. 1950).

6. S. A. Cunningham, ed., *Confederate Veteran*, 1(1) (Nashville: January 1893), p. 6.

7. Dixon Wecter, *When Johnny Comes Marching Home* (Cambridge, MA: Houghton Mifflin Company, 1944), p. 172.

8. Ibid., p. 249.

9. Jeffrey W. McClurken, *After the Battle: Reconstructing the Confederate Veteran Family in Pittsylvania County and Danville, Virginia, 1860–1900* (Johns Hopkins University, 2002).

10. Charles Phillips and Alan Axelrod, *My Brother's Face: Portraits of the Civil War in Photographs, Diaries, and Letters* (San Francisco: Chronicle Books, 1993), p. 15.

11. R. B. Rosenburg, *Living Monuments: Confederate Soldiers' Homes in the New South* (Chapel Hill: The University of North Carolina Press, 1993) p. 3.

12. Ibid., p. 162, table 2.

13. Brandt, *The Civil War Diary of Elizabeth Hatcher Simons*; and Braudaway, "The Journal of Maj. Maurice Kavanaugh Simons."

CHAPTER 4

1. Charles Phillips and Alan Axelrod, *My Brother's Face: Portraits of the Civil War in Photographs, Diaries, and Letters* (San Francisco: Chronicle Books, 1993), p. 20.

2. William H. Hodgkins, *Journal of War: The Civil War Diary of the Life of William H. Hodgkins*, ed. Robert D. Schoenthal (Scottsdale, AZ: RDSKS Publishing Co. 2002), p. 283.

3. Stephen R. Whalen, *Everything Is the Same: The Civil War Home Front in Rural Vermont* (University of Maine, 1999), p. 281.

4. Ibid., p. 282.

5. Phillips and Axelrod, *My Brother's Face*, p. 52.

6. VA Fact Sheet, August 1999.

7. The President's Commission on Veterans' Pensions, "Veterans in our society: Data on the conditions of military service and on the status of the veteran." House Committee Print No. 261, 2d Session, 84th Congress for the Committee on Veteran's Affairs (Washington: United States Government Printing Office, June 21, 1956), p. 7.

8. Ibid., p. 13.

9. Dixon Wecter, *When Johnny Comes Marching Home* (Cambridge, MA: Houghton Mifflin Company, 1944).

10. Ibid., pp. 142–146.

11. Ibid.

12. Ibid., p. 169.

13. Larry M. Logue, *To Appomattox and Beyond: The Civil War Soldier in War and Peace* (Chicago: Ivan R. Dee, The American Way Series, 1996), pp. 82–102.

14. Wecter, *When Johnny Comes Marching Home*, p. 170.

15. Ibid., p. 180.

16. Ibid., p. 172.

17. Ibid., p. 154.

18. Ibid., p. 154.

19. Logue, *To Appomattox and Beyond*, pp. 82–102; and Richard Severo and Lewis Milford, *The Wages of War: When America's Soldiers Came Home—From Valley Forge to Vietnam* (New York: Simon and Shuster, 1989), p. 138.

20. Wecter, *When Johnny Comes Marching Home*, pp. 194–195.

21. Ibid., pp. 195–196.

22. Ibid., pp. 196–197.

23. Severo and Milford, *The Wages of War*, p. 135.

24. Ibid., p. 136.

25. Bell Irwin Wiley, *Common Soldiers in the Civil War* (New York: Grosset and Dunlap, 1951), pp. 124, 310.

26. Wecter, *When Johnny Comes Marching Home*; and Wiley, *Common Soldiers in the Civil War*; and Mary R. Dearing, *Veterans in Politics* (New York: Workers Library Publishers, 1952).

27. Michael J. Bennett, *When Dreams Came True: The GI Bill and the Making of Modern America* (Washington: Brassey's, 1996), pp. 40–41.

28. Severo and Milford, *The Wages of War*, pp. 183–184.

29. Wecter, *When Johnny Comes Marching Home; and Dearing, Veterans in Politics.*

CHAPTER 5

1. Charles Johnson Post, *The Little War of Private Post: The Spanish-American War See Up Close* (Electronic Version) (Lincoln, NE: University of Nebraska Press, 1999).

2. Ibid.

3. Roger D. Cunningham, "The Black 'Immune' Regiments in the Spanish-American War" (On Point: The Journal of Army History, Spring 2005), pp. 9–17.

4. Joseph Deburgh, "A Few Reminiscences of the First Expedition of American Troops to Manila," published in *The American Oldtimer*, 1939, and on the Spanish-American War Centennial Website (www.spanamwar.com).

5. Ibid.

6. Post, *The Little War of Private Post.*

7. Ibid.

8. Ibid.

9. Cunningham, "The Black 'Immune' Regiments in the Spanish-American War," pp. 9–17.

10. Post, *The Little War of Private Post.*

11. Ibid.

12. Ibid.

13. Martin L. Callahan, "From Shiloh to Santiago" *Military Images Magazine*, March-April 1998; and Joe Petritsch contributing to the Spanish-American War Centennial Website, "Conditions at Camp Wikoff."

14. Post, *The Little War of Private Post.*

15. Bill Bottoms, *The VFW: An Illustrated History of the Veterans of Foreign Wars of the United States* (Rockville, MD: Woodbine House, 1991).

16. Richard Severo and Lewis Milford, *The Wages of War: When America's Soldiers Came Home—From Valley Forge to Vietnam* (New York: Simon and Shuster, 1989) p. 209.

17. Post, *The Little War of Private Post.*

18. Bottoms, *The VFW,* p. 1-13.

19. United States Marine Corps, *Small Wars Manual,* 1940, p 1-1.

20. The President's Commission on Veterans' Pensions, "Veterans in our society: Data on the conditions of military service and on the status of the veteran," House Committee Print No. 261, 2d Session, 84th Congress for the Committee on Veteran's Affairs (Washington: United States Government Printing Office, June 21, 1956).

21. Benjamin R. Beede, ed., *The War of 1898 and U.S. Interventions 1898–1934* (New York: Garland Publishing, Inc., 1994), pp. 402–405.

22. U.S. Congress, House Document 804, 78th Congress, 2d Session, Dec. 8, 1944.

CHAPTER 6

1. Martin Samuel Vilas, *The Veterans of the National Soldiers Home* (Burlington, VT: Free Press Association, 1915).

2. Robert Russell (AFC 2001/001/18879), "Diary of Sgt. Reese Melvin Russell," Veterans History Project Collection, American Folklife Center, Library of Congress.

3. Brigadier Peter Young, editor-in-chief, *The Marshall Cavendish Illustrated Encyclopedia of World War I* (New York: Marshall Cavendish, 1986), pp. 2009–2011.

4. Ibid., pp. 2002–2020.

5. George Lamb and Betty Boyd (AFC 2001/001/1627), "Letter Home: World War I Letters of Charles Stanley Lamb," Veterans History Project Collection, American Folklife Center, Library of Congress.

6. Rudolph Joseph Neumann (AFC 2001/001/24282), *Diary of Rudy Neumann, World War I*, Veterans History Project Collection, American Folklife Center, Library of Congress.

7. General Richard Thoumin, edited and translated by Martin Kieffer, *The First World War* (New York: G.P. Putnam's Sons, 1963), pp. 347–372).

8. Young, *The Marshall Cavendish Illustrated Encyclopedia of World War I*, pp. 2903–2911.

9. Lettie Gavin, *American Women in World War I* (Niwot: University Press of Colorado, 1997), pp. 1–119.

10. Lamb and Boyd, "Letter Home."

11. Irving W. Johnson (AFC 2001/001/7027), *Looking into the Past: Irving W. Johnson's Memories of World War I*, Veterans History Project Collection, American Folklife Center, Library of Congress.

12. Joseph J. Gleeson (AFC 2001/001/10911), *A Soldier's Story: A Daily Account of World War I*, Veterans History Project Collection, American Folklife Center, Library of Congress.

13. Will Judy, *A Soldier's Diary: A Day to Day Record in the World War* (Chicago: Judy Publishing Co., 1930), p. 173.

14. Gail Buckley, *American Patriots: The Story of Blacks in the Military from the Revolution to Desert Storm* (New York: Random House, 2001), pp. 219–220.

15. Neumann, *Diary of Rudy Neumann, World War I*, Veterans History Project.

16. Wecter, *When Johnny Comes Marching Home*, pp. 298–300.

17. Gavin, *American Women in World War I*, pp. 1–119.

18. Wecter, *When Johnny Comes Marching Home*, pp. 302–303.

19. Neumann, *Diary of Rudy Neumann, World War I*, Veterans History Project.

20. M. L. Greenquist (AFC 2001/001/9574), *Independent Research on the World War I Experiences of Corporal Lars N. Greenquist*, Veterans History Project Collection, American Folklife Center, Library of Congress.

21. Wecter, *When Johnny Comes Marching Home*, pp. 348–350.

22. Young, *The Marshall Cavendish Illustrated Encyclopedia of World War I*, pp. 3146–3147.

23. Ibid., pp. 1986.

24. Mary Frost Jessup, *The Public Reaction to the Returning Service Man after World War I* (Washington, DC: U.S. Department of Labor, 1944).

25. Gordon Stelter, *The Doughboy, the City, and the Farm after the Great War* (The University of Guelph, 1996).

26. Wecter, *When Johnny Comes Marching Home*, p. 265.

27. Edward H. Loudenbeck (AFC 2001/001/1937), *His Daily Diary of the Great War, and his Part in it*, Veterans History Project Collection, American Folklife Center, Library of Congress.

28. Stelter, *The Doughboy, the City, and the Farm after the Great War.*

29. Wecter, *When Johnny Comes Marching Home*, p. 319.

30. Severo and Milford, *The Wages of War*, pp. 239–240.

31. Ibid., pp. 249–250.

32. Wecter, *When Johnny Comes Marching Home*, p. 400.

33. Severo and Milford, *The Wages of War*, pp. 251–254.

34. Ibid., pp. 255–257.

35. Michael J. Bennett, *When Dreams Come True: The GI Bill and the Making of Modern America* (Washington: Brassey's, 1996), p. 57.

36. Ibid., pp. 65–67.

37. Severo and Milford, *The Wages of War*, pp. 269–270.

38. Loudenbeck, Johnson, and Gleeson, Veterans History Project.

39. David M. Kennedy, *Over Here* (New York: Oxford University Press, 1980), pp. 367–369.

40. Gleeson, *A Soldier's Story.*

41. Greenquist, *World War I Experiences of Corporal Lars N. Greenquist.*

42. Lamb and Ford, *Letters Home.*

43. Russell, *Diary of Sgt. Reese Melvin Russell.*

CHAPTER 7

1. Sidney Riches (AFC 2001/001/557), Collection for Center of Military History, 1996, Veterans History Project Collection, American Folklife Center, Library of Congress.

2. Judith E. Greenberg and Helen Casey McKeever, *Letters from a World War II GI* (New York: Franklin Watts, 1995), p. 95.

3. Robert and Jane Easton, *Love and War: Pearl Harbor through V-J Day* (Norman: University of Oklahoma Press, 1991), p. 334.

4. Greenberg and McKeever, *Letters from a World War II GI*, p. 96

5. Ibid., p. 111.

6. George Feldman, *World War II Almanac*, Vol. 2 (Detroit: UXL 2000), pp. 403–405.

7. Richard Severo and Lewis Milford, *The Wages of War: When America's Soldiers Came Home—From Valley Forge to Vietnam* (New York: Simon and Shuster, 1989), pp. 283–285.

8. Samuel A. Stouffer et al., *The American Soldier: Combat and its Aftermath*, Vol. 2 (Princeton, NJ: Princeton University Press, 1949), p. 552.

9. Greenberg and McKeever, *Letters from a World War II GI*, p. 115.

10. J. Giles, *The GI Journal of Sgt. Giles* (Boston, 1965), p. 337.

11. Stouffer, *The American Soldier*, p. 598-599.

12. Ibid., p. 601.

13. Ibid., p. 464.

14. *Educational Plans of Veterans*, Research Service, Veterans Administration, May 1946, Washington, DC.

15. Greenberg and McKeever, *Letters from a World War II GI*, p. 132.

16. Easton, *Love and War*, pp. 369–377.

17. Riches, Veterans History Project.

18. Robert Francis Saxe, *Settling Down: Domesticating World War II Veterans' Challenge to Postwar Consensus* (University of Illinois at Urbana-Champaign, 1999).

19. Michael J. Bennett, *When Dreams Come True: The GI Bill and the Making of Modern America* (Washington: Brassey's, 1996), p. 194.

20. Thomas A. Rumer, *The American Legion: An Official History, 1919–1989* (New York: M. Evans & Company, 1990), p. 243.

21. Ibid., p. 212.

22. Kenneth E. Cox, "The Greatest Legislation," *The American Legion Magazine*, June 2004, p. 16.

23. Bennett, *When Dreams Come True*, p. 78.

24. Ibid., pp. 94–97.

25. Ibid., p. 141.

26. Rumer, *The American Legion*, p. 243.

27. Bennett, *When Dreams Come True*, pp. 5, 13.

28. Severo and Milford, *The Wages of War*, p. 289.

29. Feldman, *World War II Almanac*, pp. 406–407.

30. Severo and Milford, *The Wages of War*, p. 294.

31. Bennett, *When Dreams Come True*, pp. 195–196.

32. Ibid., pp. 241–242.

33. Glover E. Hopson, *The Veterans Administration* (New York: Chelsea House Publishers, 1988); and Mary O'Donnell, *The G.I. Bill of Rights of 1944 and the Creation of America's Modern Middle Class Society* (St. John's University, 2001).

34. Bennett, *When Dreams Come True*, p. 8.

35. Severo and Milford, *The Wages of War*, p. 286.

36. Stouffer, *The American Soldier*, pp. 622–623.

37. Ibid., p. 635.

38. Rumer, *The American Legion*, p. 259–263.

39. Robert Klein, *Wounded Men, Broken Promises* (New York: MacMillan Publishing Co., Inc., 1981), pp. 10–12.

40. Rumer, *The American Legion*, pp. 302–303.

41. Robert J. Havighurst, John W. Baughman, Walter H. Eaton, and Ernest W. Burgess, *The American Veteran Back Home* (New York: Longmans, Green and Co, 1951), p. 23.

42. Ibid., pp. 23–36.

43. Ibid., pp. 72, 76, 82–83.

44. Judy Barrett Litoff, David C. Smith, Barbara Woodall Taylor, and Charles E. Taylor, *Miss You: The World War II Letters of Barbara Woodall Taylor and Charles E. Taylor* (Athens: The University of Georgia Press, 1990), pp. 273–276.

45. Greenberg and McKeever, *Letters from a World War II GI*, pp. 283–284.

46. Litoff, *Miss You*.

47. Harold Bond, *Return to Cassino* (Garden City: Doubleday and Company, 1964), p. 1.

48. Audie Murphy, *To Hell and Back* (New York: Holt, 1949).

49. Clarence Alvin Schutt, Jr. (AFC 2001/001/5904), Interview, Veterans History Project Collection, American Folklife Center, Library of Congress.

50. Easton, *Love and War*, p. 377.

CHAPTER 8

1. William D. Dannenmaier, *We Were Innocents* (Chicago: University of Illinois Press, 1999).

2. Don F. Adams (AFC 2001/001/1120), Interview, Veterans History Project Collection, American Folklife Center, Library of Congress.

3. Asa Charles Ball (AFC 2001/001/5944), Interview, Veterans History Project Collection, American Folklife Center, Library of Congress.

4. Sidney Riches (AFC 2001/001/557), Military History Center Collection, Veterans History Project, American Folklife Center, Library of Congress.

5. Clarence Alvin Schutt, Jr. (AFC 2001/001/5904), Interview, Veterans History Project Collection, American Folklife Center, Library of Congress.

6. Robert Leckie, *Wars of America* (New York: Harper & Row, 1968), pp. 344–345.

7. Adams, Veterans History Project.

8. Robin S. Keehan, *Dialectics of Containment: Mothers, Moms, Soldiers, Veterans and the Cold War Mystique* (University of California—San Diego, 1998).

9. The President's Commission on Veterans' Pensions. "Veterans in our society: Data on the conditions of military service and on the status of the veteran," House Committee Print No. 261, 2d Session, 84th Congress for the Committee on Veteran's Affairs. (Washington: United States Government Printing Office, June 21, 1956), p. 35.

10. Donald M. Griffin (AFC 2001/001/4925), Interview, Veterans History Project Collection, American Folklife Center, Library of Congress.

11. Richard Severo and Lewis Milford, *The Wages of War: When America's Soldiers Came Home—From Valley Forge to Vietnam* (New York: Simon and Shuster, 1989), p. 330.

12. Severo and Milford, *The Wages of War*, pp. 336–337.

13. Leckie, *Wars of America*, pp. 405–406.

14. Severo and Milford, *The Wages of War*, pp. 341–342.

15. Jeff Stoffer, "The Birthplace of Veterans Day," *The American Legion Magazine*, November 2003, p. 44.

16. Leckie, *Wars of America*, p. 407.

17. Richard K. Kolb, ed., *Cold War Clashes: Confronting Communism, 1945–1991* (Kansas City, MO: Veterans of Foreign Wars Publications, 2004).

18. Adams, Veterans History Project.

19. Janet Graff Valentine, *The American Combat Soldier in the Korean War* (University of Alabama, 2002).

20. Ball, Veterans History Project.

21. Dannenmaier, *We Were Innocents*, 1999.

CHAPTER 9

1. Lynda Van Devanter, *Home Before Morning: The Story of an Army Nurse in Vietnam* (Amherst: University of Massachusetts Press, 2001).

2. Richard Severo and Lewis Milford, *The Wages of War: When America's Soldiers Came Home—From Valley Forge to Vietnam* (New York: Simon and Shuster, 1989), p. 348.

3. Myra Oliver, writing in the Los Angeles Times; and Van Devanter, *Home Before Morning*, 2001.

4. Maxine Salvatore, *Women after War: Vietnam Experiences and Post-traumatic Stress* (Simmons College School of Social Work, 1992).

5. Paul Starr, *Discarded Army: Veterans after Vietnam* (New York: Charterhouse, 1973), p. 6.

6. James N. Wallace, "Talks with GI's on their way to Combat in Vietnam," *U.S. News and World Report*, Jan. 15, 1968.

7. Bob Greene, *Homecoming: When the Soldiers Returned from Vietnam* (New York: G.P. Putnam's Sons, 1989), pp. 88–89, 136.

8. Starr, *Discarded Army: Veterans After Vietnam*, p. 14.

9. Greene, *Homecoming*, p. 34.

10. Ibid., p. 93.

11. Ibid., pp. 40–41, 61.

12. Robert Klein, *Wounded Men, Broken Promises* (New York: MacMillan Publishing Co., Inc., 1981), p. 165.

13. Charles R. Figley and Seymore Leventman, ed., *Strangers at Home: Vietnam Veterans Since the War*, 2nd ed. (New York: Bruner/Mazel Publishers, 1990).

14. Greene, *Homecoming*, p. 184.

15. Ibid., p. 238.

16. Ibid., p. 254.

17. C. Noell and G. Wood, *We Are all POWs* (Philadelphia: 1975), pp. 55–57.

18. David Parks, *GI Diary* (Washington: Howard University Press, 1984), pp. 121–135.

19. Greene, *Homecoming*, pp. 84–85.

20. Gerald Nicosia, *Home to War: A History of the Vietnam Veterans' Movement* (New York: Crown Publishers, 2001), p. 70.

21. Ibid., pp. 217–232.

22. Greene, *Homecoming*, p. 46.

23. Ibid., pp. 80–83, 198, 217, 240.

24. Nicosia, *Home to War*, pp. 200–201.

25. Aphrodite Matsakis, *Vietnam Wives: Facing the Challenges of Life with Veterans Suffering Post-Traumatic Stress,* 2nd ed. (Lutherville, MD: Sidran Press, 1996).

26. Klein, *Wounded Men, Broken Promises*, p. 270.

27. Greene, *Homecoming*, pp. 42–43.

28. Gail Buckley, *American Patriots: The Story of Blacks in the Military from the Revolution to Desert Storm* (New York: Random House, 2001), pp. 421–423.

29. Greene, *Homecoming*, pp. 78-79.

30. Ibid., pp. 94, 104, 209, 239.

31. Severo and Milford, *The Wages of War*, p. 355; and Paul Starr, *The Discarded Army: Veterans After Vietnam* (New York: Charterhouse, 1973), p. 37, 198.

32. Greene, *Homecoming*, p. 23, 30.

33. Starr, *Discarded Army*, p. 226.

34. Greene, *Homecoming*, pp. 199–220.

35. Bill Sanders, "Coached Silence," *The Atlanta Journal-Constitution*, March 27, 2005.

36. Max Cleland, *Strong in the Broken Places* (Atlanta: Cherokee Publishing Company, 1989).

37. Starr, *Discarded Army*, p. 80.

38. Klein, *Wounded Men, Broken Promises*, pp. 22–24.

39. Starr, *Discarded Army*, pp. 43–44.

40. Cleland, *Strong in the Broken Places*, p. 155.

41. Severo and Milford, *The Wages of War*, pp. 360–361.

42. Ibid., p. 378.

43. Ibid., pp. 360–370.

44. Ibid., p. 392.

45. Ibid., pp. 404–412.

46. Klein, *Wounded Men, Broken Promises*, pp. 158, 181.

47. Thomas Rumer, *The American Legion: An Official History, 1919–1989* (New York: M. Evans & Company, 1990), pp. 444–456.

48. Greene, *Homecoming*, p. 65.

49. Ibid., pp. 162, 226–228, 247–248.
50. Ibid., pp. 151–152.
51. Ibid., pp. 268–269.
52. Jan C. Scruggs and Joel L. Swerdlow, *To Heal a Nation* (New York: Harper and Row, Publisher, 1985), p. 147.
53. Ibid., pp. 139–140.
54. Greene, *Homecoming*, p. 246.
55. Scruggs and Swerdlow, *To Heal a Nation*, p. 152.

CHAPTER 10

1. Otto Kreisher, "Desert One," *Air Force Magazine Online: Journal of the Air Force Association*, 82(1), January 1999; and Jim Greeley, "Desert One," *Airman*, April 2001.
2. Gunnery Sergeant Keith A. Milks, "Marines in Beirut," *Marine Corps News*, September 29, 2003; and Al Hemingway, "Marines Remember Beirut 20 years Later," *VFW Magazine*, October 2003.
3. Eytan Gilboa, "The Panama Invasion Revisited: Lessons for the Use of Force in the Post Cold War Era," *Political Science Quarterly*, 110(4), 1995.
4. Colin Powell, *My American Journey* (New York: Random House, 1995).
5. Gail Buckley, *American Patriots: The Story of Blacks in the Military from the Revolution to Desert Storm* (New York: Random House, 2001), p. 433.
6. Jeffrey Clark (AFC 2001/001/3232), Interview, Veterans History Project Collection, American Folklife Center, Library of Congress.
7. Cynthia B. Acree with Colonel Cliff Acree, *The Gulf between Us* (Washington: Brassey's, 2000), pp. 276–279.
8. Juanita Woodhouse Blair, *The Impact of Desert Storm on Military Wives Who Are Human Service Professionals* (The Union Institute, 1992).
9. Geoffrey A. Campbell, *Life of an American Soldier: The Persian Gulf War* (San Diego: Lucent Books—American War Library, 2001), p. 106.
10. As told to the author by Dick Goddard, Georgia Vietnam Veterans Association, 2005.
11. Buzz Williams, *Spare Parts: A Marine Reservist's Journey from Campus to Combat in 38 Days* (New York: Gotham Books, 2004), pp. 253–284.
12. Campbell, *Life of an American Soldier*, pp. 107–109.
13. Seymore M. Hersh, *Against All Enemies—Gulf War Syndrome: The War between America's Ailing Veterans and Their Government* (New York: The Ballantine Publishing Group, 1998).
14. Ibid.
15. Joyce Riley and Dave Riddell von Kleist, "Mission Statement," The American Gulf War Association, News Release, February 5, 2004.
16. Hersh, *Against All Enemies*, pp. 41–42.
17. Ibid.
18. John Pike, "Operation Enduring Freedom," Global Security.org, on line 2000–2003.
19. Judith Millidge, *Letters from the Front* (London: PRC Publishing, Ltd., 2002).
20. Greg Jaffe, "For Nate Self, Battlefield Hero, Trauma Takes a Toll," October 6, 2005, and "For Army Families, Repeat Tours Strain Life on the Home Front," December 16, 2005, *The Wall Street Journal*.

21. Steven Komaro, "Vietnam vets in Iraq see 'entirely different war,'" *USA Today*, June 20, 2005.

22. Moni Basu, "Going to war, coming of age," September 11, 2005; and "Not your mother's war," November 13, 2005, *The Atlanta Journal-Constitution*.

23. Bob Deans, "Women's combat role on front burner," *The Atlanta Journal-Constitution*, June 26, 2005.

24. Steve Fainaru, "Battle citations display valor of female troops," *The Atlanta Journal-Constitution*, June 26, 2005.

25. Edward Colimore, "Vietnam vets jolted back," *The Philadelphia Inquirer*, September 2004.

26. Basu, *Atlanta Journal-Constitution*.

27. Jim Auchmutey, "To Baghdaddy and back," *The Atlanta Journal-Constitution*, October 23, 2005.

28. Staff Sergeant Jason Adams, *Active Duty: Letters to Home from Iraq* (Fishers, IN: Learnovation Press, Thistle Ridge, 2006), p. 416.

29. Janie Blankenship, "Women change face of military," *VFW Magazine*, March 2004; and "Coming home to a changed world," June/July 2004.

30. Jaffe, *Wall Street Journal*, 2005.

31. Dave Hirschman, "I'm not going home until I've got my arm …" *The Atlanta Journal-Constitution*, October 9, 2005.

32. John Brieden, "Commander's message," *The American Legion Magazine*, December 2003.

33. Jaffe, *Wall Street Journal* series, December 16, 2005.

34. Specialist Kyle J. Cosner, "Fort Bragg releases homicide study," *The Pentagram*, Army News Service, November 15, 2002.

35. Williams, *Spare Parts*.

36. Jaffe, *Wall Street Journal* series, December 16, 2005.

37. Peg Tyre, "Battling the effects of war," *Newsweek*, December 6, 2004.

38. Tom Roeder, Writing in *The Gazette*, Colorado Springs, CO, January 26, February 13, March 14, 2004.

39. Anonymous by request from Colorado Springs, CO.

40. Don Vaughan, "Aftershock," *Military Officer*, November 2005.

41. Tim Dyhouse, "Waiting line for VA exams doubles," *VFW Magazine*, June/July 2006, p. 12.

42. Adams, *Letters to Home from Iraq*, pp. 416–417.

43. Ibid., p. 436.

44. Ibid., p. 462.

45. James V. Carroll, "When heroes come home hurt," *American Legion Magazine*, June 2006, pp. 13–16.

CHAPTER 11

1. Jonathan Shay, *Odysseus in America: Combat Trauma and the Trial of Homecoming* (New York: Scribner, 2002), pp. 245–246.

Selected Bibliography

BOOKS

Abbott, Shirley. *The National Museum of American History*. New York: Smithsonian Institution, Harry N. Abrams, Inc., 1981.

Acree, Cynthia B. with Cliff Acree. *The gulf between us*. Washington, DC: Brassey's, 2000.

Adams, James Truslow. *Album of American history, Vol. I: Colonial period*. New York: Charles Scribner's Sons, 1981.

Adams, Jason. *Active duty: Letters to home from Iraq*. Fishers, IN: Learnovation Press, Thistle Ridge, 2006.

Adkin, Mark. *Urgent fury: The battle for Grenada*. Lexington, KY: Lexington Books, 1989.

Beede, Benjamin R., ed. *The war of 1898 and U.S. interventions 1898–1934*. New York: Garland Publishing, Inc., 1994.

Bennett, Michael, J. *When dreams come true: The GI bill and the making of modern America*. Washington, DC: Brassey's, 1996.

Blizzard, Dennis F., ed. *The roster of the General Society of the War of 1812*. Baltimore, MD: Clearfied, 1989.

Bockstruck, Lioyd DeWitt. *Revolutionary War bounty land grants awarded by state governments*. Baltimore, MD: Genealogical Publishing Co., 1996.

Bond, Harold. *Return to Cassino*. Garden City, NY: Doubleday & Company, 1964.

Bottoms, Bill. *The VFW: An illustrated history of the Veterans of Foreign Wars of the United States*. Rockville, MD: Woodbine House, 1991.

Bray, Robert C. and Paul E. Bushnell, eds. *Diary of a common soldier in the American Revolution, 1775–1783: An annotated edition of the military journal of Jeremiah Greenman*. Dekalb, IL: Northern Illinois University Press, 1978.

Buckley, Gail. *American patriots: The story of blacks in the military from the Revolution to Desert Storm*. New York: Random House, 2001.

Budahn, P.J. *Veterans' guide to benefits*, 3rd ed. Mechanicburg, PA: Stackpole Books, 2001.

Butler, Steven R. *U.S. veterans of the war with Mexico*. Richardson, TX: Descendents of Mexican War Veterans, 1998.

Campbell, Geoffrey A. *Life of an American soldier: The Persian Gulf War*. San Diego: Lucent Books (American War Library), 2001.

Cleland, Max. *Strong in the broken places*. Atlanta, GA: Cherokee Publishing Company, 1989.

Coffman, Edward M. *The war to end all wars*. Lexington, KY: The University Press of Kentucky, 1998.

Commanger, Henry Steele. *The blue and the gray*. Indianapolis, IN: The Bobbs-Merrill Company, Inc., 1950.

Commanger, Henry Steele, editor-in-chief. *The American destiny, Vol. 2: The war for independence*. Danbury, CT: The Danbury Press, 1975.

Dannenmaier, William D. *We were innocents*. Chicago, IL: University of Illinois Press, 1999.

Dearing, Mary R. *Veterans in politics*. Baton Rouge, LA: The Louisiana State University Press, 1952.

Douglas, Jack. *Veterans on the march*. New York: Workers Library Publishers, 1934.

Easton, Robert and Jane Easton. *Love and war: Pearl Harbor through V-J day*. Norman, OK: University of Oklahoma Press, 1991.

Eisenberg, Ronald, M.D. *Veterans compensation: An American scandal*. Shreveport, IL: Pierremont Press, 1985.

Eisner, Marc Allen. *From warfare state to welfare state*. University Park, PA: Pennsylvania State University Press, 2000.

Feldman, George. *World War II almanac*, Vol. 2. Detroit: UXL, 2000.

Figley, Charles R. and Seymore Leventman, eds. *Strangers at home: Vietnam veterans since the war*, 2nd ed. New York: Brunner/Mazel Publishers, 1990.

Frazier, Donald S., ed. *The United States and Mexico at war*. New York: MacMillan Reference USA, 1998.

Freeman, Douglas Southall. *George Washington: Patriot and president*, Vol. 6. New York: Charles Scribner's Sons, 1954.

Gavin, Lettie. *American women in World War I*. Niwot, CO: University Press of Colorado, 1997.

Giles, J. *The GI journal of Sgt. Giles*. Boston, MA: 1965.

Greenberg, Judith E. and Helen Casey McKeever. *Letters from a World War II GI*. New York: Franklin Watts, 1995.

Greene, Bob. *Homecoming: When the soldiers returned from Vietnam*. New York: G.P. Putnam's Sons, 1989.

Greene, Jack P. and J.R. Pole, eds. *The Blackwell encyclopedia of the American Revolution*. Cambridge, MA: Blackwell Reference, 1991.

Grossman, Dave. *On killing: The psychological cost of learning to kill in war and society*. Boston, MA: Little, Brown and Company, 1995.

Havighurst, Robert J., John W. Baughman, Walter H. Eaton, and Ernest W. Burgess. *The American veteran back home*. New York: Longmans, Green and Co., 1951.

Haythornewaite, Philip J. *The World War One source book*. London: Arms and Armour Press, 1992.

Heller, Charles, E. and William A. Stofft, eds. *America's first battles*. Lawrence: The University Press of Kansas, 1986.

Hersh, Seymour M. *Against all enemies—Gulf War syndrome: The war between America's ailing veterans and their government*. New York: The Ballantine Publishing Group, 1998.

Hillard, E.B. *The last men of the revolution* (Originally published in 1864 by N.A. Moore & R.A. Moore, Hartford) Barre, MA: Barre Publishers, 1968.

Hodgkins, William H. *Journal of war: The Civil War diary of the life of William H. Hodgkins.* Ed. Robert D. Schoenthal. Scottsdale, AZ: RDSKS Publishing Co., 2002.

Hopson, Glover E. *The Veterans Administration.* New York: Chelsea House Publishers, 1988.

Judy, Will. *A soldiers diary: A day to day record in the world war.* Chicago, IL: Judy Publishing Company, 1930.

Karsten, Peter. *Soldiers and society: The effects of military service and war on American life.* Westport, CT: Greenwood Press, 1978.

Kennedy, David M. *Over here.* New York: Oxford University Press, 1980.

Ketchum, Richard M., editor-in-charge. *The American Heritage picture history of the Civil War.* New York: American Heritage/Bonanza Books, 1982.

Kim, K.H., Susan Farrell, and Ewan Clague. *The all-volunteer army.* New York: Praeger Publishers, 1971.

Kirchberger, Joe H. *The Civil War and reconstruction.* New York: Facts on File, 1991.

Klein, Robert. *Wounded men, broken promises.* New York: MacMillan Publishing Co., Inc., 1981.

Kolb, Richard K., ed. *Cold war clashes: Confronting communism, 1945–1991.* Kansas City, MO: Veterans of Foreign Wars Publications, 2004.

Leckie, Robert. *The wars of America,* Vols. 1 and 2. New York: Harper & Row, 1968.

Levitan, Sar A. and Karen A. Cleary. *Old wars remain unfinished: The veteran benefits system.* Baltimore, MD: The Johns Hopkins University Press, 1973.

Lightsey, Ada Christine. *The veteran's story.* Meridian, MS: The Meridian News, April 3, 1899.

Litoff, Judy Barrett, David C. Smith, Barbara Wooddall Taylor, and Charles E. Taylor. *Miss you: The World War II letters of Barbara Wooddall Taylor and Charles E. Taylor.* Athens, GA: University of Georgia Press, 1990.

Logue, Larry M. *To Appomattox and beyond: The Civil War soldier in war and peace* (The American Way Series). Chicago, IL: Ivan R. Dee, 1996.

Martin, Joseph Plumb, edited by George F. Scheer. *Private yankee doodle.* Boston, MA: Little, Brown and Company, 1962 (Originally published in Hallowell, ME, in 1830).

Matsakis, Aphrodite. *Vietnam wives: Facing the challenges of life with veterans suffering post-traumatic stress,* 2nd ed. Lutherville, MD: Sidran Press, 1996.

Millidge, Judith. *Letters from the front.* London: PRC Publishing, Ltd., 2002.

Monahan, Evelyn M. and Rosemary Neidel-Greenlee. *And if I perish: Frontline U.S. Army nurses in World War II.* New York: Alfred A. Knopf, 2003.

Moskos, Charles C., Jr. *The American enlisted man.* New York: The Russell Sage Foundation, 1970.

Murphy, Audie. *To hell and back.* New York: Holt, 1949.

Nicosia, Gerald. *Home to war: A history of the Vietnam veterans' movement.* New York: Crown Publishers, 2001.

Nishiura, Elizabeth, ed. *American battle monuments.* Detroit, MI: Omnigraphics, Inc., 1989.

Noell, Chuck and Gary Wood. *We are all POWs.* Philadelphia, PA: Fortress Press, 1975.

Parks, David. *GI diary.* Washington, DC: Howard University Press, 1984.

Phillips, Charles and Alan Axelrod. *My brother's face: Portraits of the Civil War in photographs, diaries, and letters.* San Francisco, CA: Chronicle Books, 1993.

Powell, Colin. *My American journey.* New York: Random House, 1995.

Purvis, Thomas L. *Revolutionary America: 1763–1800.* New York: Facts on File, Inc., 1995.

Rickey, Don, Jr. *Forty miles a day on beans and hay: The enlisted soldier fighting the Indian wars.* Norman, OK: The University of Oklahoma Press, 1963.

Rosenburg, R.B. *Living monuments: Confederate soldiers' homes in the new south.* Chapel Hill, NC: The University of North Carolina Press, 1993.

Ross, Davis, R.B. *Preparing for Ulysses: Politics and veterans during World War II.* New York: Columbia University Press, 1969.

Rumer, Thomas A. *The American Legion: An official history, 1919–1989.* New York: M. Evans & Company, 1990.

Scruggs, Jan C. and Joel L. Swerdlow. *To heal a nation.* New York: Harper & Row, 1985.

Severo, Richard and Lewis Milford. *The wages of war: When America's soldiers came home—from Valley Forge to Vietnam.* New York: Simon and Shuster, 1989.

Shay, Jonathan. *Odysseus in America: Combat trauma and the trials of homecoming.* New York: Scribner, 2002.

Shrader, Charles Reginald, gen. ed. *Reference guide to United States military history 1607–1815.* New York: Facts on File, Inc., 1991.

Starr, Paul. *The discarded army: Veterans after Vietnam.* New York: Charterhouse, 1973.

Stouffer, Samuel A., Arthur A. Lumsdaine, Marion H. Lumsdaine, Robin M. Williams, Jr., M. Brewster Smith, Irving L. Janis, Shirley A. Star, and Leonard S. Cottrell, Jr. *The American soldier: Combat and its aftermath*, Vol. II. Princeton, NJ: Princeton University Press, 1949.

Taylor, Richard. *Prodigals: A Vietnam story.* Havertown, PA: Casemate, 2003.

Thoumin, Richard, edited and translated by Martin Kieffer. *The First World War.* New York: G.P. Putnam's Sons, 1963.

Van Devanter, Lynda. *Home before morning: The story of an army nurse in Vietnam.* Amherst, MA: University of Massachusetts Press, 2001.

Vilas, Martin Samuel. *The veterans of the national soldiers' home.* Burlington, VT: Free Press Association, 1915.

Von Raumer, Frederick (translated from German by William W. Turner). *America and the American people.* New York: J. & H. G. Langley, 1846.

Wecter, Dixon. *When Johnny comes marching home.* Cambridge, MA: Houghton Mifflin Company, 1944.

Wiley, Bell Irwin. *Common soldiers in the Civil War.* New York: Grosset and Dunlap, 1951.

Williams, Buzz. *Spare parts: A marine reservist's journey from campus to combat in 38 days.* New York: Gotham Books, 2004.

Wylie, Alexander E. *Veterans and affiliated organizations arising from the Civil War.* Mendota, IL: Mendota Reporter, 1966.

Yezzo, Dominick. *A G.I.'s Vietnam diary, 1968–1969.* New York: F. Watts, 1974.

Young, Peter, editor-in-chief. *The Marshall Cavendish illustrated encyclopedia of World War I.* New York: Marshall Cavendish, 1986.

PERIODICALS

Blankenship, Janie. "Women Change Face of Military." *VFW Magazine*, March 2004; and "Coming Home to a Changed World." June/July 2004.

Braudaway, Douglas Lee. "A Texan Records the Civil War Siege of Vicksburg, Mississippi: The Journal of Maj. Maurice Kavanaugh Simons, 1863." *Southwestern Historical Quarterly*, The Texas State Historical Association, July 2001.

Brieden, John. "Commander's Message." *The American Legion Magazine*, December 2003.

Callahan, Martin L. "From Shiloh to Santiago." *Military Images Magazine*, March-April 1998.

Cox, Kenneth E. "The Greatest Legislation." *The American Legion Magazine*, June 2004.

Cunningham, Roger D. "The Black 'Immune' Regiments in the Spanish-American War." *On Point: The Journal of Army History*, Spring 2005.

Cunningham, S.A., ed. and manager. *Untitled Narrative* (Joe Petritsch contributing). *Confederate Veteran*, 1(1). Nashville, January 1893.

Gilboa, Eytan. "The Panama Invasion Revisited: Lessons for the Use of Force in the Post Cold War Era." *Political Science Quarterly*, 110(4), 1995.

Greeley, Jim. "Desert One." *Airman,* April 2001.

Hemingway, Al. "Marines Remember Beirut 20 Years Later." *VFW Magazine*, October 2003.

Stoffer, Jeff. "The Birthplace of Veterans Day." *The American Legion Magazine,* November 2003.

Tyre, Peg. "Battling the Effects of War." *Newsweek*, December 6, 2004.

Vaughn, Don. "Aftershock." *Military Officer*, November 2005.

Wallace, James N. "Talks with GI's on Their Way to Combat in Vietnam." *U.S. News and World Report*, January 15, 1968.

Widener, Robert. "America's Warriors Return." *VFW Magazine*, August 2004.

NEWSPAPER ARTICLES

Auchmutey, Jim. "To Baghdaddy and back." *The Atlanta Journal-Constitution*, October 23, 2005.

Basu, Moni. "Going to war, coming of age." September 11, 2005; and "Not your mother's war." *The Atlanta Journal-Constitution*, November 13, 2005.

Colimore, Edward. "Vietnam vets jolted back." *The Philadelphia Inquirer*, September 2004.

Cosner, Kyle J. "Fort Bragg releases homicide study." *The Pentagram*, Army News Service, November 15, 2002.

Deans, Bob. "Women's combat role on front burner." *The Atlanta Journal-Constitution,* June 26, 2005.

Fainaru, Steve. "Battle citations display valor of female troops." *The Atlanta Journal-Constitution,* June 26, 2005.

Hirschman, Dave. "I'm not going home until I've got my arm . . ." *The Atlanta Journal-Constitution*, October 9, 2005.

Jaffe, Greg. "For Nate Self, battlefield hero, trauma takes a toll." *The Wall Street Journal*, October 6, 2005; and "For army families, repeat tours strain life on the home front." December 16, 2005.

Komarow, Steven. "Vietnam vets in Iraq see 'entirely different war.'" *USA Today*, June 20, 2005.

Sanders, Bill. "Coached silence." *The Atlanta Journal-Constitution*, March 27, 2005.

Young, Stephen with Bui Tin, "How North Vietnam won the war." *The Wall Street Journal*, August 3, 1995.

VETERANS HISTORY PROJECTS

Adams, Don F. Interview (AFC/2001/001/1120) Veterans History Project Collection, American Folklife Center, Library of Congress.

Ball, Asa Charles (AFC/2001/001/5944) Veterans History Project Collection, American Folklife Center, Library of Congress.

Clark, Jeffrey. Interview by Emmy Huffman (AFC/2001/001/3232) Veterans History Project Collection, American Folklife Center, Library of Congress.

Dawson, Robert G. "Notebook Diary of Robert G. Dawson from March 1945 to March 1946." (AFC 2001/001/20682) Veterans History Project Collection, American Folklife Center, Library of Congress.

Gleeson, Joseph J. "A Soldier's Story: A Daily Account of World War I" (AFC 2001/001/10911) Veterans History Project Collection, American Folklife Center, Library of Congress.

Greenquist, M.L. Independent Research on the World War I Experiences of Corporal Lars N. Greenquist. Interview by Vernon Johnson, Evansville Historical Foundation (AFC 2001/001/9574) Veterans History Project Collection, American Folklife Center, Library of Congress.

Griffin, Donald M. Interview (AFC/2001/001/4925) Veterans History Project Collection, American Folklife Center, Library of Congress.

Johnson, Irving W. "Looking into the Past: Irving W. Johnson's Memories of World War I" (AFC 2001/001/7027) Veterans History Project Collection, American Folklife Center, Library of Congress.

Lamb, George and Betty Boyd. "Letter Home: World War I Letters of Charles Stanley Lamb" (AFC 2001/001/1627) Veterans History Project Collection, American Folklife Center, Library of Congress.

Lathrop, Eric C. Interviewed by Lawrence Molczyk (AFC/2001/001/21748) Veterans History Project Collection, American Folklife Center, Library of Congress.

Loudenbeck, Edward H. "His Daily Diary of the Great War, and His Part in it." (AFC 2001/001/1937) Veterans History Project Collection, American Folklife Center, Library of Congress.

Neumann, Rudolph Joseph. Diary of Rudy Neumann, World War I (AFC 2001/001/24282) Veterans History Project Collection, American Folklife Center, Library of Congress.

Riches, Sidney (AFC 2001/001/557) Veterans History Project Collection, American Folklife Center, Library of Congress.

Russell, Robert. "Diary of Sgt. Reese Melvin Russell" (AFC 2001/001/18879) Veterans History Project Collection, American Folklife Center, Library of Congress.

Schutt, Clarence Alvin, Jr. Interview (AFC 2001/001/5904) Veterans History Project Collection, American Folklife Center, Library of Congress.

AUDIO-VISUAL MEDIA

Miller, Daniel A. and Daniel B. Polin, writers and producers. *Crucible of Empire: The Spanish American War*. South Carolina ETV and PBS: The Great Projects Film Company, 1999.

Public Broadcasting System. "Last Battle of the Gulf War." PBS Frontline Online. Frontline Interviews, 1998.

DISSERTATIONS, THESES, AND OTHER PAPERS

Blair, Juanita Woodhouse. *The impact of Desert Storm on military wives who are human service professionals*. The Union Institute, 1992.

Brandt, Julie Lynn. *The Civil War diary of Elizabeth Hatcher Simons: Life and hardship in Texana, Texas.* Texas A&M University-Kingsville, 1999.

Sturr, Robert Doddridge. *Soldiers' stories of the American Revolution: Autobiography, politics and the patriotic ideal, 1775–1830.* University of Southern California, 1998.

Keehan, Robin S. *Dialectics of containment: Mothers, moms, soldiers, veterans and the cold war mystique.* University of California-San Diego, 1998.

Liston, Marie Claire. *Social work practice with World War II veterans: Impact of the war experience on the life course and adjustment in late life.* University of Denver, 2003.

Lynch, John T III. *A study of the current everyday coping ability of the Vietnam veteran.* The Union Institute, 1992.

McClurken, Jeffrey W. *After the battle: Reconstructing the confederate veteran family in Pittsylvania county and Danville, Virginia, 1860–1900.* Johns Hopkins University, 2002.

O'Donnell, Mary. *The G.I. bill of rights of 1944 and the creation of America's modern middle class society.* St. John's University.

Salvatore, Maxine. *Women after war: Vietnam experiences and post-traumatic stress.* Simmons College School of Social Work, 1992.

Saxe, Robert Francis. *Settling down: Domesticating World War II veterans' challenge to postwar consensus.* University of Illinois at Urbana-Champaign, 1999.

Stelter, Gordon. *The doughboy, the city, and the farm after the Great War.* The University of Guelph, 1996.

Taylor, Richard H. *The volunteer army and mobilization.* Research Report for National Defense University, Washington, DC, December 25, 1978.

Taylor, Sandra. *Front line medic.* Kennesaw State University, 2005.

Valentine, Janet Graff. *The American combat soldier in the Korean War.* University of Alabama, 2002.

Van Ells, Mark D. *To hear thunder again: The readjustment of World War II veterans to Civilian life in Wisconsin.* University of Wisconsin–Madison, 1999.

Whalen, Stephen R. *Everything is the same: The Civil War home front in rural Vermont.* University of Maine, 1999.

Wilson, John P. *Forgotten warrior project.* A partial and preliminary report submitted to the Disabled American Veterans Association. Cleveland State University, 1977.

GOVERNMENT PUBLICATIONS

Jessup, Mary Frost. *The Public Reaction to the Returning Service Man after World War I,* Washington, DC: U.S. Department of Labor, 1944.

The President's Commission on Veterans' Pensions. *Veterans in our society: Data on the conditions of military service and on the status of the veteran.* House Committee Print No. 261, 2d Session, 84th Congress for the Committee on Veteran's Affairs. Washington, DC: United States Government Printing Office, June 21, 1956.

U.S. Department of Veterans Affairs. *VA History in Brief* (VA Pamphlet 80-97-2). Washington, DC: Office of Public Affairs, September 1997.

U.S. House of Representatives. Committee on Veterans Affairs Report to the Committee on the Budget on Eliminating Waste, Fraud and Abuse in Veterans' Programs. Washington, DC: U.S. Government Printing Office, 2003.

Veterans Administration. *VA Fact Sheets.*

ELECTRONIC

DeBurgh, Joseph. "A Few Reminiscences of the First Expedition of American Troops to Manila." Published in *The American Oldtimer*, 1939, and on the Spanish-American War Centennial Website (www.spanamwar.com).

Kreisher, Otto. "Desert One." *Air Force Magazine Online: Journal of the Air Force Association,* 82(1), January 1999.

Milks, Keith A. "Marines in Beirut." *Marine Corps News*, September 29, 2003.

National Magazine. "A Revolutionary Patriot" June 1858; 12 APS Online, PG 532.

Parsons, Usher. "The Descendents of Peter Hill of York Co., ME." *The New England Historical and Genealogical Register (1847-1868)*, April 1858, 12, 2 APS Online pg. 139.

Pike, John. "Operation Enduring Freedom." *Global Security. Org.*, 2000–2003.

Post, Charles Johnson. *The Little War of Private Post: The Spanish-American War Seen Up Close* (Electronic Version). Lincoln, NE: University of Nebraska Press, 1999.

Resch, John Phillips. *Suffering Soldiers: Revolutionary War Veterans, Moral Sentiment, and Political Culture in the Early Republic.* Amherst: University of Massachusetts Press, 1999.

Roeder, Tom. Writing in *The Gazette,* Colorado Springs, January 26, February 13, and March 14, 2004.

The Spanish-American War Centennial Website. "Conditions at Camp Wikoff" (www.spanamwar.com).

VonKleist, Joyce Riley and Dave Riddell von Kleist, "Mission Statement," American Gulf War Veterans Association. News release, February 5, 2004.

Index

About the Authors

RICHARD H. TAYLOR retired from the U.S. Army as a colonel after serving around the world in war and in peace. He is the author of *Prodigals: A Vietnam Story*, a chronicle of his own experiences during that conflict, and was a contributor to the book *Shadow Wars*; he has authored articles in various military journals. He holds two master's degrees from Boston University and a bachelor's degree from North Georgia College.

SANDRA WRIGHT TAYLOR, his wife, accompanied him on most of his assignments or waited for his return from war. She holds master's degrees from Kennesaw State University and Georgia State University and a bachelor's degree from the University of Maryland.